# SCHOLASTICISM AND POLITICS

# SCHOLASTICISM AND POLITICS

## Jacques Maritain

*With a new Introduction by* James V. Schall, S.J.

*Afterword by* Waldemar Gurian

CLUNY
*Providence, Rhode Island*

Cluny Media Edition, 2018

For more information regarding this title
or any other Cluny Media publication,
please write to info@clunymedia.com, or to
Cluny Media, P.O. Box 1664, Providence, RI, 02901

As noted in the Foreword, this translation was originally
edited by Mortimer J. Adler. This new edition retains those edits,
with only minor modifications for improved clarity.

Afterword originally published in *The Thomist*, Vol. 5 (1943).
Reprinted with permission.

ISBN: 978-1944418663

Cover design by Clarke & Clarke
Cover image: Camille Pissarro, *Rue de l'Épicerie, Rouen
(Effect of Sunlight)*, 1898, oil on canvas
Courtesy of The Metropolitan Museum of Art, New York

# Contents

# INTRODUCTION

## *A* Convivium *of Temporal Activities*

"But it is no less clear that *political action*, by virtue of its definition as activity directed to the temporal good of the earthly city, aims at a common good and a common undertaking which ought to bring together in the same civil life and the same civil peace, in a *convivium* of temporal activities as harmonious as possible, all members of the temporal city, members who in fact belong to different spiritual families."

Jacques Maritain, *Scholasticism and Politics*, 1940[1]

"A general Christian education for the nation, a general development of Christian habits and Christian instincts is, in fact, a condition for the political success of democracy."

Jacques Maritain, *Scholasticism and Politics*, 1940[2]

✦ I ✦

*Scholasticism & Politics* was originally a series of lectures given by the French philosopher, Jacques Maritain, in the United States just at the beginning of World War II. To reread these lectures some eighty years after their subsequent

i

publication is to measure how much the world has changed since then. At the same time, the basic intellectual tools to understand man's ultimate destiny and the place of politics in that destiny remain pretty much the same, however seldom we hear them spelled out as we do here.

We must, while reading it, realize that this book was written before World War II was fought, with its results in the recovery of Europe and the Cold War with the Soviet Union. Maritain pays much attention to Fascism, Nazism, and Soviet Communism. Their understanding is a function of the philosophical and political theory of Western Europe. It was assumed at the time of their defeat that a more Christian and natural law foundation to public life could be established. The fact that it was not so established sets the stage for a conflict between this basis and the secularist modernity that in fact came to rule in the decades after Maritain wrote.

This book, however—how could it?—knows little of nuclear weapons, of the unification of Europe and its subsequent doubts about itself. Maritain makes a point of citing pejoratively Belloc's famous phrase "Europe is the faith and the faith is Europe." Yet, we have seen later popes insist that origins of Europe are Christian. The more recent European Union itself made every effort to deny any Christian origins to a "new" Europe even though the pioneers of European unity after World War II were Adenauer, de Guaspari, and Schuman—all Catholics.

Though Maritain deals with China, it is not the China that we have seen rise to power in our time, a communist China that has learned modern economics and technology and, with them, how to control a vast population. He would

---

1.    Jacques Maritain, *Scholasticism and Politics* (Providence, RI: Cluny Media, 2018), p. 218.

2.    Ibid., p. 113.

not have known of the computer, internet, a global economy
or space travel and exploration.

The rise of Islam, which may be present-day Europe's
most unacknowledged problem, has no mention in this book.
Maritain was aware of how much human nature could go
wrong, but he assumed the continuity of Christian habits
and instincts in Western culture. The secularization of both
Europe and America, the extent to which they have deviated
from natural law, is only touched on as a possibility. He would
be bewildered to read statistics about abortion, "legal" gay
marriages, euthanasia, transgenderism, and many other disorders centering on the family. He would not know of Vatican
II though in some sense his ideas could be called a precursor
of it. Later, when it did happen, he gradually became bewildered by it, as he tells us in *The Peasant of the Garonne.*

Though Paul VI translated two of his books into Italian,
what Maritain would make of the Church under John Paul
II and Benedict, then the contrast under Pope Francis,
recalls his own early *Integral Humanism* and his later book on
America. Maritain did have "left" tendencies in some ways.
He sympathized with the ideas of Saul Alinsky but would not
have known the tenor of these ideas under Barack Obama.
What he would have made of earth warming and ecology is
difficult to say. Maritain was an important figure in the founding of the United Nation and the theory that justified it. But
its actual record seems to have gone contrary to those things
about it which he sought to praise.

✦ II ✦

What Maritain attempted to do in this book was to lay out
the relation of Christian revelation to the political life of mortal man. He sought to give politics a proper autonomy, but one
that did not gather to itself everything about man, including

his transcendent destiny. In his basic understanding, Maritain was an Aristotelian seen through the eyes of Thomas Aquinas. This means that he could take into consideration both natural virtues—courage, temperance, justice, prudence—and supernatural virtues—faith, hope, charity. He could see how they each stood for some valid reality while properly supporting each other. He could distinguish. He respected the power of the mind to think, even about revealed things.

In this book, we find penetrating discussions of freedom, authority, and the common good. The chapter on "Action and Contemplation" is of particular importance because it deals with the natural analogate, namely, knowledge for its own sake and knowledge for the sake of doing and making. Man's ultimate destiny is contemplative; that is, it is the beholding of the highest thing, the final object of all our willing and of all our knowing. It is well to refresh our minds, as we do in these pages, on these truths. To think about politics involves thinking about what is not political. The very tendency of what is now called the modern world is to subsume the transcendent into the political; to look upon what is not Caesar's to be an impediment in the achieving what is Caesar's. Indeed, Christianity itself has often come to be seen as merely a useful tool to achieve political and economic happiness in this world.

The word "scholasticism" has gotten a bad name, probably one worse than it deserves. But, at its best, as the works of Josef Pieper, Edward Feser, and Peter Redpath have shown, it refers to a careful and systematic way to go about understanding the different levels and elements in reality.[3] The word "scholasticism" in this book accepts the wisdom that was

---

3.    Josef Pieper, *Scholasticism* (New York: McGraw-Hill, 1964); Edward Feser, *Scholastic Metaphysics* (Neunkirchen-Seelscheid, Germany: Editiones Scholasticae, 2014); Peter Redpath, *A Not So Elementary Christian Metaphysics* (St. Louis: Enroute Books, 2014), 2 vols.

found in classical and medieval thought. Moreover, Maritain systematically traces the deviations from this tradition that have ended in many of the aberrations in the modern world.

This historical understanding is why the chapter on the Thomist idea of freedom is so fundamental. For it is mostly confusion over the central meaning of freedom that modern thought has gradually substituted will for reason as the central good of politics. Aquinas foresaw much of this when he noted in his famous definition of law that the principal objection to a rule of reason is the rule of whatever the prince or political authority wishes. This basic voluntarism turns out to be the central thing that Islam and much of modern Western jurisprudence have in common.

Central to Maritain's argument is the significance of the human person. Maritain spends a good deal of time distinguishing person and individual. In doing so, he is seeking to make sense of the fact that each individual person both transcends the universe and is part of it. He is part of the political order wherein he functions as one citizen making a contribution, by his actions, to the common good. The person is a concept that has its own problems, as Charles De Koninck has long noted.[4]

Maritain discusses the person in the light of Trinitarian theology, of a person being a relation to others in terms of knowledge and love, while, at the same, time retaining its own autonomy. The effect of this understanding of the person is to establish a dignity that surpasses any good of this world. While human persons are citizens of civil societies, that is not all that they are. Each person has a supernatural destiny for which he is accountable. This transcendent orientation of his

[4]. Charles De Koninck, "The Primacy of the Common Good: Against the Personalists and the Principles of the New Order," *The Aquinas Review*, IV (1997).

existence limits the civil society and takes away any claim to
its own absoluteness.

## ✦ III ✦

Maritain spent a good deal of time on attempting to
ground this personal dignity by emphasizing "rights." In this
effort, he was seeking to find a theoretic way to accept the
concept of rights as they came to be used in modern political
documents like the American Declaration of Independence
and the French Declaration of the Rights of Man. In addition, Maritain sought to show how this dignity and these rights
argued to a conception of political order that was defined by
democracy as the best form of rule for all nations. He did not
totally rule out more aristocratic or monarchical regimes as
all bad. And he had as his model the Aristotelian notion of a
mixed regime that combined the good forms and mitigated the
bad forms.

Maritain wanted to base his conception of rights on the
natural law. Thus, the "right" to marriage, property, speech,
and liberty were grounded in an objective order. The modern view of rights, which has come to gain the upper hand,
however, was based in the will of the authority, be it prince
or democracy. It held that a "right" was what the positive
law said it was. And along this path the subsequent career of
"rights" followed. It rejected any notion that "rights" had any
unchangeable grounding in a divinely established natural law.

When it came to the use of force and state power, Maritain
was primarily a realist. He understood what might be called
the Augustinian side of human nature and civil society as
having to cope with persistent and recurring evils. He was
not a pacifist. He saw no reason why brains and force used
to restrain and settle aberrant actions of individuals or states
was not necessary. Maritain did, however, accept some of the

logic of a world order manifested in some institution like the United Nations that would presumably have enough force to deal with recurrent civil strife throughout the world. He did not show the caution about such a project that we already found in Aristotle who thought it would require a divine mind to operate such a system.

A rereading of Maritain's *Scholasticism and Politics* provides an opportunity to clear the mind about many things about the relation of man to the state and man to his transcendent destiny. Maritain sought to explain a society in which there was a living together, a *convivium*, among citizens who could agree on enough things to get along but who still might differ in their understanding of the means to achieve it. This is why Maritain frequently encouraged civic and personal friendship as also a major factor in the social order.

Finally, it must be said that Maritain's assumption that a natural order of reason would not endure without a grounding in Christian principles and practices has turned out to be essentially correct. He also assumed that the Church itself would not change to accept these tendencies of modernity. When it comes to many issues such as the meaning of human life and the nature of freedom, the laws of the democracies are, in effect, not all that different from those in the totalitarian states with which Maritain was more immediately concerned when he gave these lectures. He had a sense that this eventuality might happen. But, I suspect, he would have been perplexed to see the extent that modern society has deviated from what he understood to be a Christian culture in which reason could best affect the public order to account both for a temporal common good and a transcendent, eternal life for each person.

*James V. Schall, S.J.*
*Holy Thursday, 2018*

# Foreword

✦

This book contains the text of nine lectures which were given in the United States during the autumn of 1938. However varied the topics dealt with may be, the general purpose, which makes the organic unity of the volume, is easily perceptible. It is entirely permeated with the idea of the human person, considered in his spiritual dignity and the concrete conditions of his existence.

That which naturally forms the basis of the eminent dignity of the person is human capacity for knowing the truth (hence Chapter II). It is also necessary to determine in what personality itself consists (Chapter III); what constitutes the freedom of the human person (Chapter V); what is the meaning and the finality of his life (Chapter VII); and it is not without interest to observe the failure of the materialistic theories which sprang from a false interpretation of Freud's discoveries (Chapter VI). But the chief aim of this book is moral and practical. This explains why it opens with the author's general ideas concerning integral humanism and the crisis which the modern world is undergoing (Chapter I). It also attempts to solve some of the fundamental problems of political philosophy and of the philosophy of modern history (Chapters I, III, IV, V, VIII, and IX).[1] Generally speaking, the speculative considerations which will be found here are part of the context of practical philosophy.

To my mind, it is through a sound philosophy of the person that the genuine, vital principle of a new Democracy, and at the same time of a new Christian civilization, can be rediscovered; and this involves an extensive work of purification of the ideas that the world has received from the eighteenth and nineteenth centuries.

The dangers imperiling civilization and threatening an overwhelming crisis, due to the errors which weigh upon modern history, appear to concern Europe more immediately than the New Continent. It may be that, in America, there is still time for mankind to eliminate these errors by a creative effort of intelligence and liberty rather than by offering itself up as a victim to the forces of fatality. That is why the philosophical revival which is taking place here and there in the United States, especially among the younger generation, is, in my opinion, of particular importance for the future of civilization. If this intellectual and spiritual revival, and the historical movement of the working masses searching for a new social order, could meet and interpenetrate, the chances for a new Christendom—in the hope of which this book has been written—would be still greater.

It is a great satisfaction for me to be able to thank here the friends who, with the kindness and graciousness so characteristic of this country, have helped me with the translation of these essays and to overcome the difficulties which a philosopher necessarily encounters when expressing himself in a language which, however dear to him, is not his mother-tongue. I

---

1.    Chapter VIII is of special interest to Catholic readers.

am indebted to President Hutchins and Mrs. Robert Hutchins, Mrs. Mabel Wing Castle and Mrs. John Nef, Reverend Father Ward and Professor Earl Langwell, for having so willingly aided and encouraged me. And I am particularly grateful to Professor Mortimer J. Adler, who has sympathetically revised the whole of the volume. To him, and to all, I express here my sincere gratitude.

Jacques Maritain

# CHAPTER I

## *Integral Humanism & the Crisis of Modern Times*

### I. *The Crisis of Modern Times*

To avoid misunderstanding, I should note at once that here my point of view will not be that of the mere logic of ideas and doctrines, but that of the *concrete logic of the events of history*.

From the first point of view, that of the mere logic of ideas and doctrines, it is evident that there are many possible positions other than the "pure" positions which I shall examine. One might ask theoretically and in the abstract, what value these various positions have. That is not what I am going to do here. In brief, my point of view will be that of the philosophy of culture, and not that of metaphysics.

From this point of view, that of the concrete logic of the events of human history, I think that we may be satisfied with the following rather general definition of Humanism, which I have already proposed in another book.[1]

Not to prejudice further discussion, let us say that Humanism—and such a definition may itself be developed along quite divergent lines—tends essentially to make man more truly human, and to manifest his original dignity by enabling him to participate in everything which can enrich him in nature and history (by "concentrating the world in man," in Max Scheler's words, and by "making man as large as the world"). It demands that man develop his powers, his creative energies and the life of reason, and at the same time labor to make the forces of the physical world instruments of his freedom. Certainly the great pagan wisdom, which, according to the author of the *Eudemian Ethics*, aimed to link itself to "that which is better than reason, being the source of reason," cannot be cut off from the humanistic tradition; and we are thus warned never to *define* Humanism by excluding all reference to the superhuman and by foreswearing all transcendence.

What is it that I call the concrete logic of the events of history? It is a concrete development determined, on the one hand, by the internal logic of ideas and doctrines and, on the other hand, by the human *milieu* within which these ideas operate and by the contingencies of history as well as by the acts of liberty produced in history. Necessity and contingency are quite remarkably adjusted in this concrete logic, and to designate this logic we may use the word "dialectic" in the sense I have just indicated, a sense neither Hegelian nor Marxist.

And because we are here in the practical and existential order of human life, with the exigencies of the universe of desire and of its concrete ends, of passion and action, this dialectic involves a movement much swifter and much more violent than that of abstract logic. Positions theoretically tenable (rightly or not) are swept aside, because practically they appear at once *unlivable*, I do not say for such and such an individual, but for the common consciousness.

1.    *True Humanism* (New York: Charles Scribner's Sons, 1938).

Here we see the peculiar vice of classical humanism. This vice, in my judgment, concerns not so much what this humanism affirms, as what it negates, denies and divides. It is what we may call an *anthropocentric* conception of man and of culture. I am aware that this word is not too felicitous, but I have used it for want of a better. We might say that the error in question is the idea of human nature as self-enclosed or self-sufficient (that is to say self-divinized, for this nature has infinite longings).

Instead of an *open* human nature and an *open* reason, which are real nature and real reason, people pretend that there exists a nature and a reason isolated by themselves and *shut up* in themselves, excluding everything which is not themselves.

Instead of a development of man and reason in continuity with the Gospel, people demand such a development from pure reason apart from the Gospel. And for human life, for the concrete movement of history, this means real and serious amputations.

Prayer, divine love, supra-rational truths, the idea of sin and of grace, the evangelical beatitudes, the necessity of asceticism, of contemplation, of the way of the Cross—all this is either put in parenthesis or is once for all denied. In the concrete government of human life, reason is isolated from the supra-rational.

It is isolated also from all that is irrational in man, or it denies this—always in virtue of the very sophism that whatever is not reducible to reason itself, must be anti-rational or incompatible with reason. On the one hand, the life proper to the sphere of will is ignored; and the non-rational in the very world of knowledge is equally ignored. On the other hand, the whole world of the infra-rational, of instincts, of obscure tendencies, of the unconscious, along with that which it includes of malicious and, indeed, of demonic, but also of fecund reserves, is put in parenthesis and religiously forgotten.

Thus, little by little, will spring up the man conformable to the pattern of bourgeois pharisaism, this respectable conventional Man in whom the nineteenth century so long believed, and in whose unmasking Marx, Nietzsche, and Freud will glory. They really have unmasked him, but in the same act they have disfigured man himself.

At the same time, enormous promises have been made to man, ever since the day of Descartes, in the prediction that progressive enlightenment will automatically bring about a complete felicity of release and repose, an earthly beatitude.

This has not happened, as the unfolding of the story—of the history—has shown. Having given up God so as to be self-sufficient, man has lost track of his soul. He looks in vain for himself; he turns the universe upside-down trying to find himself; he finds masks, and behind the masks, death.

And then we witness the spectacle of a tidal wave of irrationality. Then comes the awakening of a tragic opposition between life and intelligence.

This opposition was begun by Luther, and carried on by Rousseau. But certain phenomena of symbiosis, which I have not time to analyze here, took place later.[2] Today this opposition appears sometimes in servile forms, for example, in the form of philosophy of Klages, or in the form of racism, or in the greatly simplified form of certain military men who shout: "Death to intelligence." I shall return to this point presently.

It appears also in noble and very noble forms. I am thinking of Nietzsche, of Kierkegaard, of Karl Barth, of Chestov.

---

2.    Notably in France, the Rousseauistic current was at first dissipated by a countercurrent, the current of rationalistic humanism, but this was later reinforced by the strong sentimental dynamism of Rousseauism.

But even here, no matter with what intelligence they develop the theme that intelligence comes from the serpent, and no matter with what generosity they try to salvage human values, this position unmistakably gives way to what one may call a *counter-humanism*. I am not blind to the fact that one might raise objections here, and ask whether a humanism defending man against reason is not conceivable. Nevertheless, my point is precisely that if we set out to defend man, not against a certain use of reason, but against reason itself, and against knowledge, the result—inevitably and in spite of everything—will be a counter-humanism.

Here it is evident that reason has been imperiled by rationalism, and humanism by anthropocentric humanism. Terrible voices rise up in man, crying out: We have had enough of lying optimism and illusory moralities, enough of the liberty which starves workmen and burns the stacks of grain, enough of the idealism which kills us, which denies evil and unhappiness and robs us of the means of struggling against them; take us back to the great spiritual fruitfulness of the abyss, of the absurd, and of the ethics of despair.

The lofty counter-humanism of a Kierkegaard or a Barth may be regarded as a mistaken Christian position. In Barth particularly it is a reactive and archaic position, inasmuch as it signifies a will to absolute purification by a reversion to the past—in fact, a return to primitive Reformation. In Nietzsche it was rather a confounded Christianity: no longer able to adore, it denied and blasphemed, and nevertheless it still searched and still loved. And all these lofty forms of counter-humanism—because in them is a spirit which protests against itself and destroys itself with a kind of Promethean generosity—still preserve admirable values of humanity and spirituality. But they are only of the passing moment, for they give way fatally to the servile forms of which I spoke a moment ago. Poor Nietzsche! The truly terrifying voice, the fatal voice is not the voice of Nietzsche; it is the voice of that mediocre and base multitude whose mediocrity and baseness, and disgrace, themselves appear as apocalyptic signs, the voice which scatters to the four winds of humanity the gospel of the hatred of reason, in the form of the cult of the fecundity of war or in that of the cult of race and blood.

When love and holiness do not transform our human condition and change slaves into sons of God, the Law makes many victims. Nietzsche could not bear the sight of the lame and halt of Christianity; more even than Goethe, he rebelled against the Cross; he dreamed of a Dionysian superman, who was a fiction. Dionysus! The newspapers and radio give us news of him every morning and tell us how he leads his dance through the concentration camps and the new ghettos, the cities of China and Spain eviscerated by bombs, Europe maddened in the armament race and feverishly preparing for suicide. Nietzsche could not see that man must choose between two ways: the way of Calvary and the way of slaughter. The irrational tidal wave is in reality the tragic wheel of rationalistic humanism; it reacts against a humanism of reason closed up in itself, but it does so by making man open to the powers from below, and shutting him off from higher communications and the spirit which liberates, and walling the creature up in the abyss of animal vitality.

We witness another spectacle, a spectacle quite the contrary of a continuation, aggravation, and exasperation of anthropocentric humanism in the direction which it followed from its origin, in the direction of rationalistic hopes, now constituted no longer solely as philosophical religion, but as a lived religion. This other development arises from taking all the consequences of the principle that *man alone, and through himself alone, works out his salvation.*

The purest case of this tendency is that of Marxism. No matter how strong some of the pessimistic aspects of Marxism may be, it remains attached to this postulate. Marx turned over Hegelianism; he remained rationalistic nevertheless, so much so that for him the movement proper to matter is a *dialectical* movement. In Marxist materialism, it is not irrational instinct or biological mysticism, but reason which decapitates reason.

Man alone and through himself alone works out his salvation. Hence this salvation is purely and exclusively temporal; this salvation is accomplished naturally *without* God, since man is truly alone and acts truly alone only if God does not exist; and even *against* God, I mean against whatever in man and the human *milieu* is the image of God, that is to say, from this point of view, the image of heteronomy. This salvation demands the organization of humanity into one body whose supreme destiny is not to see God but to gain supreme dominion in history. It is a position which still declares itself humanistic, but it is radically atheistic and it thereby destroys in reality the humanism which it professes in theory. It is known that dialectical materialism claims to be heir to classical humanism, and Engels used to write that the revolutionary proletariat was the heir to classical German philosophy. If it is true that this is the most pure and therefore the most active form of the spiritual impulse which appeared earlier in the quite different form of rationalistic humanism, we understand that the God of rationalism does not count in the presence of this atheism, and that what remained of disaffected Christianity in classical rationalism is in relation to such an alcohol like a cake of starch. As for the humanism to which it invites us, the way in which revolutionary, materialistic dialectic has lived for twenty years in the country it conquered, has devoured its leaders, reduced their morality to the justification of any means by the end in view, put to death or persecuted thousands of suspected men—this is sufficient to edify us on that subject.

+

There is finally a position removed as far from anthropocentric humanism as from anti-humanist irrationalism. This is the Christian humanistic position, according to which the misfortune of classical humanism was not to have been anthropocentric; not to have hoped in reason, but to have isolated reason and to have left it to dry out; not to have sought liberty, but to have orientated itself toward the myth of the democracy of the individual, instead of toward the historical ideal of the democracy of the person.

In short, in this view the modern world has sought good things in bad ways; it has thus compromised the search for authentic human values, which men must save now by an intellectual grasp of a profounder truth, by a substantial recasting of humanism. In my opinion, we have today to deal with a considerable liquidation—a liquidation of five centuries of classical culture—the culture in question being a brilliant dissolution (in which new creative forces appear) of mediaeval civilization. It is the merit of Irving Babbitt and Paul Elmer More to have called attention to the historical necessity of a new humanism, and to the responsibilities of Rousseau in the tragedy of modern humanism. What I wanted to indicate in the preceding analysis is the breadth of this tragedy, the double responsibility of the rationalistic current and the irrationalistic current (the latter nevertheless depending on the former, as reaction on action), and the breadth with which we have as a consequence to conceive a new humanism. A new humanism ought then to be new in a singularly profound sense, it ought to evolve within the movement of history and create something new in relation to these five centuries behind us; if it has not such power to renew, it is nothing.

The new humanism must reassume in a purified climate all the work of the classical period; it must re-make anthropology, find the rehabilitation and the "dignification" of the creature not in isolation, not in the creature shut in with itself, but in its openness to the world of the divine and super-rational; and this very fact implies in practice a work of sanctification of the profane and temporal; it means, in the spiritual order, the discovery of the *ways of childhood* whereby the "humanity of God our Savior," as St. Paul says,[3] finds, with fewer human trappings, a readier way into man, and causes more souls to enter into his hidden task of suffering and vivifying; it involves, in the moral and social order, the discovery of a deeper and fuller sense of the dignity of the human person, so that man would re-find himself in God re-found, and would direct social work toward a heroic ideal of brotherly love, itself conceived not as a spontaneous return of feeling to some illusory primitive condition, but as a difficult and painful conquest of civic virtue helped by grace.

Such a humanism, which considers man in the wholeness of his natural and supernatural being, and which sets no *a priori* limit to the descent of the divine into man, we may call the *humanism of the Incarnation*. It is an "integral" and "progressive" Christian position, which I believe conforms to principles representative of the genuine spirit of Thomism. And, in my country, I am happy to find in agreement with it, not all theologians (that would be too much, and is never the case) but some theologians such as Père Chenu, Père Lavaud, l'Abbé Journet, and many others.

---

3.    "Benignitas et humanitas (φιλανθρωπία) Salvatoris nostri Dei" (Titus 3:4).

In the perspectives of this integral humanism, there is no occasion to choose, so as to sacrifice one or the other, between the vertical movement toward eternal life (present and actually begun here below) and the horizontal movement whereby the substance and creative forces of man are progressively revealed in history. These two movements should be pursued at the same time. To claim to sacrifice the second to the first is a sin of Manicheism. But to claim to sacrifice the first to the second is materialistic nonsense. And the second, the horizontal movement, unless it turns to the destruction of men, is effected only when vitally joined to the first, the vertical one, because this second movement, while having its own proper and properly temporal finalities, and tending to better man's condition here below, also prepares in history for the Kingdom of God, which, for each individual person and for the whole of humanity, is something meta-historical.

## II. *Religious Significance of Racism and Communism*

To examine all the problems raised by the preceding considerations would try the reader's patience: they are in fact infinite. Let us eliminate, first of all, the problem of the chances of realization, near or remote, of an integral humanism such as I have tried to characterize. It is clear that the world's trend toward barbarism, now passing before our eyes at an accelerated speed, seems singularly unfavorable to such an occurrence. But the essential thing, if not for our dearest human interest, at least for our philosophy, is to know whether this true humanism answers to the tendencies of the creative forces which act in history simultaneously with the forces of degradation and disintegration, and more or less masked by them. If so, it will be necessary that the true humanism have its day, even though it be after a night of several centuries, comparable to the night of the early Middle Ages.

Next, it is proper to remark that the crisis of civilization, as it appears today in the concrete, is very far from being reduced to an opposition between the "pure" forms and tendencies of which I spoke in the first part of this chapter.

Moreover, if we consider that complex ensemble of forces which we may call, in a general sense, totalitarian, we need to make a very neat distinction between their principle in the pure state, and the realizations which they have or will produce in this or that place, and in which the contingency, resistance and germination of life occasion all sorts of mixtures and, sometimes, attenuations.

Then, finally, it is just to say that in many aspects communist totalitarianism, on the one hand (totalitarianism of the social community), and, on the other hand, fascist totalitarianism (of the political State) or national socialism (of the racial community)—these two opposed families of totalitarianism present profound analogies and even phenomena of osmosis: not only in the order of political techniques, but in the order of principles themselves. Yet between these principles and these philosophical roots there are profound differences. I will summarize here what I have said in another essay.

In spite of the belligerent pessimism imprinted on it by Marxism, communism has as metaphysical root an absolutely optimistic philosophy of man, that great optimistic mysticism which began with rationalism and was continued by the Encyclopedists, then by Jean-Jacques Rousseau, then by Utopian socialism, on the one hand, and Hegelian philosophy, on the other. Practically, it denies that man is a creature of God, because it is unwilling to recognize in man that which comes from nothingness. Because of this optimistic basis, it does not profess to be totalitarian; the totalitarian principle is immanent in it as a vice and fatality, which is not avowed.

Fascism on the contrary has as metaphysical root an absolute pessimism of a rather voluntaristic and Machiavellian sort. Practically, it denies that man comes from the hands of God, and that he maintains within him, in spite of everything, the grandeur and dignity of such an origin. This pessimism, which invokes incontestable empirical truths, turns these truths into ontological lies, because it is indifferent to the fact that man comes from God. Then it despairs of man—I mean of the human person, the individual person—in favor of the State. Not God but the State will create man; the State by its constraints will oblige man to come forth from the nothingness of the anarchy of the passions, and lead an upright and even heroic life.

As for national socialism, it also makes a most fundamental mistake concerning the nature of man, since in practice it basically refuses to see in man the creature and image of God, and it uses man as zoological material: man must serve the apotheosis of the telluric, primitive, and divine (demonic) element which is developed in him and by him, that is to say, in his blood and by his predestinated blood, in such a way that a quite apparently combative optimism, which is trust in force, is added to a fundamentally pessimistic conception of human nature.

Because of this pessimism, which dispenses with any hypocrisy concerning the dignity of the human person, national socialism and fascism proclaim themselves totalitarian, and the totalitarian principle is raised up by them as a shield and standard.

In a word, looking at these two opposed kinds of totalitarianism, as these two opposed faces of the same evil, we might say that practically, existentially, here we have an atheism which declares that God does not exist and yet makes its own god of an idol; and there is an atheism which declares indeed that God does exist, but makes of God himself an idol, because it denies in act, if not in word, the nature and transcendence of God; it invokes God, but as a spirit-protector attached to the glory of a people or a State, or as a demon of the race.

These remarks were made to avoid confusion. I would return now to the purely anti-Christian position of which I spoke at the outset, and which it would be better to call "anti-Christ," because it is less a question of doctrinal opposition to Christianity than of an existential opposition to the presence and action of Christ at the center of human history. To be brief, it is on the problems of the religious significance of racism and communism that I would say a few words. In this section I shall not speak of fascism, because, for various reasons on which there is not time to dwell, the religious or mystical dynamism of fascism is feeble (on the one hand, the resistance of the Catholic Church puts a considerable check to the pagan mysticism of Empire; on the other hand, the idea of the State lends itself less readily to serve as substitute for the religious communion than does the idea of the racial Community); however, because of that, it is difficult for fascism not to be influenced in this domain, by forms that are more virulent.

Let us consider, first, the racial principle in its pure state. From the point of view of the nexus of ideas, it appears that racism is, as we said, above all an irrational reaction. Think of the actual status of scholars in the country which seemed to have vowed forever to venerate them: racism is a protest of the man in the street against the scholar! More profoundly, it is pathological protest, nourishing itself on the most absurd pedantry (but, in such case, the more absurd the pedantry, the more efficacious it is), a pathological protest of nature, with all its forces of vitality and ferocity rising out of the depths of mother-earth, with its needs of health and power and physical beauty, with the implacable rage which can exalt instinct when the spirit betrays itself and becomes engulfed in animality, a protest against the messengers of the absolute and the transcendent who have not sufficiently shared the miseries of human kind.

For we should recognize the punishment wreaked upon this primacy of the ideal unfaithful to itself, and, so far, artificial and hypocritical, which was the great vice of the Kantian nineteenth century and which we may call a clericalism of the reason. The world of elementary values in nature, of physical courage, of simplicity, no matter if brutal and gross; of that sort of natural, if cynical, candor by which the animal is not ashamed to exist nor has need to justify existence; the world of primitive feelings, of pacts such as exist even in the horde, of the instinct of physical solidarity such as exists among robbers, of the need of being together and feeling together such as exists even in the great herds on the prairies—this world can indeed be disciplined by true wisdom, which does not despise it and which turns it toward transformations of the spirit. But against false wisdom which humiliates and deceives it, some day or other it takes terrible revenge.

A mystic hatred of all intellectual or moral subtlety, of wisdom and all asceticism, is thus developed; and at the same time a powerful religiosity, the natural religiosity inherent in the human substance down to its elementary physical fibers. God is invoked, but only in virtue of the testimony, if I may say so, of these elementary fibers and of the desire of nature written in the biological elements of the human being; and (because of the basic reactional process which I indicated) He is invoked *against* the God of the spirit, of intelligence and love—excluding and hating this God. What an extraordinary spiritual phenomenon this is: people believe in God, and yet do not know God. The idea of God is affirmed, and at the same time disfigured and perverted. A God who will end by being identified with an invincible force at work in the blood, is set up against the God of Sinai and against the God of Calvary, against transcendent Being, *He who is* and who dwells in inaccessible glory, against the Word who was at the beginning, against the God of whom it is said that He is Love. We are facing, not a pseudo-scientific atheism, but, if I may speak thus, a demonic para-theism which, while declining wisdom, is open to every kind of occultism, and which is not less anti-Christian than is atheism.

Of course, if it were not perverted thus, the testimony I just spoke of, that of the natural desire of God inherent in the elementary physical fibers of the human being, is in itself authentic and valid. I mean here something still deeper and more elementary than the desire of nature which intelligence awakens in the will, and through which every intelligent creature aspires, insofar as intelligent, to know the cause of being such as it is in itself. There has been many a quarrel between Thomists and non-Thomists, and even between Thomists and Thomists, concerning this desire of nature; some have sought to minimize it, to render it conditional and inefficacious *to such an extent* that, finally one might say, St. Thomas spoke of it only to say nothing, or allowed himself to be swept away by lyrical emotion, which is seldom the case with him. Others have sought to magnify this desire of nature and to make St. Thomas say much more than what he says, so much so indeed that finally St. Thomas is made to appear the disciple of Mr. Maurice Blondel, a noted French philosopher, or of Father Rousselot, a brilliant French Jesuit; and it is thought that intelligence aspires to the vision of the divine essence, as if specified by this object, as the only truly real knowledge. To my mind, St. Thomas simply wants to say that it is natural for intelligence: (1) to desire to know its object unveiled; (2) to desire to know the causes; and that it is therefore natural for intelligence, knowing things, to desire to know, unveiled and in itself, the cause of things. But as thus desiring, intelligence knows not what it wants. Grace alone tells it the name of what it thus desires, which is to see God as He sees Himself.[4]

If I may be pardoned for this digression it is not this desire of nature, proper to every intelligent creature insofar as it is *intelligent*, which I spoke of when touching upon racist religion. For, indeed, it is not with the creature insofar as it is intelligent, that we are here concerned, but rather with the creature insofar as it is stupid. Let us say that we are concerned with the creature insofar as it is animal, as it is made of flesh and blood. But even on this level, at these animal depths, there is still a desire for God, and it is this desire I spoke of. Does not St. Thomas tell us in his Treatise on the Angels, that it is natural for every creature whatsoever, intelligent or not, living or inanimate, to love God more than itself and to tend to its proper good by virtue of this love of its transcendent *Whole*? Thus, the hen not only loves its chicks and not only loves itself; it loves God more than itself. The plant tends toward God before tending toward light and air.

The stone gravitates toward the center only by virtue of its natural tendency toward God, of its natural "love" of God. And our eyes crave for light and our smallest physical fibers crave for life, by virtue of their profound tendency toward God, and of their ontological desire for God. Such is the elementary tendency which explains racist religiousness; because it grows from the most physical and least rational roots of being, because it is blind, it can easily let itself be deviated as soon as it passes into the zone of rational life; in fact, it is this

---

4.    See our *Les Degrés du Savoir* (Paris, 1932), Ch. VI, p. 562, note 1.

elementary desire, which being perverted, causes the growth of demonic para-theism which I have mentioned above.

Will this elementary desire be able someday to free itself from the unregulated affective forces which set it against the testimony of the spirit? If so, on what conditions? And by what processes? Well, in any case, racism as it exists and acts in reality today and in the minds of today will have been swept away.

Finally, if we take the point of view not only of the nexus of ideas but of society in the concrete, we see that racism is existentially bound to this demonic para-theism. Because in its reaction against individualism and its thirst for a communion, it seeks this communion in human animality, which, separated from the spirit, is no more than a biological inferno. In the metaphysics of society in the concrete, the god of the community of blood can only be the demon of the blood. Racial neo-paganism is thus lower than the paganism of classical antiquity, which was faithful to eternal laws and to the supreme Divinity. It brings into existence once more the lowest elements of paganism.

The account of atheism and communism calls for a like discussion. From the point of view of the connection of ideas, one sees that the genesis of communism in Marx is of the philosophical order; it proceeds from impulses derived from the Hegelian left and from Feuerbach; in Marx the theory of the alienation of work by private property pre-supposes *de facto*, before becoming first *de jure*, the Feuerbachian theory of the alienation of conscience by the idea of God.

And more profoundly, the discovery of historical materialism, as Marx conceived it, implies an absolutely atheistic position; because it implies a universal process of substitution of the dialectic of history for all transcendent causality, and for the universe of Christianity in general; it implies consequently an absolute naturalistic immanentism, by hypothesis exclusive of all divine transcendence.

For Marx, then, the historical and sociological action of religion works necessarily against the emancipation of the proletariat, because it is the action of a factor of the superstructure which is originally determined only by the need for justifying the economic exploitation of man by man.

If, as I think the case, the master-idea of historical materialism can be purified, so as to designate henceforth only the essential (but not principal) importance of material causality in history, it is on condition that it breaks with Marxism, and replaces the outlook of Hegelian dialectic by that of the fourfold causality of Aristotle.

This basic atheistic principle explains why the existence of class conflict (resulting from the capitalistic structure of our economy) gave rise in Marx to a theoretic and practical conceptualization turning the class-struggle into a gesture of atheism, I mean a moral secession fully accepted by the dispossessed class, by the accursed of the earth, from the political community, which, no matter how oppressive and inhuman its economic structure may be, holds its natural value from God. This same basic, atheistic principle also explains why, as the Webbs report, one of the deepest features of the new civilization worked out in the Soviet Republics is anti-godism; and why, as they also report, a formal pledge of atheism and of repudiation of every form of the supernatural is required in Russia of every adherent to the communist party, and even of every candidate for that party.

Are there yet other potentialities in Marxism? Because in Marx, as I have just tried to explain, by reason of a pre-supposed atheism—the social problem of the emancipation of the proletariat has in fact the priority over the metaphysical and religious problem, the class war over the anti-religious war, can we conceive within Marxism a development allowing a clearly affirmed dissociation between social theory and a materialistic conception of the world, and (on the other hand) a revision of the naïve atheism which Marx derived from the nineteenth century? If so, on what conditions? And by what processes? Well, in any case, communism as it exists and acts in reality today and in the minds of today would have been wiped away.

This is plain to us if, taking the point of view not only of the connection of ideas but of society in the concrete, we see that communism is existentially bound to atheism. For if it reacts against individualism, if it thirsts for communion, it does so without finding a principle superior to anthropocentric humanism; quite on the contrary, it aggravates the latter and seeks this communion in economic activity, in pure productivity, which, considered as the *locus proprius* and homeland of human activity, is only a world of a beheaded reason, of reason without God. In the metaphysics of society in the concrete, the god of the industrial community can only be human reason as demiurgic and fabricating, the titanism of industry. Communism thus transforms Christian communion into an entirely temporal and despotic communion, which is to be achieved by the abolition of private property.

Under this heading of communism and racism, we may make a concluding remark. If it is true that in the dialectic of culture, communism is the final state of anthropocentric rationalism, we see that in virtue of the universality inherent in reason—even in reason gone mad—communism is all-embracing, and sets itself against Christianity by pretending to substitute for the universalism of the Mystic Body of Christ its own earthly universalism; whereas racism, on its irrational and biological basis, sets itself against Christianity by rejecting all universalism, and by breaking even the natural unity of the human family, so as to impose the hegemony of a so-called higher racial essence.

We see also that communism fends, quite in the line of industrialistic rationalism and of capitalistic materialism, toward a transformation of economics by annihilating the ultimate frames of bourgeois society, and that its directive elements are furnished it especially by the working population, whose thought a century of socialistic tradition has disciplined in a revolutionary direction. Racism, on the contrary, and fascism do indeed exert on the energies of bourgeois society a high revolutionary pressure, and they do detest capitalism, but—being above all reactional processes—they do not go on to a social transformation destructive of the ultimate machinery of capitalistic society. It is by another road, preferably by war, that they threaten its destruction. The masses on whom they depend belong especially to the middle classes on the path to proletarianism, classes whose affective mobility is very great. The personal magnetism of the leaders plays a major part; but the leaders could not make their enterprise succeed without the aid given them by strong privileged interests blindly anxious to safeguard their own position.

## III. *Christian Conscience and the World*

A characteristic of the humanism, which I call integral, would be that, far from being limited to the elite, it would care for the masses, for their right to work and to a spiritual life, and for the movement which brings them, we may say, to a historically full age. On the social significance of such a humanism, I will simply say that it should assume the task of radically transforming the temporal order, a task which would tend to substitute for bourgeois civilization, and for an economic system based on the fecundity of money, not a collectivistic economy, but a "personalistic" civilization and a "personalistic" economy, through which would stream a temporal refraction of the truths of the Gospel.

This task is joined to a thorough awakening of the religious conscience, and I wish to insist for a moment on this point. One of the worst vices of the modern world is its dualism, the dissociation between the things of God and the things of the world. The latter, the things of the social, economic and political life, have been abandoned to their own carnal law, removed from the exigencies of the Gospel. The result is that they have become more and more unlivable; at the same time, Christian ethics, not really carried out in the social life of people, became in this connection, I do not say in itself or in the Church, I say in the world, in the general cultural behavior, a universe of formulas and words; and this universe of formulas and words was in effect vassalized, in practical cultural behavior, by the real energies of this same temporal world existentially detached from Christ. Such a disorder can be cured only by a renewal of the profoundest energies of the religious conscience, arising in temporal existence.

On the other hand, modern civilization, which pays dearly today for the past, seems as if it were pushed, by the very contradictions and fatalities suffered by it, toward contrasting forms of misery and intensified materialism. To rise above these fatalities we need an awakening of liberty and of its creative forces, we need the energies of spiritual and social resurrection of which man does not become capable by the grace of the State or any party pedagogy, but by a love which fixes the center of his life infinitely above the world and temporal history. In particular, the general paganization of our civilization has resulted in man's placing his hope in force alone and in the efficacy of hate, whereas in the eyes of an integral humanism, a political ideal of brotherly love alone can direct the work of authentic social regeneration: and it follows that to prepare a new age of the world, martyrs to the love of neighbour may first be necessary. And this also shows how everything depends here on a profound renewal of the interior energies of conscience.

Granted what I said a moment ago about the pathological process of vassalization, in the behavior of contemporary civilization, of religious formulas by worldly energies, we see that the renewal we speak of should be a kind of Copernican revolution, which would in no way affect the doctrine, not even an iota of it, but would make a great change in the relative importance of the elements in the universe of action. It would consist in general and bold acknowledgment of the primacy of the vital and the real (even the implicitly or virtually real) over matters of appearance and external trappings, let us say—for I am primarily thinking of the Christian conscience—of the primacy of the practically or vitally Christian over the nominally or decoratively Christian. Such a Copernican revolution—which is the revolution claimed by the Apostle James[5]—would have notable consequences for the question of the ways and means of political action.

Truly speaking, it is the idea of the primacy of the spiritual which here commands the debate. To say that Christianity will remake itself through Christian means or that it will un-make itself completely; to say that no good is to be expected from the enterprises of violence and constraint—with no compunction of heart and no interior reform or inner creative

---

5.   "Be ye doers of the Word, and not hearers only, deluding your own selves" (James 1:33).

principle—enterprise animated by the same spirit which is at
the elemental source of the evils actually suffered by civilization; to say that the evidence and the patient and persevering
action of the Christian spirit in the world is *more* important
than the outer apparatus of a Christian order, especially
when those who pretend to save this order bind themselves,
and also the order, either to established injustice or even to
the immense pagan energies sweeping away one part of the
actual world—this is simply to affirm that the principle of the
primacy of the spiritual demands respect in the very mode in
which men work to give it reality; it is simply to affirm that
the primacy of the spiritual cannot be realized while denying
itself.

I add that if it were true that the leaven of the Pharisees,
against which Christ puts us on our guard, represents—as
Père Fessard, a Jesuit well known in Paris, has pointed out
in one of his books—a standing temptation for the religious
conscience, and if it is true that this leaven will not be totally
expelled from the world till the end of time, then we must
say that the renewal of the religious conscience of which I
speak, will be a new step and signal victory in the never-end-
ing struggle of the religious conscience against Pharisaism. At
the same time, it seems clear to me that, in the temporal order,
an attitude corresponding to what has always been called the
liberty of the Christian, confronted by the world and the powers of the flesh, is the only one to safeguard—for tomorrow or
for the day after, either as a favorable solution of the present
crisis or as a dawn after a long night—the hope of men in the
terrestrial efficacy of the Gospel, and of reason.

# CHAPTER II

## *Science & Philosophy*

### I. *State of the Question*

I shall use the two words "science" and "philosophy" in the sense which they have acquired in modern times, according to which *science* designates above all the mathematical, physico-mathematical and natural sciences, or, as one is also wont to say, the positive sciences, the sciences of the phenomena; *philosophy* designating above all metaphysics and the philosophy of nature.

Truly speaking, the problems of science and philosophy have been renewed and have become extraordinarily complicated in our time. First, the crisis in the growth of modern physics, while launching science itself on an entirely new path, has liberated it from many pseudo-dogmatisms and much pseudo-metaphysics, and especially from the materialism of the physicists "of the Victorian age," as Eddington says, with their pretence to "explain," *someday*, the essence of bodies, according to mechanistic determinism, and even to account for the occurrence of every single event in the universe. This crisis has made physics more conscious of its own nature.

Secondly, and at the same time, a considerable work has also been accomplished by the theoreticians of science, by logicians and by logisticians. Finally, this crisis of growth has not only diminished the dogmatic pretensions of experimental science, it has also deeply transformed in this domain (and by contagion, in certain other spheres) the work and the methods of reason; it has taught reason a sort of exhilarating freedom, a *new and terrible freedom*, to repeat the words used by Dostoievsky in quite a different matter. Yes, and as it were in compensation, a tendency toward systematic interpretation, imposing very rigorous rules and seeking a sort of logical purism, has been developed by certain theoreticians. I have in mind the logicians of the Viennese School, on whose ideas I should like to dwell in the first part of this chapter.

It must not be forgotten, however, that all great movements of contemporary thought react, in the most varied way, on our notion of science. On the one hand, German phenomenology, Bergson, Whitehead, pragmatism, Thomism— each offer their general conception of the life of knowledge, and their views on the nature of knowing. On the other hand, influences of a more practical order further complicate the work of the mind; in particular, the conceptions inspired by dialectical materialism—which are the climax of modern revolutionary rationalism—exert, as from the outside, a considerable influence on certain parts of scientific thought, and cannot therefore be ignored.

By attempting to characterize the ideas of the Viennese School on the philosophy of science, I hope to present the conceptions of science and philosophy which I believe true. I will also take the opportunity to define briefly the Thomist position in regard to Marxist epistemology. The word "Marxist" has a political resonance, rendering its use somewhat irrelevant in a discussion of speculative philosophy. However, the thought of

Marx, though turned toward the practical domain, includes a philosophy whose internal power and historical importance are considerable. And we should deal with it only from this point of view.

In Professor Tawne's judgment, Marx is the last of the Schoolmen in his economic doctrine. What is definitely so serious in the occurrence of Marxism is that it offers us the case of a philosopher precipitating philosophy (Hegelian philosophy) into practical activity, social, and political, considered as its very essence, its very life, and its genuine justification. At the beginning was action, wrote Goethe. We have now the full substitution in thought itself of the Word by Action. Such a substitution leads a long way, and reaches results unsuspected by Marx himself. When a State claims the political right to impose a certain *Weltanschauung*, a certain philosophy, on all populations of the same race and blood, this pretension, to the infinite dishonour of philosophy, is the final embodiment of the concessions, which in the end—at the extreme point of Hegelianism—philosophy has had to yield to *praxis*, to the mailed fist which was at the beginning.

## II. *Logical Empiricism*

The epistemology of the Viennese School is quite different from, and even opposed to, that of Marx.

The name of "Viennese circle" was first mentioned in 1929. At the origin it was meant to designate a philosophic association created in Vienna by Moritz Schlick, who has since met with a tragic death. It now designates a group of scientist-philosophers, whose common orientation is a *logical empiricism* due to quite different historic influences, in particular to the influence of Mach and Avenarius, that of Poincaré and of Duhem, of Peano, of Russell and of James, and to that of Einstein. Besides Moritz Schlick, the chief representatives of this school are Rudolf Carnap, Philipp Frank, Otto Neurath, and Hans Reichenbach.

When, about twelve years ago, Einstein came to Paris for important discussions at the Collège de France, I was very much interested in the manner in which, in answer to questions about time and simultaneity, he invariably replied: "*What does this mean to me, a physicist?* Show me a definite method by which measurements can be made physically certain, in terms of which this or that observed result will be given this or that name, and only then will I know what you are talking about." It seems to me that the same question underlies the researches of the Viennese School: *What does this mean to me as a scientist?* The main point for this school is to distinguish those assertions which *have a meaning* for the scientist from assertions which *have no meaning* for the scientist.

In pursuing this analysis, the Viennese logicians have thrown light upon the fact that assertions which *have a meaning* for science are not those which concern the nature or the essence of that which is, but rather regard the connections between the designations or symbols, which our senses, and especially our instruments of observation and measurement, enable us to elaborate concerning that which *appears to us* in our *Erlebnisse*, as the Germans say, that is, in our lived experiences. It is not with the being of things that science is occupied; it is with the mathematical links, which can be established between these designations taken from things, and which alone make possible—I say in the proper order and in the proper plane of science—a communication or a well-established language, an *intersubjectivation*, submitted to fixed rules of signification.

If I say *this table*, these words do not mean for the scientist a hidden substance, presenting itself to me under a certain image and with certain qualities, of which substance, moreover, he can know nothing as a physicist. They mean a certain set of perceptions, linked by expressible regularities—*the permanent possibility of sensation* of which John Stuart Mill spoke—linked to a certain number of mathematical and logistic designations, which render it *intersubjectivable*.

If I say *matter*, this word does not mean for the physicist a substance or a substantial principle, about the mysterious nature of which he might question himself and, if wise, answer with Du Bois-Reymond: *ignorabimus*. For the scientist, the word "matter" only means a certain set of mathematical symbols, established by microphysics and submitted, moreover, to continual revision, wherein certain highly designable observations and measurements are expressed according to the rules of differential calculus or of tensorial calculus and according to the syntax of certain general theoretical constructions, which are also of a provisional character, such as the quantum theory or the syntheses of wave-mechanics.

All this is excellent, but we must have the courage to go to the end. An assertion such as *I am* or *I exist*, proclaimed in the manner of Descartes, for example, has no meaning for the scientist, because to have a scientific meaning an assertion must express a stable relation between designations which can finally be reduced to such or such class of sensory experiences; and *existence*, in the Cartesian formula, is not such a designation. An affirmation such as *I speak before an audience of human persons*, uttered in the manner of common sense, is also deprived of meaning for the scientist; the person is not a sensorimechanical symbol which can be handled by science. These affirmations will have a meaning for the scientist only when the words "existence" and "person," after an appropriate reformulation, will have lost all meaning for you and for me.

Generally speaking, all reference to *being*, or essence in itself, is eliminated as *lacking meaning for the scientist*; and naturally the rational necessities disappear at the same time. What philosophers call the first principles of reason express at best certain regularities likely to be verified in certain cases, and likely not to be verified in others, according to the logical treatment to which we submit our *Erlebnisse*. The discussions concerning scientific determinism and Heisenberg's principle of indetermination, have cast light on this point, insofar as the principle of causality is concerned, or more exactly speaking, so far as concerns the recasting of the idea of causality in the domain of experimental science. And I do not see at all why the principle of noncontradiction, duly deprived of all ontological meaning, should not be exposed someday to the same fate, if upon that day the introduction of the simultaneous value of *yes* and *no* in a symbolic expression should enable us to express mathematically a set of observations and measures with more elegance and ease, or to combine in a general synthesis theories drawn from different sections of science, which could not be otherwise conciliated.

All this means that the intellect is a sort of indispensable *witness* and regulator of the senses in scientific work, remaining all the while—if I may express myself thus—*external* to this work. The senses and the measuring instruments *alone see* in science, and the intellect is there only in order to transform, according to the rules of mathematical and logical syntax, the signs expressing what has thus been seen. The intellect is set up in the central office of the factory, where it checks, and submits to more and more extensive calculations, all the indications which are conveyed to it. It remains outside the quarters where the work is being directly accomplished, and is forbidden to enter.

III. *The Thomist Idea on Science*

The theory of experimental science offered by the Viennese suffers, in my opinion, from certain peculiar philosophical errors which especially concern the notion of logical work and the notion of sign. Logical work, by which the mind passes from one assertion to another by virtue of reasoning and of the connection of ideas, is not, as the Viennese believe, a simple tautological process, wherein we only transform different symbolic expressions of one same thought; it is not a simple reiteration of the same thought, for, in thinking, the mind passes from one truth to *another* truth.

The notion of sign does not concern our states of consciousness, our *Erlebnisse*, but objects independent of our subjective states, though constituted in their intelligibility proper by the activity of our intellect.

And, above all, the theory of science offered by the Viennese, suffers from a positivist purism, to which I will return later.

But, so far as a certain characteristic structure of science is concerned, this theory insists upon a fundamental truth which, in fact, the Viennese logicians have not discovered (rather they have received it from the scientists), and which is due to the self-awareness which modern science, and especially physics, has achieved. The truth is, that science—science in the modern sense of the word—is *not* a philosophy, and consequently claims, if I dare use this barbarism, to *deontologize* completely its notional lexicon.

This endeavor is more difficult than it may seem. There is something heroic about it. It implies a merciless struggle against language, because language is inevitably loaded with intelligence and with ontology. To consider, for instance, the prose of Joyce or the works of some of our contemporary poets, it is curious to observe how this desperate struggle

against language currently characterizes two of the most typical and noblest impulses of spiritual endeavor, in very different fields, the scientific and the poetic. It might be that,
truly speaking, the mystics alone are able to succeed in such
a struggle: because the mystics have no need of language, at
least in a certain zone and at certain moments of experience
and actuation.

Let us end this digression. What I should like to note relative to the precise point which I have just indicated, is that
the consideration of the sciences of phenomena, as they have
developed in modern times—novel, indeed, by relation to the
cultural state of antiquity and the mediaeval world—this consideration carried out in the light of the epistemological principles of St. Thomas Aquinas, would lead us to general views
strikingly similar to those of the school of Vienna.

Let me sum up as briefly as possible the results which I
reached myself, before having been informed of the works of
the Viennese group.

What is essential, in my opinion, is both to repudiate the
positivist conception of knowledge, which is a philosophical
error, and also to take account of the understanding of themselves which the sciences of nature have achieved, a self-consciousness which is itself a spiritual reality, an extremely
valuable fruit of experience, and which we cannot ignore
without exposing ourselves to a serious mistake.

What is important, it seems to me, is to distinguish (and
this the Viennese School has omitted to do) *two* ways of
analyzing the world of sensible reality and of constructing
the concepts relevant thereto. I have given these two kinds
of analysis of sensible reality the following names: the one,
*empiriological analysis*; the other, *ontological analysis*.

If we observe any kind of material object, this object
is, while we observe it, the meeting point, as it were, of two

knowledges: sense knowledge and intellectual knowledge. We are in the presence of a kind of sensible flux, stabilized by an idea, by a concept. In other words, we are in the presence of an ontological or intelligible nucleus manifested by a set of qualities perceived *here* and *now*—I do not say *conceived*, I say *felt* qualities, objects of actual perception and observation.

As to the sensible reality, considered as such, there will thus be a *resolutio*, a resolution of concepts and definitions, which we may call *ascendant*, or ontological, toward intelligible being—a resolution in which the sensible matter always remains there and plays an indispensable role, but indirectly and at the service of intelligible being, as connoted by it; and there will be on the other hand a resolution *descending* toward the sensible matter, toward the observable as such, insofar as it is observable. Not that the mind ceases to refer to being—for that is impossible, being always remains there—but being passes into the service of what is sensible, of what is observable, and above all, of what is measurable. It becomes an unknown factor assuring the constancy of certain sensible determinations and of certain measures. In fact, the new aspect which modern science presents is precisely this *descendant resolution*, a procedure which the ancients had not thought of making an instrument of science.

In this empiriological analysis, characteristic of science in the modern sense of the word, the permanent possibility of sensible verification and of measurement plays the same part that essence does for the philosopher; the permanent possibility of observation and measurement is for the scientist equivalent to, and a substitute for, what essence is to the philosopher. One may here behold something like an effort against the natural slope of the intellect, because one must turn back, if one is to grasp what is essential and properly constitutive here, to the act of sense itself, to a physical operation to be performed, to an observation or a measurement. It is this observation to be made, this act of sense, which will serve to *define* the object.

If one understands this, one has understood the views of an Einstein, for instance, in physics, and the opposition more apparent than real between the philosopher and the scientist on such matters as time and simultaneity. This opposition is immediately solved, because the type of definition is essentially different in the two cases. For the physicist conscious of the epistemological exigencies of his discipline, science tends to construct definitions, not by essential ontological characters, but by a certain number of physical operations to be performed under fully determined conditions. On the other hand, all science tends in a certain way, and however imperfectly, to explanation and deduction, to a knowledge of the *why*. Therefore, empiriological science will necessarily be obliged to seek its explicative deductions in mere *ideal constructions*, though founded on the real, and which can be substituted, as well-founded explicative *myths* or *symbols*, for the *entia realia*, the real entities, those causes of ontological order which the intellect seeks when it follows its natural slope. Such an elaboration of ideal entities grounded in reality, the most significant examples of which are encountered in mathematical physics, but also in such non-mathematical disciplines as experimental psychology, and through which real causes are reached in a blind fashion—such an elaboration is linked to the aspect of *art* or *fabrication*, whose importance in empiriological science has often been observed with reason. The *essence*, the *substance*, the *explicative reasons*, the *real* causes, are thus reached in a certain fashion, in an oblique and blind manner, through substitutes which are well-grounded myths or symbols, ideal constructions, which the mind elaborates from the data of observation and measurement, and with which it goes out to meet things. Thus, these basic notions, primitively philosophical, are recast and phenomenalized.

It has been justly observed that in the image which the physicist makes of the world, "certain traits really express, not nature, but the structure of the real, and in this there is a certain adequation. For instance, the atom of Bohr signifies the table of Mendelieff—the undulatory theory signifies light's interference."[1] Thanks to ideal constructions, to *entia rationis*, the real is thus grasped.

I do not know how to translate this word, *ens rationis*; it designates certain objects of thought, as the universal, the predicate, the privation, the transfinite number, and so forth, which I conceive intelligibly, but which cannot exist outside my mind. Let us say, if you like, *ideal entity* or *logical entity*, or *being of thought*, or *being made in the mind, being not expressing a reality* (though possibly grounded in reality).

Certain facile minds, which imagine themselves strong, have often scoffed at the *entic rationis* of the Schoolmen. Yet here we have seen that the theory of the *ideal entity grounded on reality* alone furnishes us with an accomplished and satisfactory interpretation of the paradoxical twofold character—at the same time *realist* and *symbolic*—of the sciences of phenomena, which makes them appear, at first glance, so disconcerting.

## IV. *The Philosophy of the Viennese Circle*

We see that the Thomist epistemological principles enable us, without forcing or warping anything, to render an account of the reflexive intuition by which modern science becomes more and more conscious of itself, and to which the school of Vienna owes its chief merit.

---

1.   F. Renoirte, in "Philosophie et Sciences," *Studies of the Thomist Society*, V, III, p. 35.

The misfortune of the Viennese is that they are philosophers. This can be immediately seen from the way they insist on the truths they have grasped, while they blunt their point, as Pascal says. By a positivist conceptualization, by a bad conceptualization the school of Vienna impairs—a phenomenon often observed—a good intuition, the reflective intuition of which I have spoken, and by which modern science becomes conscious of itself.

We must here remember, that the logicians of Vienna have conducted their analysis according to a certain philosophical spirit, which they have not bethought themselves to submit to a critical revision, and which derives at the same time from empiricism, from nominalism, and from conceptions advanced by logistics. They suffer, moreover, from many specifically modern prejudices and ignorances. On one hand, they know but one science, the science of phenomena, the science of the laboratory; and, as good disciples of Descartes, they form of this science, and of all sciences, an idea deplorably univocal. On the other hand, they know but one kind of philosophy and metaphysics, at once bookish, profoundly arbitrary and gigantically ambitious; a kind of philosophy against which they have good reason to protest. We must admit that Mr. Carnap holds a good hand against Mr. Heidegger. It is indeed easy, too easy, to indulge here in a humorous injustice, and to declare that a metaphysician is a musician who has missed his calling.

We must therefore not be surprised by the excesses of the Viennese School in the systematization which it offers of the views—just in themselves, at least partially—which I have spoken of, concerning the logical structure of the sciences of phenomena. I have already suggested that, to my mind, they do not escape the danger of a delusive purism, to which every positivist conception of science is naturally exposed.

Obsessed by that aspect of science, characteristic enough, but not exhaustive, which we have already discussed, the Viennese forget that if science reaches the being of things only obliquely and by means of merely ideal constructions, it is being in truth, which it nevertheless reaches, as Leibniz said, in an enigmatic and "blind" fashion. The school of Vienna ignores what Mayerson has so acutely pointed out: the incurably realistic tendency of the science of phenomena. If it seems to give an account of the logical structure toward which science tends, as toward its ideal limit—science as already completed, and more and more perfectly rationalized—this school neglects certain profound characters of science *in the making*, that is, of the process of research and the work of scientific discovery. However scandalous for positivist orthodoxy, this work can be performed only with a feeling for the subjacent importance of the causes and essences of things, that is, in the climate, however obscure to the scientist himself, of the ontological mystery of the universe. That is why the problem of the adequation to the real remains central, though under an enigmatic form, for scientists like Mr. Gonseth who, with a few other mathematicians and physicists, delivered a considerable blow to the dictatorial pretensions of the Viennese School, during the philosophic congress in July, 1937, in Paris. On the other hand, as the late Professor Bumstead said, "any sort of logic (or the lack of logic) is permissible" in the work of experimental discovery.

And yet it is in another field that one finds the essential error—linked to this first mistake—for which this school is to be blamed. The essential error is, as I have already said, to confuse that which is true (with certain restrictions) of the *science of phenomena*, and that which is true of *all science* and of *all knowledge* in general, of all scientific knowing. It is to apply universally to all human knowledge that which is valid only in

one of its particular spheres. This leads to an absolute negation of metaphysics, and the arrogant pretension to deny that
metaphysical assertions have any meaning.

I have earlier referred to what has no meaning *for the physicist*. If one simply suppresses these three little words—"for the
physicist"—one will declare: that which has no meaning *for the
physicist* has no meaning *at all*. This is a uniformization, a brutal way of restricting human science, which is not preceded
by a critical examination of the life of the mind, and which
cannot be so (for one would then have to enter into metaphysics in order to deny its possibility); a uniformization which,
finally, is based only on the positivist superstition concerning
positive science. But metaphysics does not let itself be done
away with so easily. Before deciding that the question, "Does
a primary cause of being exist?" has no meaning, we should
first ask ourselves whether the question, "Does the philosophy
of the school of Vienna exist?" is not a question deprived of
meaning.

The objection has been justly raised against the Viennese
position that *if* the meaning of a judgment consists in its
method of (experimental) verification—not only in the usage
proper to experimental sciences, but in an absolute manner; *if* any judgment which cannot be thus verified is devoid
of meaning, *then* this school's own theory has no meaning,
because it is incapable of being verified in this manner. It is
incapable, even in principle, of space-time verifications. The
theory of the Viennese is in fact a *philosophical* theory, a *philosophy of science*; and, in my opinion, the principle which I have
just mentioned, the principle of the necessity of logico-exper-
imental verification, is true in regard to the function of judgment in the *empiriological sciences*; but it is true *only in this domain*.
A philosophy which generalizes this principle and extends it
to the entire field of knowledge, seeing in it an exigency of the

nature of all judgments truly valuable for knowledge—such a philosophy thus destroys itself.

The Viennese entirely ignore the mode of resolving the concepts which we have described as *ontological*, and which occurs in the direction of intelligible being. They do not see that, if it is true that all knowledge properly speaking supposes an intersubjectivation submitted to fixed rules of significance, such an intersubjectivation is not met with only on the plane of scientific knowledge, but also on the philosophical plane, where it acts, however, in quite a different way, and refers above all, not to an operation of the external senses, but to an intelligible perception. The Viennese do not see that the meaning of a judgment is derived from the intelligible objects which it composes or divides in the act of being. If, in empiriological sciences, meaning implies a possibility of physical verification, it is because, in this particular case, the objects of such notions are themselves conceived in relation to the operation of the senses. The chief point in criticizing neo-positivism is a warning to us of the irremediable mistake caused by a *univocist* conception of knowledge, and as a reminder, by antithesis, of the great words by which St. Thomas condemned Descartes before his day: "It is a sin against intelligence to want to proceed in an identical manner in the typically different domains—physical, mathematical and metaphysical—of speculative knowledge."

I have spoken too much perhaps of the ideas of the school of Vienna. The reason is that such ideas—where an excessive simple-mindedness impairs much that is true—characterize rather well the average state of mind which, succeeding materialism and the older positivism, will no doubt prevail among scientists and, especially, among popularizers of science, with which we shall have to deal for some time to come. It is important to take this state of mind into account, and to consider how problems concerning the degrees of knowledge can be presented to it.

Let us start with the highest degrees of knowledge, those which deal with the supra-rational order. It is remarkable, in fact, that logical neo-positivism looks at these degrees of knowledge—of the supra-rational order—with less disfavor than at the degrees of an order entirely rational, namely, metaphysics and philosophy. Generally speaking, the school of Vienna manifests no hostility toward religion, and certain representatives of this school, perhaps in memory of Bolzano and Brentano, show a certain sympathy for the work of the theologians, whom they prefer to university philosophers.

Let us now consider how some people appear to be so ready to "compromise" things in this way.

Science (i.e., the science of phenomena) knows only the space-time connections of the observable; it does not know being. And, it is always added, there is no other science, there is no rational knowledge other than this science. Well, this brings great relief and comfort to apologetics. To every question concerning the being of things—the soul, God, freedom and determinism, nature and miracles—to all such questions, human reason must answer, in the manner of empiriological science, beyond which it cannot go: *I do not understand the question, it has no meaning for me,* and shuts its mouth. It is for faith that such questions have meaning; it is faith which must answer. By an unexpected reversion, the object which Aristotle assigned to metaphysics passes to faith. Science does not know being, but faith—at least for him, who has received this gift—does. Let us crown *neo-positivism* by *neo-fideism,* and all will go well, with, moreover, a remarkable economy of intellectual effort.

However, solutions and conciliations acquired at the expense of intelligence, are never sound. In regard to faith let us question the believers, for they are evidently competent witnesses. What do they say? They say that, for them, faith is an obscure adherence to primordial Truth, which means a certain *knowledge*, not a science, not a demonstrative knowledge (*Wissen*), but a kind of knowing (*Erkennen*); for if it is not a kind of knowing, it is nothing. Now, if all assertions of an ontological type are devoid of meaning, not only for empiriological science, but *purely* and *simply*, then how can the assertions of faith preserve their meaning? Thus faith runs the risk of being considered, according to the rationalist scheme already outlined by Spinoza, as a simple effective and practical disposition, without content of truth or value of knowledge. On the other hand, faith involves rational implications; it implies, for instance, the possibility for reason to prove the existence of God starting from creatures. And this will also perish in the neo-positivist conception of knowledge and of the life of reason.

Nevertheless, the Viennese School in general (I do not speak of this or that popularizer) recognizes that, outside the field proper to science, faith has a domain against which science as such has absolutely no interdict to formulate; to link science to a general atheistic conception, or to speak of a "scientific atheism," is from its point of view pure nonsense. In this it is drastically opposed to other tendencies, which I mentioned at the beginning, and especially to the philosophy of science proposed by dialectic materialism.

This opposition appears to me particularly suggestive, because the Viennese theory arises from the reflections, more or less well conducted, of logicians and scientists concerning the peculiar conditions of modern science. This theory is, if I may thus express myself, of endogenous origin. On

the contrary, the Marxist theory of science is of exogenous
origin; it is derived from a general conception of man and
of the world, in which the historic-social aspect is dominant,
and it is this *Weltanschauung* which imposes on the partisans of
dialectic materialism a certain interpretation of science. Let
us remember the original relations between Marxism and left-
wing Hegelianism, and we shall not be surprised if the door,
which neo-positivism leaves open to religious horizons, should
be, in Marxist epistemology, brutally shut.

## V. *Dialectic Materialism*

Here is not the place to examine this epistemology in
detail; I should like, however, to explain briefly how, in my
opinion, it should be envisaged.

There are in Marxist epistemology a certain number
of traits, which do not displease a Thomist: its aversion for
idealism, its affirmation of the reality of the external world,
the role it grants to the body in knowledge itself (in the first
degrees of human knowledge), the importance (unfortunately
principal) which it bestows upon material causality, the sense
which it possesses of historical becoming (and which, reduced
to just proportions, would be a highly philosophic sense, but
which in the Marxist theory devours everything). Marxist
dogmatism itself, even if it appears to us a counterfeit of real,
organic, doctrinal force, has at least the courage of systematic
unity. And even Marxist atheism, however absurd we may
think it, supposes at least, that human reason must answer
the question whether God is or is not without seeking refuge
in the parentheses of a science of phenomena, from which it
refuses to emerge.

Having said as much, I will indicate two highly typical
traits of Marxist epistemology: that which one might call its
*practicalism*, and that which one might call its *dialecticism*. In

both of these respects, the Marxist theory of science is, in my opinion, a destruction of science.

To sum up, Marxism not only ordains knowledge to action (which, according to Aristotle, is proper only in a *certain category* of knowledge); it makes knowledge itself consist in an activity exercised on things, in an activity of work and domination of matter, and of transformation of the world: if Aristotle is right in considering activity *ad extra*, "transitive" activity, as the mode proper to activity, not of the mind, but precisely of bodies, of physical agents—it appears that this demiurgic conception of knowledge is something like an idea of titans, still indistinct from nature and enslaved by it, and moving in the depths of the earth their members made of roots and rocks.

It is true that the practical aspect has predominated in science since Bacon and Descartes, and has imposed itself with particular force in modern times, by reason of the close relations existing between our science and industry. But this practical aspect will never succeed in excluding the irreducible speculative value of science—in other words, the *relation of truth*, with its proper criteria. Let us admit that what in the modern world interests the scientist, and gives him the courage to work at tasks which dispense but meagre intellectual delights, is the growing desire to act on the world and to transform matter; such is the aim of him who works (*finis operantis*). But the aim of the work itself or of science itself (*finis operis*), that which interests science as such—the end at which it aims insofar as it is a mathematical interpretation of phenomena—is now and always *to know*. To banish this speculative finality from empiriological sciences, to deprive them of their speculative nature, is to become immediately *extraneous* to the question. It is a sort of barbarity which, if it had the efficacious power, would dry up at its very roots the activity of knowing.

The second character of Marxist epistemology is its *dialec-ticism*. It pretends to find in the sciences themselves the typical process of dialectics, understood in the sense which Marx gives to this word; the self-movement of the concrete by negation of the present position, negation of the negation, etc.; and as this pretension cannot be achieved by merely considering the relation of science with its object, it is to the movement of science itself in time, to the *history of science*, that it must have recourse. That human science, by virtue of its structure, demands to evolve in time, to have a history; that it should consequently imply a certain dialectical movement, due to the interaction of the internal logic of ideas with the needs and dispositions of the thinking subject—this indeed is a great truth. But what I should like to note here is the typical procedure of dialectical materialism; this consists, not merely in recognizing the importance of history, but in using the *history* of a thing, first, in order to juggle away the *nature* of the thing, and then to *explain* the thing by replacing it by its history. The history of poetry presupposes poetry. Are you going to study poetry and to ask yourself *in what poetry consists* (which by the way will not hinder, and will even encourage reference to its history)? No: you will say how poetry has developed in history; thanks to a series of successive internal contradictions, oppositions and syntheses, one state of poetry engendering another state by auto-negation—romanticism spring forth from classicism, and proletarian poetry emerging from bourgeois poetry, which, by denying itself, surpasses itself, etc. And behold!—this is all. There is nothing more to say about poetry. Dialectical materialism is satisfied with this account of it. All this supposes, of course, empirical notions concerning poetry, collected more or less extensively, but no philosophical analysis whatever regarding the nature of poetry. The scientific form, which is the definitive condition of knowledge, is sought for in history.

Even if the history in question is exactly reported, the matters in question well observed and well described, all that is true in this pseudo-explanation will have served only to prevent and to annihilate the very problems of philosophy and of science concerning the nature of poetry and its constitutive truth. Moreover, the history in question *will not be apt to be exactly reported*, because it will not be content with being a history, but will make all the explicative pretensions, which it has stolen from science and philosophy, reappear in itself. It will inevitably use facts in an arbitrary manner, philosophy will oblige history to lie, and history will oblige philosophy to lie.

Thus understood and practiced, dialectic is an extraordinary instrument of illusion. I am far from being an enemy of dialectic, either of dialectic in its ancient sense as a logic, or of the dialectic of the concrete, conceived as a historical development due to the internal logic of a principle, or of an idea, in action in the human concrete. But the Hegelian dialectic is something quite different, and this dialectic has precisely spoiled everything. In a sense, Marx is, in relation to Hegel, what Aristotle is in relation to Plato; he has brought Hegelian dialectic down from heaven to earth. As a result it has become the more pernicious. It is of Hegelian dialectic, *turned over* by Marx, that I am speaking at the present moment, and I am considering the logical virtue it has in its purity. No more causes and effects in being; everything in history happens of itself, according to the play of immanent antinomies.

Now, the more this dialectic wants to be realistic and take possession of reality as of a thing to be intellectually manufactured, the more it liquefies reality in order to recompose it according to the fancy of the mind in the schemes of a logical universe, or rather of a logical becoming. I do not know whether I have explained with sufficient clearness what appears to me so marvelously sophistic in this proceeding.

Marx has spoken of the *mystification* of the Hegelian dialectic. His own dialectic, inasmuch as it imagines itself realistic, only doubles this mystification. It makes historical explanation a parasite of the knowledge of natures—a parasite which reabsorbs and annihilates in itself the parasited subject, and which having nothing left to live on, lives and prospers all the better inasmuch as it becomes ideal and delusive.[2]

Now, it is this universal process which Marxist epistemology applies to the particular case of science. In principle it admits a reciprocal conditioning between the theory of knowledge and history. In fact, it uses the latter in order to escape the authentic problems of the former. The relation of physics with reality, and the proper problems put forth by this relation, then pass into the background. And what acquires all importance for the mind is the relation of physics to itself (and to cultural and economic conditions of humanity), and the dialectic process explaining the passage of one physical theory into another physical theory. Science as a specific energy of truth, as a specific vitality of intelligence, has vanished, has been annihilated in the illusion of historical explanation; the latter can carry abundant materials and fecund views concerning the human becoming of science and its cultural connections; but, insofar as the epistemological problem, properly speaking, is considered, this explanation yields the mind only an illusory satisfaction.

---

2.  We speak here of the pseudo-explanation which serves as a logical instrument for dialectical materialism, considering this pseudo-explanation in itself. No doubt dialectical materialism as an event in history will leave important acquisitions: but that is quite another question. Darwinism (in whose logic, as Driesch has shown, one finds the same substitution of history for the knowledge of natures) has left a capital acquisition: the idea that there exists an evolution and a historic transformation of the species; but the pseudo-explanation of this fact, offered by Darwin, has precisely fallen to pieces.

Perhaps, after these considerations, we can understand better the profound opposition existing between the neo-positivist conception of science and the materialistic-dialectic conception of science. In the eyes of the logicians of the Viennese School, dialectical materialism must appear as a metaphysics of the worst kind, based on an idea of matter not only out of date but devoid of meaning. For Marxist epistemology, the ideas of the school of Vienna correspond to a "bourgeois" and undialectic conception, artificially isolating the intellect from all other faculties of knowledge, and by this very reason "incapable," as a Marxist writer tells us, "of producing a usable theory of knowledge."

In certain points, however, these two theories arrive, though for different reasons, at similar negations and refusals. I have said that neo-positivism leaves the door open to faith (on condition that it should not be a knowledge) and to theology (on condition that it should not be a science). But we have also seen that, as regards metaphysics and speculative philosophy, neo-positivism is as negative as Marxism.

## VI. *Metaphysics*

What is the position of Thomism with respect to these matters? My first answer is as follows: for St. Thomas, there are in the supra-rational order two kinds of wisdom—contemplation by union of love and discursive theology—which are, properly speaking, *scientiae*, knowledge of a well-assured and complete type (not in the modern sense of the word "science," but in the authentic and very ample sense of knowing well-founded on causes or reasons of being).

I say this first because this conveys to us the analogical amplitude of the word "science," when one returns to its genuine sense, and makes us realize what misery it is for the mind to reduce science to the type—surely noble and deserving in itself, but of all which this analogical amplitude embraces, the least elevated—to the type of empiriological science, i.e., the physico-mathematical sciences and the sciences of phenomena.

Now, if contemplation and theology can be a knowledge of well-assured and complete type, it is first of all because there can be in the rational order a knowledge which is a wisdom—a wisdom accessible to our natural powers of inquiry and demonstration. Is it possible that the intellect—which knows itself and judges itself, and which knows and judges reflexively the nature of science—should be unable to enter itself in the work of knowledge, that is to *see into* the nature of things? Can it be condemned to remain always on the outside of this work, in the role of a witness and a regulator of the senses, as happens in the science of phenomena? There must be such a science, a knowledge in which the intellect is on the *inside,* and where it freely develops its deepest aspirations, the aspirations of intellect *as intellect.* That is metaphysics.

Metaphysical wisdom is in its essence a purely natural wisdom. It is in terms of natural and rational evidences that this wisdom is entirely developed. And though, from the point of view of exercise, one should, as Plato said, philosophize with all one's soul, from the point of view of specification, it is the intellect alone of man which is here engaged. Metaphysical wisdom is illumined by the intelligibility of being disengaged and in a pure state (I mean without intrinsic reference to any construction of the imagination or to any experience of sense), at the highest degree of abstractive intuition. Its formal object is *being* according to its proper mystery—*being as being,* as Aristotle said.

If positivism, old and new, and Kantism do not understand that metaphysics is authentically a science, a knowledge of achieved and completed type, it means that they do not understand that the intellect *sees*. For them, sense alone is intuitive, the intellect having only a function of connection and of unification. Let them be silent! For we cannot say "I," we cannot utter a noun of the language, without testifying that there are objects in things, that is, centers of visibility, which our senses do not reach but which our intellect does. Of course, there is no *angelistic*, intellectual intuition, in the sense of Plato and Descartes—I mean an intuition which does not need the mediation of the senses; of course there is nothing in the intellect which does not originally derive from sensible experience. But it is precisely the activity of the intellect which disengages from this experience and brings to the fire of immaterial visibility in act, the objects which sense cannot decipher in things, and which the intellect sees. This is the mystery of abstractive intuition. And in these objects which it sees, the intellect knows, without seeing them directly, the transcendent objects which do not exist in the world of sensible experience. This is the mystery of analogical intellection. The problem of metaphysics reduces itself finally to the problem of abstractive intuition and to the question whether, at the summit of abstraction, being itself, insofar as it is being— permeating the world of sensible experience, but yet exceeding this world on all sides—is or is not the object of such an intuition. It is this intuition which makes the metaphysician. Everybody does not have it. And if we ask why positivism, old and new, and Kantism ignore this intuition, we shall be bound finally to admit that it is because there are philosophers who see, and philosophers who do not see.

As to dialectic materialism, the fact that it ignores metaphysical values not only means that there are philosophers who do not see; it means, in addition, that there are also philosophers who fabricate a world without seeing. It is especially when he criticizes, or, rather *explains*, the genesis of metaphysical reason and its future, ultimate integration in empirical knowledge, that the Marxist dialectician appears as a magician who has missed his calling.

There exists in the world—so the Marxists tell us—a vast "secteur," a vast province which is not yet submitted by science to man's domination: now, metaphysics and religion (for the Marxists do not distinguish the one from the other) are but a way of anticipating, in terms of imagination, a supremacy not yet acquired in practice. Metaphysical reason refers to the *non-dominated* province, which it pretends to construct theoretically, in such a way that it dominates it in the imagination. God and being qua being have been created for the sake of dominating this province which yet remains inaccessible. When a real and practical domination replaces this imaginary domination, the illusory constructions of metaphysics and religion will vanish of themselves. And when will this occur? No doubt when the "practical domination of the external world will be assured by such a high degree of material, productive forces, that the advent of a society without classes and without individual increase in value will enter the domain of the possible."[3]

Thus are disposed of the problems and objects which, at all times, the most universal and skilled thinkers—from Lao-Tse, Çankara, and Ramanoudja, to Plato, Aristotle, Plotinus, St. Thomas Aquinas, Leibniz, and Hegel—have considered to be the domain of wisdom. Would it be indiscreet to ask whether this historical evacuation of the universe of wisdom does not itself presuppose a metaphysical intrepidity unconscious of itself? For after all, what is it that assures the theoreticians of

---

3.    Max Raphael, *Zur Erkenntnistheorie der Konkreten Dialektik* (1934); translated into French under the title: *La Théorie Marxiste de la Connaissance* (Paris, N.R.F.), p. 121.

dialectic materialism, that the entire material world will some-day be submitted to the domination of man? Unless, per-haps this assurance is given to them by the words of Genesis: "Replenish the earth and subdue it." What is it that assures them that not only the external world, but also the internal world, the one that is inside man himself, will thus be suscep-tible to complete domination? In short, are they quite sure that there does not exist somewhere some province not subject to *domination*? It is commercial dishonesty to open a store of machine-guns and to say: "I sell umbrellas." It is intellectual dishonesty to dispense metaphysics and to say: "Metaphysics exist no more; I open a factory of social facts." We know, and we profess that our reasons are metaphysical ones. And because of metaphysical reasons which we believe to be good, we are convinced that there exists a province of reality which cannot be *dominated*. We believe it to be impossible that by the mere effort of man and of empirical knowledge, death can someday be defeated, and the eternal longings be satisfied which man bears in his intelligence and in the physical fibers of his being. We assert that the liberation demanded by man is such that the possession of the world would still leave him unsatisfied; we consider man to be an unusual animal, who will be content with nothing less than absolute joy.

The Marxist dialecticians cannot even try to establish that we are mistaken in all these assertions, for in order to pro-ceed to this demonstration they would have to indulge in an explicitly metaphysical discussion. And so long as they have not proved that in these matters their presuppositions are exact, their dialectical explanations and evacuations must be considered as a simple imposture. It is a certain satisfaction for the mind to attain to positions and oppositions so abso-lutely primordial, that whatever respect and amenity is felt for the person of their contradictors by the philosophers, the latter will have to renounce all possibility of courtesy, and to exchange offensive words. As long as one is not reduced to denying one's opponent the right to exist intellectually, there is no really radical philosophic conflict. It is perhaps by virtue of the degradation of the sense of this truth, that the use of injurious terms is so wide now in certain circles of dialectical-materialist thinkers, as it once was in certain circles of theologians. And so, let us be indulgent in regard to them. Mr. Max Raphael is a particularly distinguished Marxist philosopher. I have recently received the French translation of one of his books: *The Marxist Theory of Knowledge* (*Zur Erkenntnistheorie der Konkreten Dialektik*), accompanied by the most refined and friendly dedication. After perusing, most profitably, this interesting work, I realized that Mr. Max Raphael cannot do otherwise than classify Thomist metaphysics as a *bigoted imposture*. I highly esteem the works of Mr. Max Raphael; but I cannot help placing Marxist metaphysics in the category of *dialectical trickery*.

I should add that I am so deeply convinced of the infinite suppleness of the dialectical procedure, and of the possibility of obtaining from it, at the appropriate moment, anything one chooses, that I do not lack the hope that someday dialectical materialism will find means for explaining that it fully agrees with, and even calls for metaphysics, theodicy, and even revelation.

## VII. *Philosophy of Nature*

I still have to indicate, before concluding this chapter, that in the Thomist perspectives, metaphysics does not constitute the whole of speculative philosophy, but only its highest category.

Below metaphysics and above the sciences of the empiriological type, there exists another degree of knowledge, that of the *philosophy of nature*. The philosophy of nature knows the same world as the empiriological sciences, the world of change and movement, of sensible and material nature; but the resolution of concepts is made here in intelligible being, not in the observable and the measurable as such. Here, again, the intellect perceives being abstractively, but not, this time, being according to its proper mystery; it perceives being insofar as the latter is invested with material motion and according to the proper mystery of the world of becoming; and it is clear that, if human intelligence is capable of abstractive intuition, it must exercise this power first in that order which is most connatural to human intelligence, namely, the order of sensible nature. A philosophical knowledge of movement, of transitive action, of corporeal substance, of living organism, of sensitive life, helps thus to complete, by proceeding according to an entirely different noetic type and conceptual lexicon, the empiriological notions obtained about nature by the sciences of phenomena and of experimental detail—that is, by science in the modern sense of the word.

I will not dwell here further on the problems relative to the philosophy of nature. I shall end this discussion by repeating that, notwithstanding their opposition, neo-positivism and dialectical materialism lead, by different ways, to certain common negations. If either of them is right, there is only one science, the science of phenomena, pure and even purist in one case and, in the other case, carried away by the great dialectical fantasy. And there is no wisdom. Blinded by logical empiricism or hallucinated by historical explanation, the intellect is a slave in the service of sensitive apprehension.

If Thomism is right, all the truth that neo-positivism has discerned concerning the sciences of phenomena is maintained and saved, just as is all the truth discerned by dialectical materialism concerning the movement of history and the evolution of the social concrete. But above the sciences of phenomena, there are other categories of science which are categories of wisdom, because they reach in its very mystery, and yet in quite different ways, being itself, that being after which the intellect thirsts and hungers. And above the work of man in time, accomplished in order to subjugate material nature and eliminate from society the forms of servitude— above this work, there is the activity of man in the eternal, an activity of wisdom and of love, by which the intellect and the heart of man interiorize to themselves an infinite good, not dominated, not capable of domination, but which finally gives itself as the object of fruition.

# CHAPTER III

## *The Human Person & Society*

The subject treated in this chapter is, truly speaking, the fundamental subject of all social and political philosophy. But, at the same time, I must admit that it is an extremely difficult subject, and one which, in the beginning at least, is unavoidably arid.

Whence this aridity? It is due to the fact that it is impossible to discuss such matters without first embarking upon rather abstract philosophical considerations concerning *individuality* and *personality*—two notions which are usually confused and whose distinction I consider to be highly important.

After attempting to explain how man is as a whole an *individual* and also as a whole a *person*, and how at the same time the focus of *individuality* is quite different from that of *personality*, I will consider the applications of this distinction, especially in *social* matters. Lastly, I shall conclude by saying, that *humanism of the individual* and *democracy of the individual*, in which the nineteenth century had placed its hopes, must be replaced today—if we want to save civilization—by *humanism of the person* and by *democracy of the person*.

## I. *Individuality and Personality*

The person, is it not the *I*, the *ego*? Is not my person *myself*? Let us immediately observe the peculiar contradictions to which this word and this notion of *ego* give rise.

Pascal tells us that "the *ego* is hateful." It is a commonplace expression of Pascalian literature. And in the current language, when it is said of someone that he has a very "personal character," this usually means a character shut up in itself, imperious, domineering, barely capable of friendship. A great contemporary artist once said: "I don't like others." Such an affirmation reveals a terribly "personal" character. And, considered from this angle, one might think, that personality consists in realizing itself at the expense of others, and that it always implies a certain impermeability, or a certain selfishness, due to the fact that in a man *occupied* with himself and with his own affairs, there is no room for anyone or anything else.

On the other hand, it sounds like a bitter reproach to say of someone: "He is a man without personality." And do not the saints and heroes appear to us as the very highest achievement of personality and at the same time of generosity? Nothing great is accomplished in the world without a heroic fidelity to a truth which a man who says "I" beholds, and to which he bears witness; a fidelity to a mission, which he, a human person, must perform—of which perhaps he alone is conscious, and to which he sacrifices his life. One need only open the Gospel to see that no personality is more magnificently affirmed than that of Christ. The theologians tell us that it is the personality of the Uncreated Word itself.

And so, as a counterpart to the word of Pascal which I have just quoted, "the *ego* is hateful," we must remember the words of St. Thomas: "The person is that which is noblest in the whole of nature."

Pascal says, that "the *ego* is hateful." But St. Thomas teaches that the man who loves God must also love himself for God's sake; he must love his soul and his body in a spirit of charity.

To be wrapped in oneself—a state which contemporary psychologists call introversion—can cause much havoc. And, I believe, many people brought up in a spirit of strict Puritanism complain of the suffering and a sort of inner paralysis created by *self-consciousness*. But, on the other hand, the philosophers, and particularly Hegel, tell us that the faculty of becoming conscious of oneself is a privilege of the spirit and that the chief progress of humanity consists perhaps in this growing consciousness of self.

Concerning art, Mr. Lionel de Fonseca, an aesthetician of the East, declares that "vulgarity always says *I*." But one might answer that vulgarity says "everybody" also, and that it is the same thing. In quite a different way, poetry also, and always, says "*I*". Here again, if the selfish ego is hateful, the creative self is that which is noblest and most generous of all.

What do these contradictions mean? They mean that the human being is held between two poles: a material pole, which in reality does not concern authentic personality, but rather the material condition and the *shadow*, as it were, of personality; and a spiritual pole, which concerns personality itself.

It is this material pole, and the *individual* becoming the center of all things, that the words of Pascal aim at. And it is on the contrary with the spiritual pole, and with the *person*, source of freedom and of goodness, that the words of St. Thomas are concerned.

Herein we face the distinction, which I mentioned at the beginning, between *individuality* and *personality*.

There is nothing new in this distinction; it is indeed a classical distinction, belonging to the intellectual heritage of humanity. And the distinction between the "*ego*" and the

"*self*" in Hindu philosophy is—with other metaphysical connotations—its equivalent. This distinction is fundamental in
the doctrine of St. Thomas. The sociological problems of our
days, as well as our spiritual problems, have bestowed upon
it a fresh actuality. It is invoked by very different schools, by
the Thomists, by certain disciples of Proudhon, by Nicholas
Berdyaev and by the so-called existential philosophers. Dr.
Salazar declares himself attached to it. I remember that a few
years ago, when I was in Lisbon with François Mauriac and
Georges Duhamel, we were received by the Portuguese ruler.
And Duhamel, who is a confirmed "individualist," asked him
how could a dictatorship—even of a non-totalitarian type—
be combined with the free development of individual beings,
which alone makes human life tolerable. "Ah," answered Dr.
Salazar, "in order to explain this to you, I would have to speak
of the distinction between the individual and the person."
Mauriac fully enjoyed this philosophical answer, addressed by
a dictator to a novelist.

Does this distinction find its best application in dictatorship? I greatly doubt it. As for dictators other than Dr. Salazar,
who do not possess his culture, I would say that instead of
distinguishing personality and individuality, they precisely
confuse these two terms. I recollect that one of them, whom
a member of the French Academy visited a long time ago,
praised that which he believed was saintliness in the following
manner. "What moral strength," he exclaimed, "what prodi-
gious energy, must develop in a man who, as he gets up each
morning, says to himself: *act well, and you will be canonized!*" To
install one's *ego* on the altar is hardly the ideal of these heroic
personalities whom one calls saints.

It is therefore extremely important to distinguish the person from the individual, and it is also extremely important to
grasp the exact significance of this distinction.

Let us first speak briefly of individuality. Suffice it to recall that, according to St. Thomas Aquinas, the *individuality* of inanimate and animate things is rooted in *matter*, so far as matter has uniquely distinct determinations with respect to location in space. The word matter designates here, not a concept used in physics, but in philosophy: that of the *materia prima*, pure potentiality, able neither to *be* nor to *be thought* by itself, and from which all corporeal beings are made. Prime matter or "matter absolute" is a kind of non-being, a simple power of receptivity and of substantial mutability, an avidity for being. And, in every being made of matter, this avidity bears the imprint of a metaphysical energy—"form" or "soul"—which constitutes with matter a substantial unity, and which determines the latter to be that which it is, and which, by the simple fact that it is ordained to inform matter, is particularized to such and such a being, sharing with other beings, equally immersed in space, the same specific nature.

According to this doctrine, the human soul constitutes, with the matter which it informs, a unique substance, both spiritual and fleshly. It is not as Descartes believed: the soul is not *one* thing—thought—existing as a complete being; and the body *another thing*—extension—existing in its own way as a complete being. But soul and matter are two substantial co-principles of one and the same being, of a single and unique reality whose name is man. It is because each soul is made to animate a particular body (which derives its matter from the germinative cells from which it springs with all their load of heredity); it is because each soul has a substantial relation, or rather *is* a substantial relation with a particular body; it is for these reasons that it has in its very substance individual characteristics which differentiate it from every other human soul. For man, as for all other corporeal beings—as for the atom, the molecule, the plant, the animal—individuality has its primary ontological root in matter. Such is the doctrine of St. Thomas concerning individuality.[1]

I said that matter is an avidity for being, without determination, an avidity which receives its determination from form. One might say that in each of us, *individuality*, being in one that which excludes from one all that other men are, is the narrowness in being, and the "grasping for oneself," which, in a body animated by a spirit, derives from matter. Man, insofar as he is a material individuality, has but a precarious unity, which wishes only to slip back into multiplicity; for matter as such tends to decompose itself. Insofar as we are individuals, each of us is a fragment of a species, a part of this universe, a single dot in the immense network of forces and influences, cosmic, ethnic, historic, whose laws we obey.

---

1.　With spiritual beings, as Angels, it is not the same; their individuality is rooted not in matter (they have no matter) but in their form itself, that is to say their essence (which is pure form); each Angel being his own specific nature and differing from another Angel as the lion differs from man and from the oak. They are individuals, they are not individualized. God is at the summit of individuality, but He is not individualized. In Him, individuality and personality are one and the same, as all His perfections. In Angels as in man, the proper root of personality is not the essence itself, but a metaphysical achievement of the essence, thanks to which the essence is sealed in itself, and facing existence as a whole able to possess itself and give itself. In this essay, we consider only the individuality of corporeal beings (inanimate and animate), that is to say, individuality insofar as it involves individualization (*individuatio*).

[The present chapter was completed when, on my return to France, I read a recent publication of Father Pedro Descoqs (*Individu et Personne*, Archives de Philosophie, XIV, 2), wherein the distinction between individuality (individualization) and personality is sharply criticized. I have already noted that this distinction is difficult to make; naturally, some people have used it in very bad and inadequate formulas. Is it not sufficient to point out the great amount of nonsense which Father Descoqs gratuitously attributes to the doctrine he criticizes? Having previously written a book in order to show that he does not correctly understand the doctrine of matter and form, he now has no difficulty in showing that he does not correctly understand the doctrine of individuality and personality.]

We are subject to the determination of the physical world. But each man is also a person and, insofar as he is a person, he is not subject to the stars and atoms; for he subsists entirely with the very subsistence of his spiritual soul, and the latter is in him a principle of creative unity, of independence and of freedom.

✦

I have spoken briefly of *individuality*. Now *personality* is an even deeper mystery, whose profound significance it is still more difficult to discover. In order to embark upon the philosophical discovery of personality, the best way is to consider the relation between personality and love.

Pascal said: "On n'aime jamais personne, mais seulement des qualités. One never loves anybody, one only loves qualities." This is a false assertion. It reveals in Pascal himself the traces of that very rationalism which he fought against. Love does not aim at qualities, one does not love qualities. What I love is the deepest reality, the most substantial, hidden, *existing* reality in the beloved—a metaphysical center, deeper than all qualities and essences which I can discover and enumerate in the beloved. That is why such enumerations pour endlessly from the lover's mouth.

Love aims at this center, without separating it from the qualities—in fact, merging into one with them. This center is in some way inexhaustibly a source of existence, of goodness and of action, capable of giving and of *giving itself*—and capable of receiving not only this or that gift from another, but another self as gift and giver.

Thus, through considering the very law of love, we are introduced to the metaphysical problem of the person. Love does not aim at qualities, or at natures, or at essences, but at persons.

"Thou art thyself though," says Juliet to Romeo, "not a Montague.... Romeo, doff thy name; and for that name, which is not part of thee, take all myself.'

In order to be able to *give oneself*, one must first exist, and not only as the sound which passes in the air, or this idea which crosses my mind, but as a thing which subsists and which by itself exercises existence. And one must not only exist as other things, one must exist in an eminent way, by possessing oneself by holding oneself in hand and by disposing of oneself; that is, one must exist through a spiritual existence, capable of enveloping itself by intelligence and freedom, and of *super-existing* in knowledge and free love. That is why the Western metaphysical tradition defines the person by independence: the person is a reality, which, subsisting spiritually, constitutes a universe by itself and an independent whole (relatively independent), in the great whole of the universe and facing the transcendent Whole, which is God. And that is why this philosophical tradition sees in God the sovereign personality, since God's existence consists itself in a pure and absolute super-existence of intellection and love. The notion of personality does not refer to matter, as does the notion of individuality applied to corporeal things. It refers to the highest and deepest dimensions of being; personality is rooted in the spirit, insofar as the latter stands by itself in existence and super-abounds in it. Metaphysically considered, personality, being in one's substance a signature or a seal enabling one freely to perfect and freely to give this substance, evidences in each of us that expansiveness of being which, in a corpore-al-spiritual being, is linked to the spirit, and which constitutes, in the secret depths of our ontological structure, a source of dynamic unity and of inner unification.

Thus, personality means interiority to oneself. But precisely because it is the spirit which—in a manner unknown

to the plant and animal—makes man cross the threshold of
independence, properly speaking, and of interiority to oneself, consequently the subjectivity of the person has nothing
in common with the unity without doors and windows of the
Leibnitzian monad; it demands the communications of intelligence and love. Because of the very fact that I am a person
and that I express myself to myself, I seek to communicate
with *that which is other* and with *others*, in the order of knowledge
and love. It is essential to personality to ask for a dialogue, and
for a dialogue wherein I really give myself, and wherein I am
really received. Is such a dialogue actually possible? That is
why personality seems to be linked in man to the experience
of suffering even more deeply than to that of creative conflict.
The entire person is relative to the absolute, in which alone
it can find its fulfillment. Its spiritual fatherland is the whole
order of goods having an absolute value, and which serve as
an introduction to the absolute Whole, which transcends the
world. Finally, the human person not only bears to God the
common resemblance born by other creatures; it resembles
Him in a proper and peculiar fashion. It is the image of God.
For God is spirit, and the person proceeds from Him, having
as its principle of life a spiritual soul, a spirit capable of knowing and loving, and of being elevated by grace to participate
in the very life of God, so as to finally love Him and know
Him even as He knows and loves Himself.

Such are, if I have succeeded in describing them correctly,
the two metaphysical aspects of the human being: individuality and personality, each with their own ontological physi-
ognomy. Let us note, that we do not represent two separate
things. There is not in me one reality called my individuality
and another called my personality. It is the same entire being

which, in one sense, is an individual and, in another sense, a person. I am wholly an individual, by reason of what I receive from matter, and I am wholly a person, by reason of what I receive from spirit: just as a painting is in its entirety a physicochemical complex, by reason of the coloring materials out of which it is made, and a work of beauty, by reason of the painter's art.

Let us note, moreover, that material individuality is not something bad in itself. No, it is something good, since it is the very condition of our existence. But it is precisely in relation to personality that individuality is good; what is bad is to let this aspect of our being predominate in our actions. No doubt, each of my acts is an act of myself-the-individual, and an act of myself-the-person. But even as it is free and engages my whole self, each of my acts is drawn *either* into the movement which tends to the supreme center toward which personality strives, or into the movement which tends toward dispersion, to which, if left to itself, material individuality is bound to fall back.

Now it is important to observe that man must complete, through his own will, what is sketched in his nature. According to a commonplace expression, which is a very profound one, man must become what he is. In the moral order, he must win, by himself, his freedom and his personality. In other words, his action can follow either the slope of personality or the slope of individuality. If the development of the human being follows the direction of *material individuality*, he will be carried in the direction of the "hateful ego," whose law is to snatch, to absorb for oneself. In this case, personality as such will tend to adulterate, to dissolve. If, on the contrary, the development follows the direction of *spiritual personality*, then it will be in the direction of the generous self of saints and heroes that man will be carried. Man will really be a person, insofar as the life of spirit and freedom will dominate in him that of passion and of the senses.

Here we stand before the crucial problem of the education of the human being. Certain educators confuse person and individual; in order to grant personality the development and the freedom of expansion to which it aspires, they refuse all asceticism, they want man to yield fruit without being pruned. They think that the happiness of man consists in that joyous smile which is seen, in the advertisements, on the faces of boys and girls relishing a good cigarette or a glass of Coca-Cola. Instead of fulfilling himself, man disperses and disassociates himself. The heart atrophies itself and the senses are exasperated. Or, in other cases, what is most human in man falls back into a kind of vacuity, which is covered by frivolity.

And there are other educators and rulers who misunderstand the distinction of person and individual. They mistake it for a separation. They think that we bear in ourselves two separate beings, that of the individual and that of the person. And, according to these educators: *Death to the individual! Long live the person!* Unfortunately, when one kills the individual, one also kills the person. The despotic conception of the progress of the human being is not better than the anarchic one. The ideal of this despotic conception is first to take out our heart, with anaesthetics if possible, and next to replace it by the heart of an angel. The second operation is more difficult than the first one, and is but rarely successful. Instead of the authentic person, imprinted with the mysterious face of the Creator, there appears a mask, the austere mask of the Pharisee.

In reality, what is especially important for the education and the progress of the human being, in the moral and spiritual order (as well as in the order of organic growth), is the interior principle, that is to say, nature and grace. The right educational means are but auxiliaries; the art, a co-operating art, at the service of this interior principle. And the entire art consists in cutting off and in pruning—both in the case of the person, and of the individual—so that, in the intimacy of our being, the weight of individuality should diminish, and that of real personality and of its generosity, should increase. And this, indeed, is far from easy.

## II. *Applications to Social Matters*

Before undertaking the second part of this essay, I wanted to say these few words concerning the moral development of the person. Let us now approach the problems which concern society and its relation to the person.

We have noted, in discussing the typical character of the person, that it is essential for personality to tend toward communion. We must insist on this point which is often forgotten: the person, by virtue of his dignity, as well as of his needs, requires to be a member of a society. Animal societies are improperly called societies or cities. Society, properly speaking—human society—is a society of persons. Insofar as a city deserves this name, it is a city of human persons.

And why does the person demand for himself life in society? He demands this, first, by virtue of the very *perfections* which are inherent in him, and because of the fact of this being open to the communications of knowledge and of love, of which I have spoken, and which require an entrance into relation with other persons.

Taken in the aspect of its radical generosity, the human person tends to super-abound in social communications, according to the law of super-abundance which is inscribed in the very depths of being, of life, of intelligence, of love.

And, secondly, it is because of his needs that the human person demands this life in society. Taken in the aspect of his indigences, he demands to be integrated to a body of social communications, without which it is impossible for him to attain to his full life and achievement.

Society thus appears as furnishing the person with the conditions of existence and development which he definitely needs. The human person cannot achieve his fullness alone, but only through receiving certain goods essential to him from society.

I do not mean only material needs, of bread, of clothes and lodging, for all of which man depends upon the aid of his fellows; but also, and first of all, the need of their aid in acting according to reason and virtue, which corresponds to the specific character of the human being. In order to attain to a certain degree of elevation in knowledge and perfection of moral life, man needs the education and the aid granted by his fellows. It is in this sense that one must give a very strict meaning to the words of Aristotle, that man is naturally a political animal. He is a political animal because he is a reasonable animal, because his reason seeks to develop with the help of education, through the teaching and the co-operation of other men, and because society is thus required to accomplish human dignity.

Yet we must not say that the aim of society is the individual good (or the mere collection of individual goods) of each person who constitutes it! This formula would dissolve society *as such* for the benefit of its parts, and would lead to the "anarchy of atoms." It would mean either a frankly anarchic conception or the old disguised anarchic conception of individualistic liberalism—according to which the entire duty of society consists in seeing that the freedom of each should be respected, though this permit the strong freely to oppress the feeble.

The end of society is its *common good*, the good of the body politic. But if one fails to grasp the fact that the good of the body politic is a common good of *human persons*—as the social body itself is a whole made up of human persons—this formula may lead in its turn to other errors of the collectivist or totalitarian type. The common good of society is neither a simple collection of private goods, nor a good belonging to a whole which (as in the case of the species in relation to its individual members) draws the parts to itself, as if they were pure means to serve itself alone. The common good is the *good human life* of the multitude, of a multitude of *persons*; it is their communion in the good life; it is therefore common *to the whole and to the parts*, on whom it flows back and who must all benefit from it. Under pain of being itself denatured, such a good implies and demands the recognition of the fundamental rights of the person (and of the rights of the family, in which the persons are engaged in a more primitive mode of communal living than in political society). It involves, as its chief value, the highest possible accession (an accession compatible with the good of the whole) of persons to their life as persons, and to their freedom of expansion, as well as to the communications of goodness which in turn proceed from it.

The end of the state is the common good, which is not only a collection of advantages and utilities, but also rectitude of life, an end good in itself, which the old philosophers called *bonum honestum*, the intrinsically worthy good. For, on one hand, it is a thing good in itself to insure the existence of the multitude. And, on the other hand, it is the just and morally good existence of the community which may thus be insured. It is only on this condition, of being in accordance with justice and with moral good, that the common good is what it is: the good of a people, the good of a city, and not the "good" of an association of gangsters or of murderers. That is why perfidy, the contempt of treaties and of sworn faith, political murder or unjust war—all these can be *useful* to a government, and procure, if only for a time, *advantages* to the peoples who have recourse to them; but they debase and destroy, as far as in them lies, the *common good* of these peoples.

The common good is a thing ethically good. And this common good itself includes, as an essential element, the greatest possible development of human persons, of those persons who form the multitude, united, in order to constitute a community, according to relations not only of power, but also of justice. Historical conditions, and the present inferior state of humanity's development, make it difficult for social life fully to attain its end. But the end toward which it tends, as is shown in another chapter,[2] is to procure to the multitude the common good in such a fashion that the concrete person gains a real independence regarding nature, which is insured through the economic guaranties of labor and of property, through political rights, the civil virtues, and culture of the mind.

I have insisted upon the sociability of the person and on the properly human nature of the common good, which is a good according to justice, which must flow back to the persons, and whose chief value is the accession of persons to their freedom of expansion.

But I have not yet entered into what one might call the typical paradox of social life. Here we shall find once more

2.    Chapter V: *The Thomist Idea of Freedom.*

the distinction between individual and person. For this paradox is linked to the fact that each of us is altogether an individual and altogether a person.

The person, as such, is a whole—a whole open and generous. Truly speaking, if human society were a society of pure
persons, the good of society and the good of each person
would be one and the same good. But man is very far from
being a pure person. The human person is an unfortunate
material individual, an animal who is born in an infinitely
more depraved state than all the other animals. If the person,
as such, is an independent whole, and that which is noblest
in all of nature, yet the human person is placed at the lowest
degree of personality. He is destitute and miserable—an indi-
gent person, full of needs. Because of these profound indigences—deriving from the matter of which man is made and
from material individuality—and because of the limitations
of his perfection itself, which also, in another way, derive from
material individuality, it so happens that, when such a person
enters into the society of his fellows, he becomes a *part* of a
whole, a whole which is larger and better than its parts, insofar as they are parts. According, not to his entire self, but to all
the complements which he receives from society, and without
which he would remain, so to speak, in a state of latent life,
the human person is part of a larger whole, a whole which
surpasses the person insofar as the latter is a *part*, and insofar
as the common good is other than the good of each (and than
the sum of the good of each). And yet, it is by reason of personality, as such, and of the perfections which it involves as an
independent and open *whole*, that man must enter into society; so that it is necessary for the good of the social whole, as
I have said, to flow back in a way to the person of each of its
members. It is the *human person* which enters into society. And
insofar as he is a *material individuality*, he enters into society as

a part whose good is inferior to the good of the whole; nevertheless, this good itself of the whole, in order to be what it is—that is to say, superior to the private good—must necessarily profit individual persons and be redistributed to them, in respect of their rights and their dignity. Because, finally speaking, society, being a whole of persons, is a *whole* of *wholes*.

On the other hand, by reason of his destination to the absolute, and because he is called upon to fulfill a destiny superior to time—in other words, according to the highest exigencies of personality as such—the human person, as spiritual totality, referring to the transcendent Whole, *surpasses* all temporal societies and is superior to them. And from this point of view—in other words, as regards the things that are not Caesar's—it is to the perfect achievement of the person and of its supra-temporal aspirations, that society itself and its common good are subordinated, as to the end of *another* order, which transcends them.

A single human soul is of more worth than the whole universe of bodies and material goods. There is nothing above the human soul—except God. In regard to the eternal destiny of the soul, and its supra-temporal goods, society exists for each person and is subordinated to it.

It is thus in the nature of things that man sacrifices his temporal goods, and if necessary his life itself, for the sake of the community, and that social life imposes upon the life of the person, taken as part of the whole, many a constraint and many a sacrifice. But even as these sacrifices and constraints are demanded and accepted by justice and by friendship, even so they raise the spiritual level of the person. When man gives

his life for the community's sake, he accomplishes, through
an act of such great virtue, the moral perfection by which
the person asserts his supreme independence as regards the
world. By losing himself temporally for the city's sake, the
person sacrifices himself in the truest and most complete fashion, and yet does not lose the stakes; the city serves him even
then, for the soul of man is not mortal, and there is an eternal
life.

In brief, while the person as such is a *totality*, the individual as such is a *part*; while the person, as person or as totality,
demands that the common good of temporal society should
flow back to him, and while through his ordination to the
transcendent whole, he even surpasses the temporal society,
the same person, as an individual or as part, is inferior to the
social whole, and must serve the common cause as a member
of the whole.

We thus perceive the state of tension and of conflict,
which human society inevitably involves. Social life is naturally
ordained—in the measure in which I have tried to define—to
the good and to the freedom of the person. And yet there is
in this very social life a natural tendency to enslave the person
and to diminish him, insofar as this person is considered by
society as a simple part and as a simple material individual.
"Every time I have been amongst men," said Seneca, "I have
returned a diminished man."

The person—so far as a person—wishes to serve the
common good freely, by tending at the same time toward its
own plenitude, by surpassing himself and by surpassing the
community, in his proper movement toward the transcendent Whole. And, insofar as he is a material individuality, the
person is obliged to serve the community and the common

good by necessity, and even by constraint, being surpassed, by
them, as the part by the whole.

This paradox, this tension and conflict, are something natural and inevitable. Their solution is not static, it is dynamic,
*in motu*. For thus is provoked a double motion, surely a deeper
one than the dialectic motion of the Marxists. The first of
these motions is a movement of progression of temporal societies, which operates above all through the energies of spirit
and freedom, and which is continuously thwarted by forces of
inertia and degradation: this movement tends to bring the law
of personality to prevail over the law of individuality in social
life. In other words, it tends toward the realization of man's
aspiration to be treated, in social life itself, as a whole and
not as a part. Such a formula offers to us a very abstract but
correct definition of the supreme ideal toward which modern
democracies are aspiring, and which has been betrayed by a
false philosophy of life. This ideal is to be completely achieved
only at the end of human history; it requires the climate of a
heroic conception of life, fixed on the absolute and upon spiritual values. It can be progressively realized only by means of
the development of a sacred feeling, as it were, for justice and
honor, and by the development of law and of civic friendship. For justice and law, by ruling man as a moral agent, and
appealing to reason and free will, concern personality as such,
and transform into a relation between two wholes—the individual and the social—what must otherwise be a mere subordination of the part to the whole. And love, by assuming
voluntarily that which would have been servitude, transfigures
it into freedom and into free gift.

The second motion is a motion which one might call vertical, the motion of the life of persons themselves inside social
life. It is due to the difference of level between the plane on
which the person has the center of its life as person, and the

low-water mark, where it constitutes itself as a part of a social community. By reason of this difference of level, the person always claims society and yet tends to surpass it.

✦

But let us return to the complex relations of structure which we have tried to characterize. One could, it seems, apply the following formulas.

The human person is a *part* of the political community and is inferior to the latter, according to the things which compensate in him the needs of material individuality: that is to say, according to the things which, in him and of him, depend as to their very essence on the political community, and can be called upon to serve as means for the temporal good of this community. Thus, for instance, a mathematician has learned mathematics thanks to the educational institutions which social life alone has made possible; this progressive formation, received from others, and attesting the needs of the individual, depends on the community. And the community is entitled to ask the mathematician to serve the social group by teaching mathematics.

And, on the other hand, the human person, as a superior *whole*, dominates the political community according to the things which belong to the ordination of personality as such to the absolute: that is to say, according to the things which, in him and of him, depend as to their very essence on something higher than political community, and properly concern the supra-temporal achievement of the person as person. Thus, for instance, mathematical truths do not depend on social community, and concern the order of absolute goods of the person as such. And the community will never have the right to ask a mathematician to *hold as true* one mathematical system in preference to another one, and to teach such mathematics as may be considered more suitable to the law of the social group; for example, and to speak madly, *Aryan* mathematics or *Marxist-Leninist* mathematics.

Man is constituted as person, made for God and for eternal life, before being constituted part of a human community; and he is constituted part of familial society before being constituted part of political society. Hence, there are primordial rights, which the latter must respect, and which it dare not wrong when it demands for itself the aid of its members because they are its parts.

To sum up: on one hand, it is the person itself, which enters into society; and, on the other hand, it is finally by reason of its material individuality that the person is in society as a part, whose good is inferior to the good of the whole. If this is the case, we understand that society cannot live without the perpetual gift and the perpetual surplus which derive from persons, each *irreplaceable* and incommunicable; and that, at the same time, what in social use is retained from the persons is transmuted into something communicable and *replaceable*, into something ever individualized and yet depersonalized.

We could also say that society—its life, its peace—cannot exist without the efficient causality of love, which is essentially personal, and yet the formal structure of society is constituted by justice, which is essentially measured according to things, and merits, without respect for persons.

### III. *Democracy of the Individual and Democracy of the Person*

Now let us briefly turn our attention to the materialist philosophies, the materialist conceptions of the world and of life. And let us ask ourselves what happens to the person according to these views. We must not forget, however, that when one deals with a philosophy, there are three things which should be distinguished regarding it. First, the values of sentiment, which exercise a seduction over the minds of its followers, and the simple human aspirations which the latter actually obey, perhaps even without knowing it. Second, what this philosophy *says*. Third, what it *does*, and the results to which it leads.

We shall then observe that the materialist philosophies of man and of society, are subject *in spite of themselves*—I mean because of the actual aspirations of their followers who are men—to the attraction of the proper values and the proper goods of personality, which they desire obscurely even when they ignore them. Hence, in practice, these doctrines can act upon men, only through invoking justice, liberty, the goods of the person.

But what do they perceive, what are they capable of perceiving and of saying, insofar as they are doctrines? Recognizing only that which belongs to the world of matter, blind to the realities of spirit, they perceive in man only the shadow of real personality—the material individuality. And of man they can only tell us this much. Thus, what they do, the result to which in fact they lead, is to deteriorate, to vilify and to enslave the person, either by dissolving it in anarchy, or, as inevitably happens under the natural necessities of political life, by submitting it entirely to the social body as Number, as Economic Community, or as State.

I can only indicate briefly the criticisms to which we should submit the materialist philosophy of society, considered under its three chief forms: bourgeois individualism, communist anti-individualism; and the combined anti-individualism and anti-communism of the dictatorial or totalitarian type.

These three doctrines equally ignore the *human person*, and are reduced to considering instead the *material individual* alone.

As one has often observed, bourgeois liberalism, whose pretension it is to base everything on the individual considered as a little god, and on his caprice, on the absolute liberty of property, of commerce and of the pleasures of life—this liberalism inevitably ends in étatisme, the hypertrophy and absolute primacy of the State.

The rule of numbers produces the omnipotence of the State—a State of the ruminant or plutocratic type. If, in fact, one wants to build up a city, with individuals free *in this sense* that their first duty is *to obey only themselves*—it will be possible only upon condition that each one relinquishes his own will to the General Will. Man, considered in his material individuality, being only a part and not a whole, the individual will finally find himself entirely subjected to the social whole by the mechanical connections which insure his junction with it. No doubt, his freedom will remain full and complete, but in an illusory mode and in the world of dreams. Or else he will anarchically refuse the conditions of social life, and there will be the insurrection of the parts against the whole, mentioned by Auguste Comte.

Communism can be regarded as a reaction against this individualism. Its pretension is to aim at the absolute liberation of man, who will become the god of history. But, in reality, this liberation, supposing it were achieved, would be the liberation of collective man, and not of the human person. And even supposing that the *political* State were finally abolished, Society, as an *economic* community, would in turn subjugate the entire life of the person. Why? Because the reality of the person as such has been ignored from the very beginning and, with it, the very function of civil society—to procure a common good essentially human, whose chief value is the freedom of expansion of persons, with all the guaranties this entails. Under the pretext of replacing the government of men by the administration of things one transforms this administration of things—that is, economic functions of production and distribution—into the *chief* work of civil society. But, according to the nature of things, the work of civil society mobilizes for itself the human life of persons, and therefore this life, being no longer mobilized for a common work whose chief aim is the freedom of expansion of persons—but only for the economic output—will find itself inevitably referred in its entirety to this output and to the society which procures it.

As to the anti-communist and anti-individualist reactions of the totalitarian or dictatorial type, it is not in the name of the social community and of the freedom of collective man, but rather in the name of the sovereign dignity of the State or in the name of the spirit of a people, the *Volksgeist*, or in the name of race and of blood, that they seek to annex the entire man to a social whole, composed of a multitude of material individualities, and not of genuine persons. And it is in the person of a master—the only person in political life who remains facing a regimented world of material individualities—and, as it were, absorbed in the unique person of this master, that the multitude will become conscious of itself and will realize its almightiness.

In all three cases, we behold the conflict of the whole with the parts, of social life with man, considered as material individuality. That which is inherent in the human person as person, and that which is inherent in society as a community of persons, have equally disappeared.

Let me add that we seem to witness today a sort of tragedy of these three opposite forms of social and political materialism. The tragedy of bourgeois individualism appears but too clearly in the crisis of morality of our Western civilization and in the disastrous spasms of liberal and capitalist economy.

The tragedy of communism is above all manifest in the interior failure to which its first realizations have led of themselves in Russia, and in the inner conflicts which it cannot help engendering. The successive waves of terrorism in the Soviet Republics have, from this point of view, an extraordinary significance for the philosopher: communism, which is a sort of economic theocracy, requires an extremely rigorous and tense discipline. But it can only seek this discipline through *external methods* of pedagogy and constraint. Now, without some sort of *interior* ethics, implying and respecting the aspirations of the soul and of the person, without a vivid faith which communicates its fervor to the minds of people, no strong social discipline is really possible. And thus is inevitable the internal conflict between an anarchy of passions, ambitions, individual energies, employing no matter what means—an anarchy continually reborn—and an "order" which ignores the very principle of order.

Finally, the tragedy of totalitarian States seems to us especially manifest in the fact that, requiring for themselves the total devotion of the person, yet having no respect for the person and its inner reserves, they fatally seek a principle of human exaltation in the myths of external greatness; in an effort toward prestige and external power, never to be achieved. And this inevitably leads to war and to the self-destruction of the civilized community.

Thus, materialistic conceptions of life and of the world—philosophies which do not recognize in man the eternal, the spiritual element—are incapable of guiding man in the building up of a society, because these philosophies are incapable of respecting the exigencies of the person, and this means that they cannot understand the nature of society.

If this spiritual, this eternal element, is recognized, then one also recognizes the aspiration immanent in the person to surpass, by reason of what is highest in it, both the life and the conditions of temporal societies. But then, and at the same time, temporal society can be built up according to the proper order of its being. Its nature as a society of persons is understood, and the natural tendency of the person toward society, and the fact of its belonging morally and legally to the society of which it is part, are equally understood.

This means, definitely speaking, that the relation of the individual to society must not be conceived according to the atomistic and mechanistic type of bourgeois individualism, which suppresses the social organic totality; neither must it be conceived according to the biological and animal type, characteristic of the communist and totalitarian doctrines, which engulf the person, as a histological element of Behemoth or of Leviathan, in the body of the social community or of the State, and which enslave it to the work of this totality. The relation of the individual to society must be conceived according to type irreducibly human and specifically ethico-social—that is, both personalist and communal—and this will then mean an *organization of freedoms*. Now this is strictly inconceivable without those *moral* realities which are called *justice* and *civic friendship*, the latter being a natural and temporal correspondence of that which, in the spiritual and supernatural plane, the Gospel calls brotherly love.

It thus appears that the most excellent common work toward which, as toward a heroic ideal, the city of our desires must tend is the arduous instauration of this friendship between brothers in labor and hope of the earthly community, which is not granted ready-made by nature, but which can be achieved by virtue.

Here we find once more the considerations which we have expressed earlier concerning the way in which (through a movement of progression which will never find its terms on earth) is solved what we have called the paradox of social life. There is a common work to be accomplished by the social whole as such, by that whole of which human persons are parts, and which is not "neutral," which is itself engaged, held by a temporal calling. And thus the persons are *subordinated to this common work.* And yet, not only in the temporal order itself, is it essential for the common good to flow back to the persons; but in addition, with regard to an altogether different order, concerning what is deepest in the person, his eternal calling, with the goods attached to this calling—there is in each human person a transcendent end, *to which society itself and its common work is subordinated.*

Do not forget that society's common work itself has its chief value in the freedom of personal expansion, with the guaranties it involves and with the diffusion of goodness which proceeds from it. Because the temporal common good is a common good of human persons, it happens, by the grace of justice and friendship, that through subordinating himself to the common work, each one still subordinates himself to the good of persons—that is, to the accomplishment of the personal life of *others*—and at the same time to the interior dignity of his own person. But this solution can acquire a practical value only if the real nature of common work is recognized, and if at the same time there is recognized, as Aristotle taught, the political value and importance of the virtue of *friendship.*

It is difficult not to think that the temporal advent of such a city of persons would come as a consequence and an earthly effectuation of this consciousness of the dignity of the human person and his eternal calling in every man whomsoever, which has forever penetrated, through the Gospel, into the heart of humanity.

Democracy inspired by Rousseau, which is now threatened in the world, suffers from a philosophy of life which

attempted an illusory naturalization or secularization of evangelical truths. Rather, is not human history laboring to achieve
another sort of democracy, which would be an *evangelization
of nature?*

In his book on *Two Sources of Morality and Religion,* M.
Bergson emphasized the originally religious character of the
democratic ideal; in a formula charged with sense (and even
with opposite senses), he writes that one must perceive "in
the democratic state of mind a great effort whose direction is
inverse to that of nature."

This can mean that it is an effort finally *contrary to nature;*
which, to my mind, exactly qualifies *false democracy,* such
as bourgeois individualism originating from Jean-Jacques
Rousseau's conceptions, and which bases everything on the
native goodness and native freedom of the *individual*—a fictitious individual, shut up in himself. But it can also mean
a properly human effort to *redress* nature, an effort which is
linked to the developments of reason and of justice, and
which is to be achieved in humanity under the influence of
the Christian leaven; an effort demanding that human nature
should be super-elevated in its proper order, in the order
of the movement of civilization, through the action of this
Christian ferment. And I think this is true of *genuine democracy,* of organic democracy, ordained to the human expansion
of concrete and open persons. It is such a democracy, to the
preparation for which a well-founded philosophy of history
and of society invites us to labor.

Democracy of the individual and humanism of the individual arise from an anthropocentric inspiration. Materialism,
atheism, dictatorship, are their fatalities. By saying to men,
you are gods by your own essence and will, they have debased
men. Practically they have left to men no other internal weight
than flat egoism and longing for material possessions.

Democracy of the person and humanism of the person spring forth from a theocentric inspiration. Conquest of freedom in the social and political, as well as the spiritual order, is their aim—I mean freedom of expansion, exultation, and autonomy, so far as it conforms to the image of God. They say to men: you are gods by the gifts and the calling of God, gods in becoming and in suffering and in hope; gods by means of humility, virtue, and grace. Their weight in men is the weight of love. They dignify the creature really—in God and as made by God and for God; not illusively—as a god itself. They know the grandeur of man, and they know his misery. They respect human dignity, not as something abstract, timeless and non-existent, ignoring historic conditions and historic diversities and devouring men pitilessly. They respect human dignity in each concrete, and existing person, in its flesh and blood and in its historical context of life.

It is to the democracy of the person that one must apply, I think, and not without certain comments, the thought of M, Bergson when he writes that at the extreme limit one might say, "democracy is evangelic in its essence, and that its motive power is love."

I do not mean, in quoting this formula of M. Bergson, to link religion and the Gospel to any form of government whatsoever. The Christian religion is not enslaved to any temporal regime. It is compatible with all forms of legitimate government. It is not its business to determine which one of them must be adopted by men *hic et nunc*. It imposes none of them upon their preference. Neither does it impose—so long as certain superior principles are safeguarded—a particular philosophy. In contrast with individualist democracy, inspired by Rousseau, certain implications of which (as, for instance, the idea that law holds its force from the Number and not from justice) cannot be reconciled with Christian principles, I am convinced that there is nothing in personalist democracy which is not in accordance with the common doctrine of the Catholic Church. Both Rousseauist and personalist conceptions are very general conceptions of political life, reconcilable to a monarchic as well as to a strictly democratic form of government; but, contrary to the conception of Rousseau, the personalist conception of democracy is first of all determined by the idea of man as God's image, and by the idea of the common good, of human rights and of concrete liberty; and it is based on Christian humanism. I do not pretend at all, however, that personalist democracy may ever impose itself in the name of the Christian creed, no more than, in the speculative order, Thomist metaphysics can impose itself in the name of this creed.

But the relation which is noticed—I believe justly—by M. Bergson, between the Gospel and democracy, is not a relation of *right*, which would oblige us, in the name of Christian doctrine and of the Kingdom of God, to recognize a certain temporal conception and a certain social and political philosophy. It is a relation of *fact*, which concerns only—as in the question of slavery—the germinations naturally reduced in the depths of profane and temporal conscience itself under the influence of Christian leaven. It is from the historical and cultural point of view, from the point of view of the philosophy of history and culture, that things are here considered. Even under mixed and aberrant forms, and even in the Rousseauist tendency to naturize (and denaturize) the Gospel, is it not the Christian leaven that is still seen fermenting in the bosom of human history, while the unhappy adventure of the individualist democracy is unfolding itself? Under purer forms, and tending this time, as I have said before, to evangelize nature, is it not always, and more truly, the Christian leaven that is at work in history, preparing in it a personalist democracy?

In brief, the question is to know whether, in fact, in the historic development of humanity, a slow work is not being performed, a slow and spontaneous activation of the human mass and of profane conscience, tending to bring the temporal regime of men closer to an order, of which democracy of the individual was but a counterfeit, and which I call here democracy of the person. And the question is also to know whether this democracy of the person is not inconceivable without the super-elevation which nature and temporal civilizations receive, in their proper order, from the energies of Christian life.

These reflections induce me to think that the drama of modern democracies is to have sought, without knowing it, something good: the democracy of the person, disguised in an error, viz., the democracy of the individual, which leads by itself to serious failures. If democracies are still able to escape grave dangers, it is by turning themselves decisively in the direction of an essentially different type—the democracy of the person, discovered in its real significance. And this presupposes, truly speaking, something quite different from a simple weakening or a simple extenuation of the errors of the democracy of the individual; it means an internal transformation, a complete turnabout toward spirit.

Is not the tragedy of our age to be found in the fact that modern democracies have lost all confidence in themselves? Their vital principle is justice, and they do not want to run the risks of justice. They do not want, it seems, to run any risks whatsoever. They invoke justice, but they pursue purely utilitarian politics, and they pursue them inefficiently and clumsily.[3]

---

3.   This was written before the second European war. In the face of catastrophe, the Western Democracies have been compelled by the force of things to choose finally, and courageously, to struggle for justice, at the risk of unheard of sacrifices.

During the same period, totalitarian dictatorships, which put Machiavellian policies much better into practice, have the fullest confidence in their principle, which is barbaric force, and they risk everything thereon.

Modern democracies suffer from a philosophy of life which undermines and annihilates their vital principle from within. If they must refind the sense of justice, and of risk, and of heroism, it is under condition of rejecting their materialist philosophy, and of viewing in full light a personalist conception of life and of society.

To the unhuman humanism of the individual would thus succeed a new humanism—the integral humanism of the person, open to that which surpasses it and leads it to achievement, and open to the common service of justice and friendship.

# CHAPTER IV

## *Democracy & Authority*

### I. *Preliminaries*

I know not whether the question to be examined in this chapter presents itself to American opinion in the same way as it does to French opinion. On one hand, the crisis of political ideas is, as is well known, extremely acute in Europe, where democracies have to face both their own internal difficulties and the obstinate opposition of totalitarian propagandas; the latter imagine they offer a better principle without being aware that they are themselves but the fruit of the most morbid elements which affect modern democracies. On the other hand, the very word of democracy covers, in the historical concrete, extremely different realities.

In Europe, the Helvetic Democracy represents a very genuine democratic type, whose sources go as far back as the Christian Middle Ages. British Democracy rather appears— so it seems to me—as a singular combination of an aristocracy, whose hierarchies satisfy the people's pride and whose activity serves it, and of a plutocracy, whose appetites have coincided for a long time with the national interest. A vivid sense of personal freedom and of the importance of public opinion are linked in that country with an immense and admirable heritage of antique forms and structures, whose preservation is assured by a sort of plant-like perseverance. French Democracy conceptualizes and disguises in the consecrated formulas of an ideology, which corresponds above all to a ritual satisfaction of the mind, psychological and moral realities which have little relation to these formulas: I mean a deeply rooted sense, linked with the peasant's and artisan's life, of the freedom to judge, to criticize, to work according to all resources of personal ingenuity, and to economize in the same way; virtues of civilization, embodied in the very depths of popular life, which constitute a source, perhaps inexhaustible, of human energy, and which accommodate themselves quite well—maybe too well—with age-old negligences and most apparent disorders; and obstinate opposition against any eventual return to domination of social classes privileged in the past—an opposition inscribed in the very fibers of collective memory—which may become implacable, if it feels itself threatened, and whose natural political expression in such a case is Jacobinism. All these traits are combined, on one hand, with the cultural legacy of the oldest and most active Christian civilization and with the political heritage of the French monarchy and centralized State; and, on the other hand, with the internal logic of the democratic principle, taken in the very special and morbid form which we have inherited chiefly from Jean-Jacques Rousseau.

In the Democracy of the United States, I believe that the ideology of the eighteenth century and of Rousseau also plays a certain role, but much less than in France; yet the mental disposition to dislike any human hierarchy can be connected with this ideology. But, I think, it is the ideology of Locke rather than Rousseau which has predominated in the American case. Moreover, in America democracy is based on human realities, wherein the sense of individual freedom, of initiative, of trust in the chance of every man, are fundamental. To this profound democratic sense—nourished by the heroic memories of an epic which taught the world how peace can be established on a continent—corresponds a political constitution, usually recognized as an excellent type of Constitution. Its structure owes little to Rousseau, if I am to believe some Dominican friends of mine that this Constitution has rather some relation to ideas which presided in the Middle Ages at the constitution of St. Dominic's Order. When America criticizes herself, I suspect that she has to deal much less with the political structure of her democracy than with the practices of politicians, or with the social and spiritual evils inflicted either by modern capitalism or by the philosophical and religious disorder of our age.

I have begun with these preliminary remarks in order to notify the reader that my exposition will inevitably be set in the perspective of those historical debates with which I am most familiar: debates and conflicts of the old continent. Nevertheless, I shall not concern myself, even in these perspectives, with particular realizations, full of contingent circumstances. My point of view is rather a philosophical one, and I shall try, therefore, to disengage certain pure forms of the democratic principle, beginning with those I consider false, and ending with one I believe true. One could say of this true form of democracy what Lord Acton said once of the Whigs: "that not the devil, but St. Thomas Aquinas was the first Whig." Indeed, there is a delusive form of the democratic principle—that of Rousseau; and a true one—that based on the principles of St. Thomas.

I will not speak of democracy in general, but of the special problems concerning the relation between democracy and authority, and I will discuss authority in democracy from

the point of view of political functions (the government of
men). As to the question of authority and democracy from
the point of view of economic functions (the administration
of things), it would lead us to considerations of quite a different order, which concern rather the philosophy of labor and
the problem of servitude. These I shall not consider in this
essay.

✦

I will thus examine, from the point of view of philosophical principles considered in themselves, a subject which
awakens so many passions: democracy and authority. Need
I excuse myself? There is no question that it is philosophy
which this subject needs the most, but the philosophy of this
subject is far from easy.

Let us posit, first, two definitions. I shall mean by "authority" the *right* to direct and to command, to be listened to or
obeyed by others. And I shall mean by "power" the force,
which one can use, and with the aid of which one can oblige
others to listen or to obey. The righteous man, deprived of
all power and condemned to hemlock, does not diminish—
he increases—in moral authority. The gangster or the tyrant
exercises power without authority. There are institutions—the
Senate of Ancient Rome, the Supreme Court of the United
States—whose authority is the more manifest because these
institutions do not exercise determined functions in the field
of power.

This distinction between *auctoritas* and *potestas*—authority and power—must not be exaggerated into the sort of
systematic separation urged by certain German writers
who, for instance, grant the Church an *auctoritas* in temporal
things, when they involve values of eternal life, but refuse it
a corresponding *potestas*. All authority, insofar as it concerns

social life, demands to be completed (under some mode or other, which need not be juridical) by power, without which it threatens to become useless and inefficacious among men. All power which is not the expression of authority is iniquitous. Practically, it is normal that the word authority should imply power, and that the word power should imply authority. Insofar as it has power, authority descends into the physical order; insofar as it has authority, power is raised to the moral and legal order. To separate power and authority is to separate force and justice.

Nevertheless, what is of absolutely *primary* importance is authority. To "gain power" is important for him who wants to act on the community. To possess or acquire authority—the right to be followed by the minds and by the wills of other men (and consequently the right to exercise power)—is more important still.

## II. *Masked and Open Anarchic Democracy (Democracy of the Individual)*

Let us consider first the peculiar form which Rousseau gave to the democratic principle. Democracy, conceived in the manner of Rousseau, *suppresses authority and preserves power.* It is this type of Democracy which for almost two centuries now has prevailed in the ideology of Western peoples. One may call it liberal or bourgeois democracy, or masked anarchic democracy. Its root proper is in the following principle: since each individual, as Rousseau tells us, is "born free" (it is clear that each individual is born endowed with *free will,* but it is evidently not the latter which interests Rousseau; he is equivocal as to the word "free," and means a certain condition of existence, a *freedom of independence)*—since every individual is born free, his dignity demands that he should *obey only himself.* Naturally, as everything immediately gets out of

order, and as one must live all the same, and as, moreover, the
bourgeois class needs order so that it may prosper in business,
the dialectic of this democracy leads to the formula of the
*Social Contract*: "to find a form of association...through which
every man, united with all others, should nevertheless obey
only himself and remain as free as before." This formula inevitably leads to the myth of the General Will, in which the will
of each is mystically annihilated in order to arise transfigured;
to the myth of Law as the expression of Number, and not
of reason and justice; to the myth of authority considered,
not only as coming from the multitude, but as the proper and
inalienable attribute of the multitude; and, finally, this formula leads to totalitarian dictatorship.

To declare that authority resides in the whole multitude
as in its proper subject and without being able to emerge
from it and to exist in such or such responsible men—this is
a trick permitting irresponsible mechanisms to exercise *power*
over men, without having *authority* over them. Thus, power
(the power of the State) masks anarchy. But, as in every case
where nature is violated, such power tends to become infinite.
Concentrating all their attention on the question of the origin
of power, and reassured by the idea that in the democratic
regime the power of the State emanates from the people,
democracies of the Rousseauist type not only grant the State
all the usurpations of power, but they tend toward these very
usurpations. Proudhon admirably described and predicted
this process.[1] Moreover, the mass as such is by hypothesis the
subject proper of sovereignty and yet lacks political discern-
ment, except in quite simple and fundamental matters where
human instinct is surer than reason. This results in an original
equivocation, because those delegated by the multitude will

---

1.    *Principe fédératif*, pp. 96–97.

actually direct it, but only *as if* the multitude were directing
itself. Above all, the exercise of sovereignty under such conditions will require *myths*. Now, to dispense myths and collective
images, can anything be more useful than a dictatorship—a
dictatorship where the entire sovereign multitude is reab-
sorbed in the unique person of a half-god, sprung forth from
this multitude? Thus, through an inevitable dialectic, and
so long as a new fundamental principle has not been found,
democracies of the bourgeois liberal type tend to engender
their contrary, the totalitarian State.

The ruin of authority and of the principle of authority—to the benefit of power without authority, without the
foundations of justice and law and without the limit—is con-
summated in the totalitarian State. A great number of our
contemporaries complain with reason of the crisis of authority. Let them not be deceived by the outward appearances
of a tyrannical order: this crisis is at its maximum limit, or
rather it ends in complete dissolution, in the regimes of violence which call themselves "authoritarian democracies."
Ask the Austrians of 1938; ask the countless men, despoiled,
downtrodden, thrown into concentration camps, condemned
to abject humiliations, to slow death, to despair—ask them
what they think of the "community of the people," and of a
Power which carries to an absolute extreme its contempt for
the human person? Such totalitarianism is the ultimate fruit
of masked anarchic democracy.

The common conscience of the Party, being itself identified with the State, or with the Nation, or with the proletarian Jerusalem, and with their biological destiny, becomes
the supreme rule of good and evil, of truth and error. Thus,
from transmutation to transmutation, the Rousseauist principle ends, by way of an almost continuous series, in communist sociolatry, or through a reactive backward movement, in

totalitarian statolatry. It has, as its ultimate term, the complete disintegration of authority as a moral principle, to the benefit of the absolute of power as a constraining force. To the extent that anarchy devours the substance of authority, the mask of power becomes the only reality. These considerations explain why, in the European democracies, the process of abolition of the sense of authority, of the civic sense, however advanced it may be elsewhere, reaches its maximum in those circles of opinion and of the press which are in sympathy with totalitarian ideology—fascist or communist—and aspire to a dictatorship of violence. The American people have perhaps the opportunity of observing similar phenomena.

Here we face many paradoxes: dictatorial anti-democratism is both the fruit and the destruction of masked anarchic democracy. The hypocrisy which satisfied the old theoreticians of absolutism (to manage things in such a way that force should appear just), is thus replaced by an open contempt for justice and real authority, and by a pure exaltation of force and of power, without any authority other than itself. And the democratic state of mind which, by virtue of its most genuinely human sources (I do not here mean Rousseauism, I mean far deeper sources) aspires to place the whole of social and political life under the authority of justice and law, and which is linked to the respect and the love of the human person—the democratic state of mind seems to end and to dissolve in a perfect practical negation of justice and law, and of human dignity.

At the source of this paradox, there is no doubt a latent contradiction. Is it the tendency expressed in the middle of the nineteenth century by the French socialist Proudhon, is it democracy of the Proudhonian type which will solve this contradiction? I am thinking here of a democracy which, while *suppressing authority, would at the same time also suppress power* and

which one might call *openly anarchic*: all power and all authority exercised by man over man, and by the community over
its parts, being considered contrary to justice. I think that
this type of democracy, by virtue of its Utopian background,
played and still plays a major role in the socialist forms of the
labor movement, even those most remote from Proudhon. It is
summed up in the famous formula: "to substitute the administration of things for the government of men." Its root proper
is, to repeat the words of a French contemporary philosopher,
M. Gurvitch, the idea of "a non-hierarchic totality." Engels,
so much opposed to Proudhon in other questions, here seems
to agree with him, for he says that "the State will disappear at
the same time as the classes. A society which reorganizes production on the basis of the free association of all producers on
a footing of equality, will relegate the governmental machinery to the place where it belongs—the museum of antiquities,
together with the spinning wheel and the bronze axe."

However useful may be many of Proudhon's intuitions
and critiques, this idea of open democracy, which I am here
considering alone, must be regarded as a capital error. A totality without hierarchy—a whole without subordination of the
parte to the whole—such a supernatural marvel can only be
found in the Divine Trinity, in Uncreated Society, where the
Persons are precisely not parts.

The necessity of authority in the political community, as
the necessity of the State itself, is inscribed in the very nature
of things. The political community having, insofar as it is a
whole, its own reality, its own unity, and its own life, is by
this very fact superior to its parts as such, and demands a
hierarchic distribution of its organs; hence, furthermore, it
demands that certain of its parts should have as their proper
work those functions which concern the unity of the whole
and the direction of the common work and common life, and

that they should consequently possess an authority over the others. Moreover, since the common work and the common good of the multitude must be procured in a world of contingency and singularity, which is the world of existence and of history, the agreement of minds cannot there be simply achieved by virtue of objective causality (as in speculative matters, considering mathematical essences). It demands a practical direction proceeding from minds invested with a judgment and a command of operations. Even if all individuals possessed perfect reason and perfect rectitude of will, the unified conduct of social affairs would still require a political authority and a hierarchy. That is why St. Thomas Aquinas teaches that even in the state of Adamic integrity political authority would have had to exist in order to direct *free men* toward the good of the social community. The leader himself exists as such only for this good, and finally, is the latter's victim as well as its ordinator.

## III. *Organic Democracy (Democracy of the Person)*

The misfortune of democracy of the anarchic type (masked or openly anarchic) is that it has sought, without being always aware of it, a genuine good (the freedom of expansion of the real and open person), but has sought it under the form of an error: the deification of the fictitious individual, shut up in himself. The contradiction from which such democracy is dying has been precisely the fact that it was anarchic, that in principle it refused men the right to be obeyed by other men, while at the same time seeking political regulation, which in reality can exist only through an organization and, therefore, a hierarchy of freedoms. Now, such regulation entails ordination, the sort of commands which are issued to free men (that is to say, to men masters of their own life), and issued for the sake of a good common aim, the achievement of the work of the "whole of persons," of which these free men are parts.

More profoundly speaking, the internal contradiction of the delusive democracies, which I described, is to want to build up a work of justice and of law, of respect for the human person, and of civic friendship; and, at the same time, to refuse in this work all traces of transcendence of the supreme foundation of justice and personality; in short, to wish to be surpassingly human, and also practically atheistic.

It would be unworthy of man to renounce aspiring to a regime surpassingly human; what he should renounce is atheism. In brief, there is a democracy other than the democracy conceived according to Rousseau or to Proudhon. It is, to my mind, the true substance on which the Rousseauist and Proudhonian ideologies have lived as parasites. It is toward this *other* democracy, the Democracy of the Person, that the ascending movement of history tends, and for the sake of which so many brave men have given their lives. It would be a disastrous folly to reject this other democracy—communal and personalist—in a blind reaction against the errors of the nineteenth century, and because of the confusion with anarchic-individualist democracy.

This organic democracy does not suppress, even in principle, either authority or power. It wishes both to come from the people and to be exercised in its name. At its root we find the idea that man is not "born free" (independent), but must conquer freedom, and that in the State—a hierarchic totality of persons—men must be governed as persons, not as things; and toward a common good truly human, which flows back to the persons, and whose chief value is the latter's freedom of expansion. Naturally, democracy thus understood is a concrete historic ideal, which still needs many centuries of human education before it will take on all its dimensions in history. But this tendency is precisely in line with a rational nature's aspirations toward its perfect accomplishment.

As I have pointed out in the preceding chapter, I consider such a democracy inconceivable without the super-elevation which nature and temporal civilizations receive, in their proper order, from the energies of the Christian leaven. Does not M. Bergson tell us, in a formula which has been quoted above, and which should be correctly interpreted, that democracy is "evangelic in its essence"?

Joseph de Maistre wrote, on the other hand: "Man, in general, if reduced to himself, is too wicked to be free.... The world, until the time of Christianity, has always been full of slaves, and the sages never condemned this institution... Government alone cannot govern... It needs either slavery which reduces the number of acting wills in the State, or divine force which, through a kind of spiritual *graft*, destroys the natural harshness of these wills and permits them to act in common without hurting each other." Thus, the tendency toward atheism, inherent in democracy of the anarchic type, appears as one of the absurdities through which the latter destroys itself; while, in the political order, as I have observed, its internal dialectic carries it, by virtue of this very same absurdity, toward dictatorship which is its own negation.

An organic democracy will not efface from its ideology the notion of authority. It will, on the contrary, make it evident, because it will admit the following double truth of common sense: first to obey, according to the just measure by virtue of which such a right is exercised in such a case—to obey him who really has the right to direct action—is in itself an act of reason and of freedom; and second, to thus obey him, who really fulfills the duty to direct the common work toward the

SCHOLASTICISM AND POLITICS

common good (as in a game of football or hockey a player obeys his captain) is to act as a freeman—as a man who is not in the service of another man (nor in the service of a monster, where the State and political power outrun their nature and reduce everything, not to the common good, but to their own good, resulting in the enslavement of men to the State-Idol— which is essentially *anti-political*).

But such an organic democracy will also understand that the power of constraint—that power to which nowadays everything is monstrously reduced, and which is extended to the very heart of peoples through the poisoning process of Propaganda, of Pedagogy, and of the lies of the State-Idols— that the power of constraint is not the substance of authority. It is only an attribute, which authority needs to complete itself in order to be efficacious among men, especially as regards children, or the vicious and obstinate. Organic democracy will understand, moreover, that if the vicious and obstinate are numerous, thus requiring the enforcement of sanctions which are good only if they are vigorous, nevertheless the essential office of the law (receiving its authority from justice and not from Number, and being nothing if it is unjust), is an office of pedagogy of freedom, tending to render the constraints of law superfluous. Lastly, that which organic democracy will wish to efface from existence by its very root, is power without authority. This is precisely what must be suppressed, and cannot be suppressed by a mere declaration of principles, for it is continuously reborn. Legal formulas do not suffice. An appeal to the initiative of the State aggravates the evil. The only efficacious means is the enlargement of rights and of the power of action of persons, and spontaneous groups of persons, and the state of tension thus developed.

Thus the whole question turns on the justice immanent in authority. The principle of an organic democracy does

not pretend to suppress authority. It demands that authority should be just, which means an authentic authority. It
demands this, not as a simple moral wish to whose inefficiency
one is resigned, but as something which must be brought into
existence and be continually conquered (and it is really this,
which every confirmed "anti-democrat" regards as "the sur-
est way to miss everything"). Organic democracy holds that
an unjust law lacks foundation in authority and hence does
not oblige man in conscience. If, in certain cases, conscience
requires one to obey an unjust law (it being supposed, of
course, that this law does not prescribe the performance of
an act morally bad), it is for a different reason, an extrinsic
reason depending on a higher justice, that conscience makes
this demand. The reason is that, in such a case, to disobey
the law would bring upon the human community an even
greater evil. So that, finally, whether the law be just or unjust,
free men obey it only because *it is just to obey*, just by a justice
intrinsic to the law or just—in certain cases—by an extrinsic
and, in a way, accidental justice.

At the origin of the democratic sense, taken in its human
truth, there is not the desire to "obey only oneself," but rather
the desire to obey only *whatever it is just* to obey.

## IV. *The First Origin of Authority*

The inevitable philosophical question concerning the first
foundation, or the first origin, of authority involves a general conception of man and of the world. How can a morally binding relation, according to which the one commands
and the other obeys, be established among individuals of the
same species and therefore equal in nature? As long as one
considers only the human species and its individuals, the question remains in suspense. One must, as in all ethical questions,
consider man in the midst of the cosmos, and the real in its

relation to that which gives irrational value. If in the cosmos, a nature, such as human nature, can only be preserved and developed in a state of culture, and if the state of culture necessarily entails a certain condition—the relation of authority among men—this relation is demanded by natural law. I mean here the relation of authority taken as yet indeterminately, and not in the sense that *some* in particular must command and *some* in particular must obey; but rather in the general sense that there must be people who command and people who obey, the mode of designation of those who shall command being a different matter to be determined later and according to reason.

It is by virtue of these considerations that all *non-materialist* conceptions of the world, be they religious or simply philosophic, admit in one way or another that authority among men has its original foundation in the origin of nature itself and in the primordial root of the world's intelligibility. This idea in the Christian tradition is classically expressed by the Pauline principle that all authority derives from God as from its primordial source.

An organic democracy will not commit the folly of rejecting this idea. It needs it more than any other regime. Even if, invoking in the name of the most elementary natural philosophy, and one least tinged with the theology, the rule of respect due in conscience to authority, it would in any case agree regarding this subject with an essential theme of Christian philosophy and theology.

I do not ignore the fact that, whereas the early Christians heroically obeyed this rule concerning their imperial persecutors, there are many today who, while invoking the claims of religion, scoff at this very rule when it does not benefit their politics.

And yet, this rule of the respect due in conscience to authority exists, and its value is independent of the opinion

of people. It has no theocratic value whatever. It has a twofold meaning: first, hierarchic differentiations within the social
totality are required, as I have already observed, by the latter's
very nature; second, men being equal in essence, this exigency
of the political totality—that one should be placed above the
other to guide the common work—can establish a genuine *right*
to be obeyed, only if nature itself is considered, not as a simple collection of phenomena, but as the work and the created
participation of a supreme ordinating Law, "justified in itself"
because identical with the absolute Good. An integral realism understands that, in the physical order, the action of no
being whatever can be exercised except as deriving from the
motion of the primordial Agent. In the same way, we grasp in
the moral order that no man possesses authority over another,
except as this authority derives from the sovereignty of the
Cause of being, and—though also coming from the multitude—has in God the immediate ground of its moral value.
Thus, not only the kings by divine right of ancient Israel, but
also the unstable legislators and ministers of our own day—
whose speeches and fleeting pictures are generously conveyed
to us by our newspapers—possess an authority founded in
God, demanding an obedience consented to by conscience.

And so, not only is it a moral duty to give external submis-
sion to a *de facto* power, supposed to be tyrannical and deprived
of genuine authority, as long as one has not practically ascer-
tained whether insurrection would not result in a greater evil
for the community; but regarding *legitimate* power, actually
invested with authority (no matter whether this power is of
monarchic or democratic type, whether government is exercised by the prince or by men elected by the people), this moral
duty implies the recognition of a *right* to be obeyed, intrinsically residing, according to the measure and the degree of
their attributions, in the persons of those who govern.

Such are, in the perspectives of Christian realism, the philosophical reasons of the practical rule, which an organic democracy ought to assert vigorously, and to assert even more than any other regime, because its rulers are regularly renewed and hold their authority only from the designation of the people. But, on the other hand, such a democracy not only recognizes what is true for all regimes, whatever they are, namely, that by reason of the *consensus*, which lies at the origin of the fundamental rule or constitution of the political community, the authority which derives from the principle of being, as from its transcendent source, also derives from the people as passing through it in order to reside in its legitimate holders; it not only recognizes that the prince governs as representing in his person the entire people, *ut vices gerens multitudinis*:[2] but it makes of this *vicariousness* the typical law of its peculiar authoritative structure, in such a way that authority passing through the people rises, degree by degree, from the base to the summit of the hierarchic structure of the community; and so that the exercise of power by men, in whom authority is brought periodically to reside through the designation of the people, attests the constancy of the *passage* of sovereignty through the multitude.[3]

Finally, organic democracy excludes the paternalist domination of any social class over the mass of the people,

2.   St. Thomas Aquinas, *Summa Theologiae* (hereafter *ST*), I-II, q. 90, a. 3.

3.   According to this doctrine, the right to direct and to command, which is authority, is not granted to its holders by the choice of the multitude; it is granted to them by the Source itself of being and of all Nature (cf. Leo XIII, *Diuturnum illud*; Pius X *Letter upon the "Sillon"*). But the designation itself of the holders of the authority by the people involves the passage of this right through the people. "Political authority is immediately from God, and yet to kings and supreme senates it comes not immediately from God, but from men." Suarez, *Defensio*, lib. III, cap. 2, 5. Cf. Bellarmine, *De Laicis*, cap. 6. Quoted by Wilfrid Parsons, *Which Way, Democracy?* (New York: Macmillan, 1939).

considered as under age, and demands that an essential parity
in the common condition of men destined to labor, should
form the base of the relations of authority and of the hierarchy of temporal functions, be it political or any other sort of
social authority. In this "homogenetic" conception of temporal authority, the holder is as a companion who has the right
to command his fellows. "All medals have a reverse. Order,
necessary to political life, being more difficult to obtain in a
community where authority works in one and the same 'social
race' than in a community where it descends from a superior
'social race,' the weight of social life would be in the first case
heavier, and the discipline tenser."[4] This is the ransom of a
regime where *class divisions* would be abolished (in the strict
sense which this word should convey, implying a permanent
and hereditary condition based on the possession or the lack
of transferable goods); where an authentic sense of the dignity of the human person and of the dignity of the people
would replace the contempt of the owning classes for the
manual laborer, and the hatred of the crowds for all values;
and where this sense would permit a spontaneous development of popular elites.

In his famous address delivered in 1863, Abraham Lincoln
declared "that government of the people, by the people, for
the people, shall not perish from the earth." Let us observe,
in this formula, that the words *"by the people"* need comment
in order to avoid all ambiguities and to prevent Rousseauist
interpretations. Taken in their genuinely concrete sense, I do
not think that these words mean a government exercised by
the people, whose elected representatives would then serve as
a pure instrument, but rather a government exercised by the
*representatives* of the people, or by the people in the person of

---

4.    *True Humanism.*

its representatives; a government exercised in the virtue of the people's mission, in the virtue of the popular designation of authority, which passes authority over to its holders, according to the duration, the measure, and the degree of their attributions. One might think that between these two interpretations of Lincoln's formula, there is only a nuance. In reality there is a fundamental difference of political philosophy.

## V. *Aim and Mode of Authority*

*For the people.* The question of the origin and of the subject of authority, on which modern democracies hypnotize themselves, is certainly not the only one. The question of the authority's finality, and the problem of its mode, are no less important. I will only briefly mention them here.

So far as the finality of authority and of political society are concerned, I shall make the following remarks: it is not for the external power of the people—regarding either other peoples or forces of nature to be subjugated through work and industry (these ends being in no way negligible, but of secondary importance)—that authority must first of all be exercised. Nor is it, according to a very just remark of Etienne Gilson, for a platonist "Democracy-in-itself," conceived as an ideal, or idealistic, or idolatrous form (dissembling in reality the concrete interests of possessing classes), which the people should be destined to serve and for the sake of which it should be obliged to sacrifice itself—as if democracy were, in the manner of God, the separated (transcendent) common good of mankind. Democracy is only real if it is *immanent* to the people itself, and ordained to the *immanent* common good of the people.

As has been explained in the preceding chapter, the common good, which authority aims at, is a common good of human persons, whose chief value is the accession of persons to their freedom of expansion. An organic democracy is a *personalist* democracy. That which law and authority place before themselves first of all, is the conquerable freedom by which free men are made, that is, men, accomplishing from themselves, and not by fear and constraint, that which belongs to law and justice; and sufficiently provided with bodily and spiritual goods to attain a genuine independence regarding nature. Civic friendship, which is a profane image of brotherly love, is, in the same way, not an original state, granted ready-made; it is something to be conquered ceaselessly and at the price of great difficulties. It is a work of virtue and of sacrifice, and in this sense it is that we behold therein the heroic ideal of such a democracy.

In regard to the mode of authority (or to the form according to which it is exercised), we must observe the following: the means being normally the end itself in the state of becoming, and the end of authority in an organic democracy being chiefly, as we have said, the freedom and the friendship of persons, it is normal that, in order to achieve this aim, the means of authority, however vigorous the latter may be, must, be to look after the realization of freedom and friendship, rather than after the fulfillment of discipline of a military type. On the other hand, and this idea seems to me of central importance, an organic democracy should be a pluralist democracy. And the form, according to which authority should be exercised therein, should be determined by this pluralism. Except for the functions concerning the totality of the community and of its life, and which depend on the State as such, authority would thus be distributed according to the ascending degrees of the different social bodies inferior to the political community, and assembled in the latter, starting from the natural basic community (familial society). The role played by the State being above all in this domain a role of arbitrage, which prevents the animating tension thus created from turning into conflict and disorder.

As wrote M. Yves Simon, a young French philosopher whose works I particularly appreciate, "the tendency to restrict the attributions of the State—disquieting and dangerous, as long as it is accompanied by any sort of hostility regarding the temporal supremacy of the State—becomes purely and simply salutary, as soon as the just notion of the State and its supremacy is duly re-established. This restrictive tendency then only expresses the fundamental idea of all philosophy of autonomy, to wit, that in a hierarchic whole, every function which *can* be assumed by the inferior *must* be exercised by the latter, under pain of damage to the entire whole. For there is more perfection in a whole, all of whose parts are full of life and of initiative, than in a whole whose parts are but instruments conveying the initiative of the superior organs of the community."[5] This very pluralist conception demands the simultaneous development of the compensatory authority of the institutions, "where the resistance of just freedoms" is exercised not only against the usurpations of the State, but also against that of inferior social bodies (for the tendency to invade is natural to all social bodies). One of the essential functions of the personal property appears here at the same time.

Finally, the rights of the human person—from the very base and through the whole system—must be recognized and guaranteed in such a way that an organic democracy should be by essence the city of the rights of the person. The "Rights of Man and of the Citizen" have been compromised in minds which imagine themselves strong, by the Rousseauism whose traces are to be found in the French declaration of 1798. To deny for this reason the existence of these rights would be as

5.    Yves Simon, "Notes sur le fédéralisme proudhonien," *Esprit*, April 1, 1937.

unwise as piously to despise poetry because certain poets are drunkards. If the human person is without rights, then rights and, consequently, authority exist nowhere. In reality, the primordial rights of the person, insofar as the latter is a member of the State, express the inalienable *authority* of the image of God. And a just democratic mind demands that to this authority—so constantly ignored and insulted by men—should correspond a certain power on the part of civic organizations.

Now, are you wondering what is the nature of the primordial rights of the human person? I shall quote to you the words of Pope Pius XI: "the right to live, to bodily integrity, to the necessary means of existence; the right of man to tend toward his ultimate goal in the path marked out for him by God; the right of association and the right to possess and use property."[6] To which should be added: the right not

---

6.    "Man has a spiritual and immortal soul. He is a person, marvelously endowed by his Creator with gifts of body and mind. He is a true 'microcosm,' as the ancients said, a world in miniature, with a value far surpassing that of the vast inanimate cosmos. God alone is his last end, in this life and the next. By sanctifying grace he is raised to the dignity of a son of God and incorporated into the kingdom of God in the Mystical Body of Christ. In consequence he has been endowed by God with many and varied prerogatives: the right to live, to bodily integrity, to the necessary means of existence; the right to tend toward his ultimate goal in the path marked out for him by God; the right of association and the right to possess and use property.... God has likewise destined man for civil society according to the dictates of his very nature. In the plan of the Creator, society is a natural means which man can and must use to reach his destined end. Society is for man and not vice versa. This must not be understood in the sense of liberalistic individualism, which subordinates society to the selfish use of the individual; but only in the sense that by means of an organic union with society and by mutual collaboration the attainment of earthly happiness is placed within the reach of all. In a further sense, it is society which affords the opportunities for the development of all the individual and social gifts bestowed on human nature. These gifts have a value surpassing the immediate interests of the moment, for in society they reflect the divine perfection, which would not be true were man to live alone. But on final analysis, even in this latter

to be an Aryan or a fair dolichocephalus; not to put on a shirt of brown, black, red, green or the devil's color; not to be re-educated in a concentration camp; not to be killed by the air-bombing of the new Western civilizers; the right to dislike and despise every form of totalitarian dictatorship.

Let us observe, finally, that a just pluralism seems to furnish the most normal remedy for the difficulties inherent in all democracies. We know, indeed, that evil and foolishness are more frequent among men than intelligence and virtue. How then is it possible to call them all to a political life? Those who will try to discover in this remark a decisive argument against universal suffrage are not aware that in this case it would be still more dangerous to recognize the right of every man to found a family and to exercise an everyday authority over his children. Furthermore, experience shows that in politics (as in all spheres where the affective dispositions and the collective interests play an essential role), persons of education and refinement are no less often mistaken than the ignorant; the errors of the latter are vulgar, those of the former are intellectualized and documented, like the persons themselves. In these matters, if the central virtue of the leaders is political prudence—which is rare and difficult to acquire—what matters most in the rest are right instincts. And this confirms, we may point out parenthetically, the view that a general Christian education for the nation, a general development of Christian habits and Christian instincts is, in fact, a condition for the political success of democracy.

---

function, society is made for man, that he may recognize this reflection of God's perfection, and refer it in praise and adoration to the Creator. Only man, the human person, and not society in any form, is endowed with reason and a morally free will" (Encyclical *Divini Redemptoris*, §§27, 29).

The truth is that, in any case, *some* element of risk is inevitable; at least, it should not be too great. Universal suffrage, as it works at present, has especially a symbolic democratic value. Because it offers the people a recourse against political enslavement; perhaps particularly because of its value as a symbol; and because it attests, according to the specific law of democracy, the right of human persons to political life, and of the multitude to the constitution of the authoritative organism of the city—it is because of all this that modern peoples are so strongly and so justly attached to it. But, to my mind, universal suffrage will acquire a genuine value, equal to its symbolic one, only if it is itself engaged in a pluralist organization, and completed by the representation of various social bodies: communities of labor, spiritual families, regional institutions, etc. The object saves the subject. Taken as a participant in the humblest common work (I mean a work measured according to the real and implying genuine responsibilities), it is according to what is least bad and most wise in him that man has a chance to express himself. At present, I vote as an abstract atom, geographically situated in this or that electoral district. Suppose that all citizens should be grouped in communities (professional or otherwise), each electing a number of representatives proportional to the number of its members, and suppose that I vote as member of one of these communities. In this second case, my vote has a better chance of being reasonable than in the first one.

Today in Europe, if only with the intention of founding a unique Party (in which the defects of partisan spirit are carried to the utmost point)—political parties are often criticized; and the truth is that they deserve these criticisms. Yet, in itself, the existence of parties seems normal in all democratic regimes, in so far at least as a party groups its members precisely on the one basis of a certain political conception. If one recognizes that human persons have the right to possess a political thought and to seek legitimately to make it prevail, one must then recognize their right to constitute parties. However unsatisfactory this may appear, such parties—on condition that they correspond to their destination and are not reduced to vast coalitions of interests, from which all political thought is absent—outline moreover a certain political education of men. They at least develop a sort of tradition, and those instincts and reflexes, which reason governs without being able to replace, and which are necessary to the stability of political life. Dr. Salazar sees in the suppression of parties the salvation of the State. I believe that it is important not to suppress parties, but to suppress that which corrupts them and turns them into instruments of corruption of the public good. To achieve this aim, it is necessary to render the State, and government itself of the city, independent of these political parties. I do not think that this result could be attained without a recasting of political structures, and of the notion itself of party, the latter becoming rather a political "school" than a political "party" of the sort which we know actually. Such a reform would replace, by a new representative regime, the parliamentary system of the British type, which has served as a model to our European democracies, and which suited the age of liberalistic individualism. And I think that this transformation—far from being incompatible with the democratic principle—would on the contrary assure the normal application of the latter.

I will not attempt to explain here how I imagine this representative system.[7] I am no legislator, nor an inventor of

---

7.    However, in order to prevent the suspicion that I have no definite idea of what such a system might be, I will give, as simple indications, the following details:

constitutions. I will only say, to conclude this chapter, that in
European democracies the discussion of these subjects is, in
my opinion, impaired in a twofold manner by the neighbor-
ing totalitarianisms: first, because of the invidiously menac-
ing atmosphere which the latter create around them; second,
because in democracies themselves, which rightfully detest
totalitarianism as the abasement of man and the triumph

In an organic democracy, political life would involve, I think, two very
distinct orders of functions, concerning, on the one hand, the *preparation*
and the *maturing* of authoritative decisions (*consilium*); and, on the other
hand, those decisions themselves (*judicium ultimum* and *imperium*). And this
splitting would again be found in each one of the pyramids rising from
below and upwards, according to an order of increasing importance,
from the smallest communal organization to the most general and highest
structure of the State.

Thus we could conceive, at each level, an assembly invested with the first
order of functions (preparation and deliberation), and an "executive" or
"praesidium" invested with the second order of functions (decision and
execution), composed of men who would not be elected by the given
assembly, but *proposed* by the organ of the superior order, and *accepted* by
the popular vote of the area which would thus be governed. (If somebody
thus proposed is not accepted, another will be proposed, until acceptance
by the people is reached.)

A similar form would occur for the highest structures of the State.
The first order of functions, rising from the base of the pyramid to the
summit, would depend on representative assemblies, the first and most
direct expression possible of the political thought and the concrete
interests of human persons, individually taken, and of various social
bodies: their duty would be to prepare the legislative and executive work
in close collaboration with the governmental organs and to exercise
an office of control and of regulation (for instance, by the vote on the
budget, the right to demand in certain determined conditions the revision
of a law or the rejection of a man, the right of sovereign decisions in
certain cases concerning in a major manner the life of the nation...). The
second order of functions descending from the summit of the pyramid
would belong to governmental organs free from all preoccupations other
than the common good, and for that very reason independent of the
representative assemblies. These governmental organs, which would
assume the ultimate decision (legislative and executive) would depend
upon a supreme organ (where a partition could be conceived between
a part assigned especially to command and designated for a shorter time

of death, it suffices to call "fascist" any technical measure of reform of structure, having nothing whatever to do with fascism, to render it odious and impossible. Certainly, the question is serious. If democracies are not able to rediscover and purify their own vital principle, and to apply it vigorously with the free and active co-operation of working classes, they run the risk that certain technical measures, necessary in themselves, which ought to be a road, perhaps arduous, toward a new social order, should in fact be disturbed by the fear which privileged interests are feeling, and become a road toward a kind of germinating "fascisation" from inside.

But I am convinced that if these obstacles, due to historical circumstances, were suppressed, there would still exist in democratic countries sufficient material and moral resources, sufficient possibilities of spiritual reform, to permit democracy to return to organic forms; this process being achieved thanks to very general, very deep, and substantial transformations; and these organic forms of democracy consisting in pluralist and personalist structures fully evolved; where authority would be exercised by popular elites; where parties, rejected from the proper sphere of the government of the State, will serve to assure the political formation of the masses, and

---

and a part especially assigned to continuity and designated for a longer time), this supreme organ emanating itself from the multitude, but in an indirect way (one could conceive it as being designated and proposed by the representatives of consultative assemblies and by the principal organs of the life of the country, and this designation or proposition being subjected to the sanction of a popular referendum).

The governmental organs would thus be a second—indirect—expression of the political thought and of the concrete interests of human persons and social bodies. Independent of the representative assemblies, they would at the same time be independent of political parties. And these parties, not being able to hope to lay a hand on the State and on the advantages born from such a seizure, would themselves be saved from the principle of corruption which today renders them pernicious.

where money would be entirely subordinated to man—not by enslavement of both man and money, to collective Man or to the State, but by the real guarantees that accession of work to property should offer to human persons and their freedom.[8]

---

8. As regards the reconstruction of the political philosophy of Democracy, I am happy to be in agreement with John U. Nef's clarifying essay *In Defense of Democracy*. It also seems to me that the self-interrogation to which American Democracy is invited by men so different as Robert Hutchins and Mortimer Adler, Stringfellow Barr and Scott Buchanan, Reinhold Niebuhr and Waldo Frank, and some liberals disgusted with liberalism, and some Catholics aware of their social responsibility, shows evidence of the preparation of a new political philosophy of Democracy.

# Chapter V

## *The Thomist Idea of Freedom*

### I. *The Two Kinds of Freedom*

I would like to note at the very beginning of this essay that the word *freedom*—like all big words for which men are ready to die, and which are laden, not only with the riches of the object, but with the desires, the dreams, and the supreme generosities of the subject—the word freedom conveys a great number of meanings; and yet these meanings, though widely different, have something in common.

If we seek to limit ourselves to the essential, we shall behold, by attentively considering this variety of meanings, two directions, two principal lines of significance. One of them concerns freedom as an *absence of constraint*; as a bird is *free* when it is not in a cage, which does not mean that the bird possesses free will. The other concerns freedom as an *absence of necessity* or of *necessitation*, which is precisely the case of free will: when Samuel Adams decided to throw the tea of the East India Company into the waters of Boston Harbor, his decision was not only a spontaneous act, an act without constraint, but it was also an act which neither outer nor inner circumstances, motives, impulses, inclinations, etc., had necessarily determined; he could indeed have made a contrary decision. What he did was an act of free will; no outer or inner necessity determined it.

One of the causes of obscurity and confusion in the elaborate discussions of freedom and grace which occupied the seventeenth century was the fact that the two lines of significance which I have mentioned were not clearly distinguished. It is these two lines and these two primordial meanings of the word, and of the concept, of freedom—freedom of choice (absence of necessitation) and freedom of spontaneity (absence of constraint)—which we must first of all distinguish. It is perhaps suitable to observe, concerning these two kinds of freedom, that the specialists in knowledge—I have in mind the philosopher and the theologian—are mostly interested in the freedom of choice, in free will, no doubt because this subject gives rise to the most arduous problems. Whereas the average man is mostly interested, not in free will—about which he troubles himself very little, knowing he possesses it—but in the other kind of freedom, the freedom of spontaneity in its highest forms, where it means emancipation and personal independence (in this case we shall call it freedom of autonomy and freedom of exultation); and this interest arises from the fact that this kind of freedom must be dearly and strenuously bought, and because it is continuously threatened.

## II. *Freedom of Choice*

Let us now, by placing ourselves in the perspective of Thomist philosophy, consider the mysterious nature of the *first freedom*, or human free will. I shall not discuss here its existence, as each of us knows by experience the existence of his own freedom. Moreover, the way in which St. Thomas clarifies for us the nature of free will, is at the same time the proof that the latter necessarily exists in every intelligent nature. Let us try to scrutinize the nature of the freedom of choice.

The ancients took care to emphasize primarily the *transcendence of the intellective appetite*, or of *the will*, with regard to every sort of good except happiness.

For St. Thomas, the will is an appetite, a power of desire and of inclination, creating in the soul spiritual weights which attract the whole of it; its primordial act is to love.

Now, all appetite is rooted in knowing or awareness. What the scholastics call sensitive appetite, the power of desire and emotion which is common to men and animals, has its root in the knowledge of the senses.

The will, that is, the power of spiritual appetition, is, on the contrary, rooted in the intellect. And it is because the intellect possesses the notion of *what is good*, of the good in itself, abstracted in its proper objectivity and in its universality, and co-extensive with the notion of the being—it is for this reason that in every intelligent nature, there must exist a power of desire and of love essentially distinct from the sensitive appetite, and tending toward the good known as such, insofar as it transcendentally imbibes all good things, toward the good intelligibly grasped, and not toward this or that particular good thing known only through the senses. And this power of desire and love is the rational appetite or will which has its root in the intellect.

Thus the will is grounded in nature and is itself a kind of *nature*. Hence it must have, as all nature has, a necessary determination—*natura determinatur ad unum*. It must have an operation which is produced in a natural way, and as such necessarily determined. There is something which it must desire by virtue of what it is, something which it desires necessarily. As God loves necessarily His being and His goodness, because to love the infinite goodness, which is Himself, is His very essence; so also the intelligent creature necessarily loves, not this or that good, but the Good (I do not say the moral good, which relates to whatever suits the intelligent creature in the line of *its own final end*; I say the metaphysical good, which relates to what is capable of satisfying desire and of bringing joy in every line, and which is as boundless as being itself). Thus, what the will necessarily desires by reason of what it is, is a good which satisfies every desire, a good which suits in every respect all human aspirations: in short, beatitude. The most unhappy creature necessarily desires happiness and, no doubt, that is why he is so unhappy; for his plight is such that, according to natural conditions, he is normally led to despair of ever reaching this happiness. If I properly understand the thought of St. Thomas, it is in his view only through a revelation of faith that we can tell ourselves that someday we shall really be able to become *perfectly, absolutely happy*. This is astonishing news: "Thou wilt be with me in paradise."

Strictly speaking, if St. Thomas insists much more than Aristotle upon the absolutely plenary character of the good to which we naturally aspire, it is because he knows through faith that we can really aspire to it—by means of divine grace, because it is supernatural. Necessarily and naturally we desire a *happiness that is absolute*: *happiness* by virtue of a desire which is *unconditional* and connatural, or tending toward something required by the capacities of our being; *absolute* happiness, by virtue of a desire which is *conditional* and transnatural, tending toward something superior to our natural limitations and concerning the constitution of which, consequently, nature cannot possess the idea.

It is with the help of these distinctions that we have to understand the assertions of the Thomists concerning the human will.

But let us return to the nature of human will. It necessarily desires—it cannot, as soon as it exercises itself, help desiring—beatitude. That which *necessarily determines* it (even before knowing where this good is to be found, or whether it is possible to achieve it) is the absolute and complete good, happiness saturating every desire.

And what follows? Simply this, that toward every good which is not this absolute good, the will of man is naturally *undetermined*, is without natural and necessary propensity. If that which necessarily determines my will is a limitless good, an absolute good which completely satiates all my capacities of desire, it is evident that whatever is not this limitless, absolute good, cannot determine my will necessarily.

This is a surprising consequence! St. Thomas deduces freedom (here) from necessity (there). Because the will is *internally and naturally necessitated* to absolutely satisfying happiness, it is free with respect to everything else; that is to say, with respect to everything it can desire here on earth—for where on earth is this perfect happiness, this complete satiety of desire?

It must be made clear that not only particular and partial goods, offered us by the finite world, but all the concrete goods which we may love and desire in this life, are thus the object of the will's free choice. Even the noblest good, even the divine good, is thus, and for the same reason, the object of the will's free choice. According to the teaching of the theologians, when the human intelligence shall behold God, not only will it know that for us beatitude can consist only in seeing God (I know this already through reason and faith), but it will grasp God, it will see Him and possess Him as He is actually in Himself; it will behold Him as actually satisfying, up to repletion and super-repletion, all the possibilities of desire of the human person, leaving him nothing, not even the shadow of a shadow, to be desired apart from Him. Then the will shall love God in a necessary manner, as necessarily and even more necessarily than it loves happiness on earth. But as long as God is not beheld face to face in the Beatific Vision, we may know well enough, through reason and through faith, that He is the absolute Good and that He is our real last end, this beatitude is not yet in our possession; the intellect does not grasp God as the beatitude which actually beatifies us; it knows Him through abstract knowledge as a beatitude which will beatify us. And there are many kinds of good, real and apparent, which for the time being we will have to renounce in order to attain to God. Many good and desirable things will continue to attract us outside the narrow path of the goods which are better for us, and which are directed toward God as the apex of the moral order.

By an apparent paradox, which it was the object of my previous remarks to explain, we necessarily desire the absolute Good (beatitude in general); and yet God—this hidden God, who is the absolute Good and the subsistent beatitude and who, existing as the (transcendent) Whole and common Good of the universe, is naturally loved by every creature more than itself, even in spite of itself—this God is longed for by us, and loved efficaciously above all, as being in His very nature Sanctity itself and the end of our life, and the goal of the whole order of our acts, yet only by virtue of a free option, which remains in our power to decline.

Here occurs a point of doctrine which clearly shows, it seems to me, the truly human amplitude and the universal bearing of the thought of St. Thomas. He teaches[1] that we make our first decision concerning our last end at the time when the life of reason and of personality matures in

---

1.   *ST*, I-II, q. 89.

the child. This act can be accomplished in utter silence in our very depths, but it is in itself an extremely great event. And each time that a man takes himself in hand in order to deliberate over his ultimate end and to choose his destiny, he recovers in this act something of the absolute beginnings of his childhood. Now, when a man deliberating about his life chooses to love that which is good in itself, the *bonum honestum*, in order to link his life to it, it is toward God, whether he knows it or not, that he turns himself. And then, St. Thomas says, this man, whether grown up in the Christian faith or among the idolatrous and nourished in wild forests, has the grace of God, without which our wounded will cannot turn itself efficaciously toward God as the supreme end of our life.

Let us add that if the ethics of St. Thomas is an ethics of beatitude, it is nevertheless something entirely different from an interested eudemonism, because it is also an ethics of love; and, when we act rightly, that in which our happiness consists (which is to say, God, the transcendent whole), is loved by us for Himself, not for ourselves, and He is loved above all else, loved more than ourselves; it is by virtue of our love for him that we ourselves want to be happy.

I have insisted upon the universal capacity of the will, on its infinite capacity to love, which is a consequence of the universal capacity of the intellect; and I have also insisted upon the indetermination or absence of a necessary propensity, which inevitably belongs to the will in respect to all good things which are not Beatitude, grasped as actually beatifying and saturating every desire.

This "indifference" or indetermination (it is highly important to understand this) does not coincide at all with the potential or passive indetermination of that which, being imperfect and as if expecting a determination, can become this or that, can receive this or that actuation. Insofar as there is such passive determination in the human will it testifies to the imperfection of all that is created. It does not constitute the freedom of human will.

There is in the human will a certain passive indetermination, from which it emerges sometimes *without our wishing it* (by non-deliberate movements for which we are not responsible and which surge up before we reflect at all, at the simple perception of some good); and sometimes *by our wishing it*, by an act of free will; such a potential and passive indetermination is a mark of the weakness of the created being. It does not constitute liberty; it does not exist in the divine will.

The indetermination which is identical with free will is quite another kind of indetermination, *an active and dominating* indetermination. It consists in *the mastering by the will of the practical judgment which determines it.*

Though, in fact, the intellect may speculatively declare that such or such an action must be accomplished by virtue of a law or of a rule which applies to human action in general (the scholastics called this a speculatively-practical judgment), yet this does not suffice to make me take a decision in favor of this action. I need a practical decision, a practical judgment of the intelligence, bearing upon the action to be accomplished insofar as it is *properly mine*, as a concrete and singular action related to my end and to my personal and singular desire of my end, in the singular circumstances in which I find myself (the scholastics called this a practically-practical judgment).

Now, if the intellect were left to itself, this practically-practical judgment which is the immediately determining principle of my act of willing, would itself remain undetermined. Such a judgment bears on the relation between my act considered *hic et nunc* and that which I, who produce this act, necessarily desire. Now, what I desire necessarily is Happiness. And the act concerning which the intellect deliberates is a particular good, which consequently lacks certain aspects of good, and therefore takes on the significance of non-good; it is a good under one aspect and a non-good under another aspect. I may continue to desire (that is to say, continue to desire Happiness), without wishing for that particular good, and the entire set of goods to which it is related, and which I can challenge, if I wish, without ceasing to desire Happiness. In one way it suits me to accomplish this act, in another it suits me not to accomplish it; that is all that the intellect alone, as a pure faculty of knowledge, can say to me. Using the intellect alone, it is impossible for me ever to decide: "I must absolutely, here and now, accomplish this act"—this is due to the *invincible determination* which characterizes the relation between this particular good considered in itself and the only thing which I necessarily desire—Happiness.

Now, the will triumphs over this indetermination of the intellect. It determines *itself*; that is, the will brings the intellect to pass from the speculatively-practical judgment, incapable of determining efficaciously the act of willing, to a practically-practical judgment, which alone is capable of determining the act efficaciously. It is the will which intervenes by an act which rises from the depths of personality, *by an act of the person insofar as it is person*, and in which the practical *fiat* bears, in the creature, the greatest possible resemblance to the creative *fiat*. It is the will which intervenes and which, by its own exercise, specifies the practical judgment, the very judgment which determinates it.

Here, indeed, is the very kernel of the problem of free will.

The intellect can express a practically-practical unconditioned judgment only as a function of the actual exercise and the actual movement of the will; as a function of *what is* actually the desiring and willing subject (not only in its natural being, but in the ultimate actuality of its spiritual being, and of its will); as a function of the line of finality to which it adheres and of the decisive proprieties that it thereby establishes between itself and such a good, or such a line of goods. And the will can exercise this actual movement only by being formally determined by the judgment which the will itself mates efficacious in this way. *Causae ad invicem sunt causae.*

As Aristotle said, the diverse causes that co-operate in producing one and the same act cause one another from different points of view. The free act appears thus as the common offspring of the intellect and the will vitally enveloping each other in one and the same instantaneous co-determination. The intelligence determines the will in the order of objective or formal-extrinsic causality; the will determines the intelligence in the order of efficient causality; or, to put it another way, *specification* (of the will by the intelligence) itself depends on the *exercise* of the will. The judgment which, insofar as it is efficaciously expressed, specifies and determines the act of willing, derives its actual value of existential efficacy from the will itself, which transfers, so to speak, to the particular good in question the excess of motivation which fills it through its determination by the infinite good. To be free means to be master of one's judgment. The will is master of the very judgment which determines it, and *thus* has full mastery of its own actions.

It is not easy to draw an image from the spectacle of sensible things which can illustrate this metaphysical process. Let us, nevertheless, try to find a metaphor, however inadequate.

Every river flows between two banks; and it is determined by them, that is, by the conformations of the earthly crust. Well, let us imagine a spiritual river, which as yet exists only in the thought, and which is ready to spring forth into existence.

Let us imagine that everything which concerns realization in existence also depends on it. Let us imagine that before it springs forth, angels present to it various conformations of soil, diverse possible banks. It cannot spring forth without being contained or determined by one or another pair of banks. But at the precise moment when it springs forth, it is the river itself which brings into existence, amongst the various possible courses presented to it, this or that earthly course and the banks which encase the waters. This image represents the act of free will. The will is as a torrent, mastering the banks which contain it.

We perceive in what sense it is correct to say with M. Bergson (yet in quite a different metaphysical context than the one he uses), that "our motives are what we make them." And, also, that "our reasons determine us only at the moment when they have become determining, that is, at the moment when the act has been virtually accomplished." This is because, truly, in the act of freedom, the will goes out to meet halfway an attraction which is incapable of quite reaching it by itself; and this is because the free act is a gratuitous answer, which has sprung forth from the very depths of the will, toward a powerless solicitation of a finite good. In the act of free will, wrote Cajetan, the famous commentator on St. Thomas, the *will bends the judgment in the direction it desires.*

Such is the character of the active and dominating indetermination which is free will, due to the spiritual amplitude of that which, put into action and into appetite by an infinity of joy, has no necessary connection with every object which is not presently infinite joy. Insofar as one comprehends this notion of an active and dominating indetermination, one understands free will, the freedom of choice.

One understands that the free act is *in itself and essentially* something impossible to *foresee.* Given all the inner and outer circumstances, all the instincts and inclinations, of a human being, all his motives and impulsions; given the speeches he delivers to himself, and the exhortations which carry him hither or thither, and the graces of God which attract him, and the passions which solicitate him; you may foresee what he is going to do with more or less probability. Moreover, if you deal with averages and large numbers, you can predict with certitude that in a town where all the citizens are ill-tempered, there will surely be some quarrelling. In a country where everyone has an inferiority complex, and manifests fear and trembling in the presence of corporals and captains, there will someday be a dictator. But to foresee with *certitude* what this *particular man* will do after inner reflection and deliberation, and by the exercise of his *free will*—that is something which you cannot do. It is this man's *absolute secret*, and it is a secret even *for himself*, a secret which he will learn only at the very moment when he makes his decision. The free act is not only the act of the person as such, it is moreover—and this is perhaps the same thing—the revelation of the person to itself. Even with a "super-comprehension of the causes," however perfect it may be supposed, you cannot foresee this act. Even God cannot do so. To be precise, God does not *foresee* our free acts, He *sees* them, all the moments of time being present to His creative eternity. And insofar as our free acts are good, He works them with us and causes them, for He is the primary cause of being. We have the initiative and the free initiative of our good acts and of our good acts in their entirety, but this is a *secondary* initiative, and not the *primary* one; the latter belongs to God alone. Our good acts are thus wholly from God as primary cause, and wholly our own as due to a secondary free cause. And this is easy to comprehend, once we have understood that freedom consists in an active and dominating indetermination and the mastery of will over judgment. How could this mastery and this high activity exercise themselves in me without the activating influx of the first Cause within me? And how could this activating influx, descending from the Life in Pure Act, destroy or diminish in me this dominating activity, at the very instant when it activates and vivifies it? It is great folly to seek the freedom of our will—which is a supreme degree of activity—in I know not what *asides*, isolating us from Him, without whom we can do nothing but evil and nothingness.

*Sine me, nihil potestis facere*—"Without Me you can do nothing." This text can be read in two different senses, and so it illuminates the problem of created freedom in relation to the Divine liberty. Without Me, you can do nothing: without Me you cannot execute the slightest movement which conveys being and goodness. So much for the line of good. But for the line of evil, this text must be read differently, *Sine me potestis facere nihil*: without Me nothingness, or nothing itself can be done by you. Without Me you can introduce into act and into being this *nothingness*, which wounds them, and which constitutes evil.

### III. *Freedom of Spontaneity*

To be free, generally speaking, is to suffer no hindrance, is to be not bound. But this general notion can be realized, as I observed at the beginning of this chapter, according to two specifically different types. There is freedom which consists in the *absence of necessity*; it is the freedom which I have just described, the freedom of choice. It implies not only spontaneity, but it also implies the absence of all necessity, even internal, and of all determinism.

There is another freedom which, on the contrary, consists merely in the *absence of restraint*, a freedom which is not

a freedom of choice, not a free will, but which, however,
deserves, in quite a different sense, the name of freedom. It
is the degrees of this second freedom, the freedom of spontaneity, which I shall now consider.

One will agree that a stone *falls freely* when nothing hinders it from obeying the law of gravitation, which is a law of
its nature. We are here at the lowest degree of spontaneity.

A second degree of spontaneity is represented by organic
bodies having vegetative life; a third, by organisms possessing
sensitive life. The animal is free with respect to the *structural
conditions*, or the constitutive structures, which it has received
from nature, in the sense that its activity in space depends on
forms or patterns of movement which are perceptions, that
is, acts of sensitive knowledge. Thus, says St. Thomas, the
animal puts itself into motion by means of a form, serving
as the principle of its movement, which it bestows upon itself
through the immanent activity of its senses.

But it does not give itself the *ends* of its own activity. They
are pre-established by nature. So the bird's flight, which we call
free and which depends on the bird's perceptions, is accomplished according to the psychic structures and the instincts,
which form a part of the *structural conditions* with which nature
endows the bird.

The fourth degree of freedom of spontaneity is that of
intellective life. The human being not only acts according to
forms and patterns of activity which are not pre-established
by nature, but which result from his own cognitive activity;
in addition, the *ends of his acts* are not imposed upon him by
nature, as in the case of the animal instinct. Able to exceed
the realm of the sense, able to know being and intelligible
natures, he knows both what he does and the ends of his
activity, as such. By means of his own intellectual operations,
he is able to envisage the ends of his activity.

Starting with this fourth degree of spontaneity, we enter into the world of spiritual things, which forms the supreme level of creation.

At this point, freedom of spontaneity becomes freedom of independence, for at this point we are concerned with persons endowed with free will, and masters of their actions—persons, each of whom is as a whole or as a universe.

Through the intellect and the will, the entire universe enters the soul, becoming there, while existing according to intentional being and in an immaterial mode, the form and interior principle of the actions which the soul will freely proceed to carry out. The supra-physical nature of that which is intelligent and loving as such, will flourish in such a creature in an activity of superabundance, free from all external constraint; it will even be free, if I can speak thus, from that interior constraint constituted in each created being by its nature, its constitutive structure. Every external reality interiorizes itself in such an activity. "Let all my activity spring from myself as from its source, and be regulated by me; let me be sufficient unto myself in order to live"—this is what the person demands, according to an inefficacious metaphysical aspiration. "Let the supreme condition of the operation of intelligence and of love in its living flame be the condition of my entire existence!"

Independent in its metaphysical root, because it appears in creation as an intelligent substance and is endowed with liberty of choice, the person—insofar as it is concerned in the pure line of its aspirations as a person—wishes thus to pass to an ever higher degree of freedom of spontaneity and independence.

It seems to me that sometimes not enough emphasis has been laid on the dynamic aspect of the thought of St. Thomas. St. Thomas says clearly that a donkey does not have a natural desire to become a lion, because this would involve a desire to destroy what it is, that is to say, a donkey. But intelligence, love, personality, are not destroyed in passing from an inferior to a superior degree of being. Far from being destroyed, these transcendental perfections are then more than ever themselves. That is why there exists in us, as reasonable animals, a natural desire, which is not exactly of ourselves but of a transcendental element within us, to pass beyond the human condition: which does not take place, of course, without some accidents, and which too often makes us want to be unreasonable animals. But precisely because these desires to pass beyond the human state are not desires of our own specific nature, but are only the product of a transcendental element in us, they remain inefficacious and conditional. We have no right to have them granted; if they are granted to some extent it is only through grace. These aspirations tend to the superhuman; they torment us without satisfying us. We cannot rightfully claim their fulfillment, because they are not specific (connatural) aspirations of human nature, but only metaphysical (transnatural) aspirations of a transcendental element within us. Truly speaking, it is only in God himself, in the uncreated Being, that these aspirations find their fulfillment.

At the fifth degree alone—which is the divine degree—freedom of spontaneity and independence, as well as personality, is absolutely perfect. Freedom as well as personality are perfect only when they are in pure act. God exists by Himself, by His own essence. What the theologians call *aseitas* is His privilege. His very essence is His very act of intellection and of love. There is for Him no specifying object, no rule other than Himself. And through faith we know that He is a Trinity of Persons, each of whom is so purely person, and so free of all shadow of dependence, that he does not participate his essence, but *is* this essence itself. He is Freedom of Autonomy in self-subsistence; He is Personality in an absolutely pure state.

As to the human person, he is but a person in embryo. He is, as with all created persons, not only subject to realities other than himself as to the specifying objects of his knowledge and of his will, but he is also subjected to laws he has not made, as measures regulating his actions. And this is the first defeat, inflicted upon the aspirations of the person as such, a defeat far deeper in men than in angels.

Moreover, the human person is involved in all the miseries and fatalities of material nature—the servitudes and the needs of the body, heredity, ignorance, selfishness, and the savagery of instincts. This is the second defeat, inflicted upon the person as such, and this defeat originates not in the transcendence of God, but in the burden of nature. The human person! This unfortunate being, threatened by the entire universe, which seems ready to crush him, pretends to be a whole, to be a person! He is, indeed, a whole and a person! He is a person in the metaphysical root of personality. But for subjects both spiritual and bodily, which participate in the same specific nature, which are opaque to themselves, and whose normal state is movement, this metaphysical root, hidden in the depths of being, manifests itself only through a progressive conquest of itself by itself, accomplished in time. Man must win his personality, as well as his freedom, and he pays dearly for it, and runs many risks. He is a person in the order of doing only if his rational energies, and virtues, and love, give such a face to the torrential multiplicity which inhabits him, and freely imprint on him the seal of his radical, ontological unity. In this sense, the one knows real personality and real liberty, while the other does not.

Personality, which it is metaphysically impossible to lose, suffers many a defeat in the psychological and moral spheres.

It risks contamination from the miseries of material individuality, from its pettiness, its vanities, its bad habits, its narrowness, its hereditary predispositions, from its natural regime of rivalry and opposition. For the same being who is a person, and subsists through the subsistence of his soul, is also an individual in a species, and dust in the wind.

## IV. *The Dynamism of Freedom*

These things being understood, one immediately perceives the consequence they entail from the point of view of what one can call the *dynamism of freedom*. The first freedom (freedom of choice) exists for the sake of the second freedom (freedom of spontaneity or of independence) toward which the aspirations of personality themselves tend. I have called this second freedom, freedom of spontaneity or of independence. In order now to describe it more clearly in its relation to the aspirations of the person, we can also call it *freedom of exultation* and, in the Pauline, not the Kantian, sense, *freedom of autonomy*.

The freedom of choice, the *free will*, is not its own end. It is ordained to the conquest of freedom in the sense of freedom of *exultation* or *autonomy*. And it is in this conquest, demanded by the essential postulates of human personality, that the dynamism of freedom consists.

In this dynamism are involved two essentially distinct forms, which I can only briefly discuss; a *social* form and a *spiritual* one. If we remember what has just been said about the two defeats inflicted in us in respect to the claims of personality in its pure formal line—one by divine transcendence, and the other by the burden of nature—we can say that the object of the social form of the dynamism of freedom is to remedy the defeat inflicted by nature; while the object of the spiritual form of this dynamism is to remedy the defeat inflicted by the transcendence of God.

In the order of social life, it thus appears that the end of civil life is a common earthly good and a common earthly undertaking, whose *highest values* consist in aiding the human person so that it may free itself from the servitudes of nature and achieve its autonomy in regard to the latter.

Civilization has its origin at once in the exigencies of our rational nature and in freedom, in the sense of freedom of choice or free will, thanks to which the constitution of the political community—commenced, prepared and dictated by nature—is completed as a human achievement of reason and virtue. And, through the *dynamism of freedom*, civilization, taking thus its point of departure in nature and liberty, tends toward freedom in the sense of *freedom of autonomy*—the expansion and growing realization of human nature. It tends toward a *terminal freedom*, which is terminal only from a certain point of view and in a certain order of things (since it concerns but an infravalent or intermediary end), which, as I have already indicated in another chapter, can be described as follows. Civilized life tends to grant the human person—that is, the concrete person of each member of the multitude—an increasingly larger measure of independence from the external and internal constraints of Nature; an independence growing according to the very tendencies and the intimate law of human nature itself, as human and endowed with reason; and assured by the economic guarantees of labor and property, by political rights, by civil virtues, and the culture of the mind. In this way, certain conditions and certain means are prepared, and certain beginnings of spiritual freedom, of the freedom *purely and simply terminal*, whose conquest and achievement transcend the proper order of nature and the civil community.

✦

Thus we return to those considerations of political philosophy which have been already expounded, and we see how they have their root in a general philosophy of man and life.

With reference to a strictly theological question, concerning the kind of life mankind would have led, had Adam not eaten of the forbidden fruit, St. Thomas enunciates principles which, in my opinion, most usefully enlighten social philosophy and the problems of liberty and authority.

He asks: In the state of innocence would man have had an authority over man, one commanding and the other obeying? And he replies that the rule or authority of man over man can be understood in two ways: either as it is exercised over free men, or as it is exercised over men in a state of servitude.

The free man (in the sense of liberty of spontaneity or of autonomy) is one who disposes of himself and has mastery over his own life; the slave, the man in the state of slavery, or more generally, the man in the state of servitude, is one who is referred to or ordered to another man and to the proper good of this other man.

And thus one man commands another as a free man, when he directs him, not toward the good peculiar to him who is directing, but toward the common good of the body politic. Such authority is required by the nature of society insofar as it is human and that is why, according to St. Thomas, it would have existed even in the state of innocence. The children of an innocent Adam would have been governed, governed as free men, and directed toward the common good of the city. Such authority would have existed among them. I suppose, for the sake of my philosophy, that they would have lived under the regime of personalist democracy which I have described in this book: the privilege of the state of innocence (a privilege, I fear, we must regard as definitely lost) being manifested in the fact that the best and wisest would always have been chosen to govern the others.

But there is another sort of rule or authority of man over man: it is that which is exercised, not over free men, but over men in the state of servitude. This occurs when he who directs refers the one directed to his *own* utility, to the utility peculiar to the *director himself*. And that is a real affliction for the person directed, says St. Thomas—to give over to the good of another the good which ought to be his own. That is why such a domination of man over man is a punishment following on sin; it would not have existed in the state of innocence.

It seems to me that these remarks go very far. They pose, in the most precise way, the problem of servitude, a problem which I did not touch in the preceding chapter, and which concerns authority considered in the economic order, in relation to the administration of things and the functions of work. In Thomistic perspectives, I believe it must be said that slavery, or more generally servitude, taken in the most philosophical sense of this word, is a state where one man serves the *private utility* of another man, and in this respect becomes, as it were, *a part* or an organ of this other man; and that, although human work has always been bound, in a more or less extended way and in different degrees, to some form or other of servitude—slavery, strictly speaking, serfdom, domesticity, proletariat—nevertheless, this condition of servitude is repugnant to human nature. It is an affliction for man, which runs contrary to the aspirations proper to the person. As much as Karl Marx, St. Thomas is cognizant of the humiliation inflicted on man by what Marx calls the alienation of work for the profit of another, and which St. Thomas called more simply servitude. As much as Marx, he renders intelligible this desire which possesses us, this nostalgia for a state where human work would be liberated and all servitude abolished.

But, in contra-distinction to Marx, he makes us understand that if the progress of human societies is to proceed in
the direction of this liberation, it would be fully attained—
that is, every form and modality of servitude, of service to
another for the peculiar or private good of another, would be
abolished for all men—only at the termination of the movement of human history. This will not be accomplished by a
quick change and a messianic revolution abolishing private
property, but by better and more human arrangements of private property. This progressive escape from servitude among
men depends, on the one hand, on technical progress, notably on the services rendered by the machine, and on certain
transformations and transferences in the regime of property;
but it necessarily demands also, on the other hand, a progressive spiritualization of humanity caused by the forces of the
soul and of liberty, and the gospel leaven at work in human
history.

✦

Thus I have outlined what constitutes, in its most general
features, the dynamism of freedom in the order of social-temporal life. In the order of spiritual life this dynamism tends—
by virtue of grace—toward what I called a moment ago
freedom purely and simply terminal. Such a freedom coin-
cides with the plenitude and perfection of love. St. Paul and
St. John of the Cross teach us what is the supreme freedom
of exultation and of autonomy by saying that where the spirit
of God abides, there is also liberty (2 Cor. 3:17), and that if
you are led by the spirit you are no longer under the law (Gal.
5:18); that those that are moved by the spirit of God, being
really sons of God, are really and perfectly free, and that they
enter into the very life of the Divine Persons. Such then is here
below the term of the progress of the soul, the penultimate

end, wherein even before having that vision, which union of a corruptible body forbids, time joins eternity. It is the freedom of God Himself that the perfect spiritual man enjoys, being independent of all external constraint insofar as he depends only on the divine causality, which is extraneous to nothing. He is sufficient unto himself because he has lost himself, and his life is the life of the subsistent Love, living in Him. Far more than the pagan sage, he is a whole unto himself, because he forms but a single spirit and a single love with the Divine Whole. "Two natures in one single spirit, and love," as St. John of the Cross puts it.

Thus we understand that freedom of choice is not an end in itself, but that one chooses in order, finally, not to have to choose. Freedom of choice tends, as to its end, to the terminal freedom (terminal from a certain point of view and in a certain order of things) which, in the order of social and political life, remedies the defeat inflicted on the connatural aspirations of the person by the burden of Nature; and to the freedom purely and simply terminal which, in the order of spiritual life, remedies by sanctity the defeat inflicted on the transnatural aspirations of the person by the transcendence of God. Freedom of choice is *freer* than the freedom of exultation or of autonomy, since it is free not only from constraint, but also from all necessity. It is *less perfect*, however, since it is itself ordained to this other freedom.

Truly and definitively speaking, being or actuality, according to all the analogical amplitude of the internal perfections which it bears, is best of all. It is better than freedom. One does not die in the name of free will; one dies in the name of freedom of autonomy or exultation. And when a man dies in the name of freedom, although he sacrifices his existence to it, this sacrifice is made in the name of a better existence for his fellow-men. For this freedom, the freedom of exultation and of autonomy, is but another name for the plenitude and superabundance of existence. God exists *necessarily*. He knows Himself and loves Himself *necessarily*. And this infinite necessity is an infinite *freedom of independence*, of exultation and of autonomy. It is *aseitas*, the freedom of independence subsistent by itself.

To return, in conclusion, to metaphysical considerations: the creature has necessarily two origins—God and nothingness; and St. Thomas reminds us that "things which are made of *nothing*, tend by themselves toward *nothing*."

From this point of view one can say that freedom of choice is linked to nothingness in quite a special way, since it cannot exist in a creature without peccability and without the possibility of making nothingness. Herein consists evil.

The creature can enter into the joy of God only if it can love God as a friend; and it can love God as a friend only if it is an image of God, endowed, as God is, with the freedom of choice. And it can be endowed with the freedom of choice only if it possesses a fallible freedom, that is, if it can converse with God, not only obeying the flux of divine actions and motions, but also by resisting them, by saying No, impeding in itself the action of God.

It is this very condition of created freedom that God wishes to turn to good account. When by the virtue of God's grace and by means of this fallible and peccable free will, a creature will attain the ultimate term and will gain a consummate freedom of exultation and autonomy, and a freedom of choice henceforth supernaturally impeccable, then nothingness itself will have been conquered in the very line of freedom of choice.

# CHAPTER VI

## *Freudianism & Psychoanalysis*

### I. *Preliminaries*

In one short chapter, it is not easy to treat problems as numerous and complex as those which Freudianism raises. The matter is rendered even more complicated by the fact that interest in Freud's discoveries and theories exists not only among psychologists and psychiatrists, but seems even greater and, I should say, more fervent, in less competent circles. Literary men have played a most important part in the diffusion of Freudianism. It is a great ordeal for a scientific doctrine, or one which presents itself as such, to owe its success to literary men and to the public at large. In such cases, the serious and objective discussion of a new teaching is drowned in a buzz of interfering noises. In this din, it is not the voice of disinterested intelligence which makes itself heard most clearly; but rather the voices of many obscure tendencies to self-justification, revindication, and curiosity more or less pure. Freud himself gives rise to this confusion by the vivid passion which animates his talent as an investigator. And what shall we say of his disciples? Yet the more a philosopher is surrounded by confusion, the more inescapable is his obligation to try, with even greater persistence, to clarify matters. It seems to me that all discussions on this subject are bound to fail as long as one does not strictly distinguish between *psychoanalysis* as a method of psychological investigation and psychiatric treatment, on the one hand, and Freudianism as a philosophy, on the other. And even this is not sufficient. A threefold division is necessary:

+ *Psychoanalytical method.*
+ *Freudian psychology.*
+ *Freudian philosophy.*

And I would begin by saying, that in the first case (psychoanalytical method) Freud appears to me as a genius of investigation and discovery. In the third case (Freudian philosophy), he seems in some way an obsessed mind. In the second case (Freudian psychology) I regard him as a very valuable psychologist, whose ideas, activated by an extraordinary instinct of discovery, are obscured by a radical empiricism and an aberrant metaphysics, unconscious of themselves.

It will be seen that my point of view in examining the work of Freud differs from that of my friend, Professor Mortimer Adler. In his remarkable book *What Man Has Made of Man*—in which the equivalences between the analytical vocabularies of ancient and modern psychology are so acutely indicated—Professor Adler prefers to consider Freud's work chiefly from the point of view of its philosophical and ethical significance, whereas I should rather place myself on an epistemological ground.

Since Freud's ideas are more or less familiar to everyone, it is unnecessary to give a historical and doctrinal account. Let us immediately enter into the heart of the subject.

## II. *The Psychological Method and the Investigation of the Unconscious*

It is well known that Freud is a determined defender of the *psychological unconscious*. He even refrains from using the word "subconscious" no doubt in order to avoid the risk of encouraging the tendency "to consider the unconscious only as a residuum of conscious activity." That which, according to Freud, characterizes the *unconscious*, properly speaking, is not the fact of being absolutely inaccessible, but of being inaccessible to voluntary evocation. For him, the unconscious embraces all that is inaccessible to voluntary evocation, the term *pre-conscious* being used only for those non-conscious elements which voluntary evocation can draw into consciousness.

Thus, the first problem is to discover whether there exists a *psychic life* which escapes consciousness, and whose emergences alone reach this lighted zone. We consider that this question must be answered in the affirmative, thus admitting that here Freud is right. If the problem has been confused by professional psychologists, some of whom for years have admitted only a purely physiological unconscious, while others have appealed to a notion which I consider extremely debatable—of a plurality of centers of consciousness—it is the fault of the philosophers, and primarily of Descartes who, because of an idealistic postulate, identified *psychological fact* and *fact of consciousness*.

For St. Thomas Aquinas, not only is the human soul obscure to itself—knowing its own concrete existence only by reflection upon its acts—not only are its basic tendencies, called powers or faculties, among the realities whose intimate nature escapes introspection, but, in addition, the instincts, the inclinations, the acquired tendencies, the *habitus* or internal improvements of the faculties, the virtues and the vices, the deep mechanisms of the life of the spirit—all these constitute a world of reality whose *effects alone reach conscious-ness*. Whether or not the will suffices to evoke them, it is under a psychic form, that the crowd of memories and images is preserved in us in a latent state; and many psychic operations, even operations of knowing, as those of the external sense, can be performed by us without our being explicitly conscious of them by a reflective act of intelligence, turning back on them and taking hold of them in order to express them to itself. It is a sort of primitive notion, due either to a summary psychology or to idealist or rationalist prejudices, to believe that we bear in ourselves only that which we can tell ourselves about ourselves, and that we think and love only that which we think we know and love. The least attentive observation of our own behavior, and that of others, suffices to illuminate this subject for us.

"The unconscious," writes Freud in the *Interpretation of Dreams*, "is the psychic itself and its essential reality. Its inti-mate nature is as unknown as that of the external world, and consciousness informs us about it as incompletely as our sense organs inform us of the external world." We can subscribe to this formula, taken in itself; but a qualification must immedi-ately be added. It would be a mistake to say, no doubt, that Freud ignores the efficacy of consciousness, since he considers that the healing of neurosis is achieved by a transference from the unconscious to the conscious. But what he does ignore is the *life proper* and the *energy proper* of that whole region of the psychic to which consciousness is necessarily linked, namely, the *rational* part of the soul. The judgments of the mind, the free choices of the will—these are necessarily and in them-selves conscious, and they are essential to our behavior. In contrast, there is, for Freud, no free choice; even the highest functions of the mind can be accomplished in the uncon-scious like the rest. If there is any efficacy in the conscious, it consists only in the fact of becoming known. Thus, for Freud, the unconscious is the principal part in man, if not the whole of his energies. Man is led by the unconscious; and the enlightenment of consciousness, when it works satisfactorily, only serves to prevent internal conflicts between unconscious energies from disturbing this leadership too much.

But let us put an end to this digression. Suffice it to remember that the psychic unconscious exists. It is the problem of exploration of this unconscious which now concerns us.

Here we are indebted to Freud for discoveries whose immense importance it would be unjust to ignore.

The primary step in exploring the unconscious is the disrupting of the control and inhibitions normally exercised by the superior psychic functions over the inferior ones; in other words, it is necessary to suspend this control for a while in order to obtain an emergence of inferior psychic states into the field of consciousness. This is what is known in the Freudian language as functional "liberation." Several stratagems have been used to get this result: some psychiatrists tried to use anaesthetics; others used hypnotism.

But it was a stroke of genius on Freud's part that he discovered how to achieve this result by producing a voluntary suspension of the exercise of self-criticism and self-guidance. As is well known, this is the essential characteristic of psychoanalytic method—the technique of free association. The patient must for a time be made to lose his head, as it were, in order to confess what he himself does not know. The best way, of course, is to obtain his consent for the undertaking. He then voluntarily submits himself to an experiment whereby his mental life will disintegrate in a way, will become liquefied—will pass into a state very much akin to that of hypnotism or of dream-life. Reclining in semi-obscurity, unable to see the doctor standing behind him, who puts him through an exercise in word-association, the patient abandons himself to words and images which rise in him one after the other, with the complete relaxation of logical thought and voluntary self-control. Then, after a more or less prolonged period, the whole fauna of memories and unknown thoughts engulfed in the depths of the unconscious, rise to the surface. This does not happen without crises and agonies, for it is necessary to break, as if by force, active and tenacious resistances, which frequently have become automatic, as well as to break down mechanisms built up by neurosis precisely to permit the unconscious jealously to guard its secrets.

To the process of liberation must therefore be added the process of interpretation. It enlightens the repressing element and transfers it to the field of consciousness, where it loses its automatic character and is disintegrated. Thus, the liberation of the repressed material and its entrance into consciousness are made possible. Once this first act of liberation is started, the psychic unblocking is pursued step by step, liberation and interpretation conditioning each other. It is in the technique of interpretation, and especially in the use of symbolism, that Freud and his disciples have been led to the profusion of the arbitrary, of obsessional dogmatism and of pedantry, which might perhaps discredit psychoanalysis and which far outdo the best jokes of Aristophanes and Molière. And this has caused certain people to say that psychoanalysis has no worse enemies than psychoanalysts. On the other hand, the spread among the public at large of Freudian interpretations, and especially of the vocabulary of symbolism, has had the effect of creating in people the very phenomena which one seeks to discover in them, and, into the bargain, has resulted in poisoning their imaginations. Nevertheless, it remains true that one does not judge a method by the way men abuse it, but by the positive results it is capable of producing. And, to my mind, not only can the principles and rules of Freudian interpretation be saved by a rigorous and precise methodology, but also the central idea which Freud gives us—an idea of great interest, almost unrecognized before him by professional psychologists. Roland Dalbiez, in his remarkable book on Freud,[1] called it the notion of *psychic expression*. A psychic state is determined not only by the foreground—that is, by the object which presents itself to the psychic energy; but it is also determined by the *background*—that is, by other, earlier states or psychic dispositions of the subject itself. The psychic foreground is both the effect and the sign of these unconscious states and dispositions. It is their "psychic expression." This is especially true in the case of psychic products which are not centered in reality: dreams, hallucinations, neurotic symptoms.

Psychoanalysis, practiced according to rigorous rules, very often fails to reach results. When it achieves a result, this more frequently belongs to the order of probability, than to that of certitude. In any case, what is learned is a knowledge of the individual case, explaining the individual present in the individual past. All this means that psychoanalysis belongs, not to the realm of speculative science, but to the realm of medicine, and that it suffers the imperfections inherent in the logical instruments of such a science. Freud very justly observes "that psychoanalysis is not an impartial scientific research, but a therapeutic act; it does not seek to prove something, but to modify something." The exploration of the

---

1.   Roland Dalbiez, *La méthode psychoanalytique et la doctrine freudienne* (Paris: Desclée de Brouwer, 1936).

unconscious by the associative method constitutes the essential factor of psychoanalysis, while the symbolic method, as Freud has often said, plays a secondary role. Within the limits I have just mentioned, the combination of these two methods with the interpretation of dreams, produces facts sufficiently well-established to permit this technique for the exploration of the geological depths of the soul to be considered as a discovery of the highest importance. "The essential character of Freud's work is to have thus created an entirely new method for the exploration of the unconscious."

However, as the text of Freud very usefully reminded us, the psychiatrist has recourse to psychoanalysis in order to heal. Now, what is the therapeutic value of psychoanalysis? Without entering here upon a detailed discussion, I would offer the conclusions, to which, it seems to me, a serious study of collected data must lead. Not only do I believe that the psychoanalytical method is an instrument of investigation capable of yielding rigorous results, notwithstanding the extremely unfinished logical form that Freud, like nearly all great initiators, has given to his discovery; but also, in my opinion, it can, in certain cases, lead to the healing of neuroses. It would be absurd to regard psychoanalysis as the only therapeutic instrument for healing neuroses. It is but *one of the therapeutic instruments* for the healing of *certain* neuroses. The mechanism of this healing is of special interest to the philosopher. "As soon as the unconscious processes become conscious," writes Freud, "the symptoms disappear." The liberation has brought back to light, not an abstract notion of the past, but the concrete past itself, with that existential certainty which belongs to the intuition of memory, and this is indispensable. "The artificial bringing about of the phenomena of hypermnesia remains," as it has been said, "one of the pillars of the psychoanalytic edifices." The patient now sees his own unconscious, his own unhappy past, his own psychic wounds. But the hypermnesia thus provoked is not sufficient; intelligence must intervene. The interpretation, made by the patient, or recognized by him as correct, uncovers for him the causal relations between the materials—the experiences—of his past life and the ailment from which he is suffering. It is most important to grasp the fact that this conscious, intellectual realization is by no means an abstract deduction, but is an intuition that exercises its hold on the very fibers of the psychic tissues of the subject. By this simple fact of realization, the automatic connections which the unconscious had created, are automatically loosened. The light of intelligence dissolves them. Any healing of a neurotic symptom by psychoanalysis is proof of the basic wholesomeness of intelligence and of consciousness.

Let us note here that this act of straightening things out can be spontaneous. I will describe a case which has come directly to my knowledge. A young girl experienced symptoms of anxiety each time that she found herself in an enclosed space—for instance, in a locked room or a railway carriage—and these symptoms became more painful from year to year. She had a frank, open nature, and was accustomed to look boldly into her soul. One day as she was taking a walk in the country, she said to herself: "It is impossible, there *must be* some explanation!" And she tried to remember.... Suddenly, a *completely forgotten* memory of her early childhood came to mind. Her father had been separated from her mother. She saw him rarely, and she feared him greatly.

When she was three years old, she had found herself in a room with her father. She had tried to leave the room, but as she was turning the door handle, the father pushed the bolt, which was placed too high for the child to reach. She rushed to the window, but the father closed it and stood before it. The child felt that she was imprisoned, and was filled with anguish, humiliation.... It was now easy to grasp the relation between this incident of early childhood and the anxiety experienced by the young girl as soon as she found herself locked up. The neurosis which was forming itself disappeared completely and definitely. This young girl, who at that time knew nothing of psychoanalysis, had worked, without suspecting it, a psychoanalytical cure, just as in Molière's play, M. Jourdain, without knowing it, had spoken prose all his life.

The psychoanalytic cure essentially consists in dissolving morbid habits by reducing them to a memory of the events which gave birth to them.

As Mr. Roland Dalbiez very justly remarks, "the key to the psychoanalytic cure is the distinction between habit and memory. It has always been observed that the training of a movement of dexterity—that is the formation of a motor habit—is achieved only when consciousness is entirely withdrawn from the movements, and they become integrated in automatic action. Conversely, it has been observed, that a conscious attempt to reconstruct the various details of the phenomena profoundly disturbs the motor habit and disrupts its automatic character. The pianist, the typist, the fencer, rely entirely upon automatic action. They are bewildered as soon as they try to analyse their movements." In similar fashion, consciousness disintegrates the morbid psychic habits which lie at the psychogenesis of neurosis.

It is known that the Viennese doctor, Joseph Breuer, discovered in 1880–1882, that the reintegration of a traumatic memory in the field of consciousness had a curative effect, which he called *catharsis*, or cleansing of the soul. This discovery consisted in applying to morbid affective habits a general rule of psychic dynamism. Freud's personal achievement was to create an entirely original exploratory technique—the analysis of spontaneous associations, of dreams, of failures and slips—and to have been the first to observe the pathogenic importance of unsuccessful repressions. But the discovery of the fundamental therapeutic principle of analysis, that is, the disintegration of habit by conscious remembering, belongs properly to Breuer, as Freud himself has continually proclaimed.

Psychoanalysis can cure certain neuroses, whose origin is not organic but psychodynamic, and primarily all hysteria, psychogenetic states of anxiety, and obsessional neurosis. Let us add immediately that it can also aggravate them, and expose to neurosis, and to even worse effects, the unfortunate, sane individuals who are enticed by snob-appeal or by a reckless curiosity to visit the psychoanalyst. All who have studied this question know of persons whose moral and mental life was ruined in this manner. This proves that, from the point of view of therapy, or from the point of view of simple exploration of the unconscious, the psychoanalytical method is a difficult and dangerous method. If one must investigate a thousand doctors to find a good doctor, certainly one must consider ten thousand psychoanalysts to make sure of one good psychoanalyst. A discovery can be excellent in itself, yet difficult to handle, and even dangerous, therefore demanding extra precautions. This indeed, is the case with many of inventions. The psychoanalytical method is dangerous both for the patient and the doctor. I should like to give a few explanations of this point.

Psychoanalysis—and this is precisely its scientific value—makes us cross the forbidden zone. There is always a danger in disturbing *established relations* between the conscious and the unconscious; it is always perilous to enter into passive states that are thus evoked. One steps over a border on the other side of which one cannot expect the protection of reason. One is in the midst of a savage world. Who knows whether the dreamer, wandering at random, will ever find the door of his old home again? The peril, which we are considering, already exists to a certain extent when a patient practices the psychoanalytical method on himself. This peril is far greater in the employment of psychoanalysis in the full sense of the word, that is, when there are *two*—the doctor and the patient—entering into the unconscious of the patient.

Now, what seems to me to be a novelty, which perhaps has not been made sufficiently clear, is that psychoanalysis transforms the relation formerly established between doctor and patient. *Before*, the doctor was only the representative of a certain art, which he applied to the patient, while effacing himself as much as possible behind this art. If his personality appeared and acted (and here was perhaps the most efficient element of its action), it was in spite of himself, and by passing instrumentally through his art. And such is also the case of the priest who receives confessions. *Nowadays*, on the contrary, the treatment, the medical act, becomes a singular combat between two personalities, both making their way side by side toward the regions of the internal inferno. This duel and this involvement impose upon the doctor an extreme and exhausting strain, if he wishes to preserve his independence and his detached control. There is some danger of his own health breaking down under this strain. As to the patient, he is *patient* in a sense far more real and dreadful than this word connoted in former days. If the experience fails, he is exposed to disorganization, to an even deeper ruin of his psychic life. It is sometimes said that psychoanalysis is a substitute for, the "ersatz" of, the confessional, as that is practiced—especially in the Catholic Church. This seems to me completely inaccurate. On the one hand, it would be an illusion to think that confession exercises a curative power on neuroses and psychoses. Its aim and object are not therapeutic. Moreover, the memories which the penitent imparts to his confessor, belong by definition to the sphere of the conscious or of the pre-conscious, and depend upon voluntary evocation. If the penitent scrutinizes himself and strains his will to go further, he risks suffering from being overscrupulous: he does not enter the world of the unconscious. Far from uncovering the roots of his neurosis or of his frenzy, a neurotic who goes to confession overwhelms his confessor with the deliverances of his neurosis.

On the other hand, confession is in itself an act of reason and of will, in which the two personalities facing each other are as much as possible closed to each other. It is characteristic of the relations between confessor and penitent, that the penitent unveils the secret of his heart to the priest as to the instrument of God; while the confessor subordinates all his personality to his ministry.

If one bears in mind the importance in psychoanalysis of this singular combat between two human personalities, which I have just described, two characteristic traits of psychoanalytical treatment will acquire a special significance. The first is the fact that, as a general rule, and in order to avoid certain risks of nervous disorder, a would-be psychoanalyst must begin by getting psychoanalyzed himself. It is only after this sort of previous initiation and psychic cleansing, that he will be able to undertake in turn the psychoanalysis of others. The second typical trait is the law of *transference*, that is, the inevitable manifestation of the patient's morbid habits, and especially of his erotic tendencies, toward the psychoanalyst himself. No doubt, all those whose duty it is to receive intimate confessions—priests, doctors, lawyers—are likely to become the object of the passion of the neurotic persons who

confide in them. But here we have to deal with a much deeper
and far more typical law: the transference is a necessary stage
of the neurosis in the process of psychoanalytical dissolution.
"A psychodynamic neurosis," according to Freud's scheme, "is
a system of repressed morbid habits, discharging themselves
in an aberrant manner. One of the first consequences of the
(psychoanalytic) cure will be that these habits, instead of man-
ifesting themselves toward the environment, will exteriorize
themselves toward the doctor,"[2] and will try to fix themselves
upon him. "An analysis without transference is an impossibility," writes Freud. But if that is necessarily so, is it not the
result of the very particular relation binding the two personalities of doctor and patient in psychoanalysis, and does not this
appear as a typical manifestation of this intromission, which
we have noted, of one into the soul of another?

This very special relation which places the psychoanalytical act, not in the realm of the (practical) science which
is medicine, but in the realm of a conflict between two persons—where the individual event and accidental aspect are
much more absorbing—would perhaps also explain why psychoanalysts more than others usually find it difficult to observe
the canon of objectivity in scientific method. "The psychoanalysts," wrote Claparède, "give me the impression of being
the owls of psychology. They see in the dark. This, of course,
is a great advantage. But this advantage has its reverse side:
being accustomed to night, they seem incapable at times of
tolerating daylight and of presenting their concepts clearly."

The remarks I have just made should not be interpreted
as condemning the psychoanalytical method. They only tend
to show the dangers which are inherent in this method—the
reasons for which I have tried to explain. It is obvious that in

2.    Dalbiez, *La méthode psychoanalytique et la doctrine freudienne.*

certain cases it may be necessary to use a dangerous medication. When an abnormal link between the conscious and the unconscious appears in the form of a neurotic symptom, which plays havoc with human life, one must not hesitate to use psychoanalysis, if the indications call for a psychoanalytical treatment, and if, furthermore, one can find a good psychoanalyst. But to use psychoanalysis in the same way that one takes a tablet of aspirin is a naïveté for which one may pay dearly.

## III. *Freudian Psychology*

I have spoken of the *psychoanalytical method*. Considering now the *Freudian psychology*, we must, to my mind, credit this psychology with the notion of psychic dynamism. Other psychologists, in particular M. Bergson, have already thrown light upon this notion, and with much more philosophical force, but Freud made an extremely fruitful application of it in the realm of psychiatry and empiriological knowledge. The deep life of the unconscious appears to him as made up of tendencies, desires, instincts, and impulsions comparable, not to mechanical forces, but to vital energies oriented from within toward a goal, and each of them working with the savage tenacity, the suppleness and the cunning of life, in order to achieve this goal. Freud, perhaps, has indulged himself in many exaggerations here, yet this restitution of dynamism and finality has great value, from the standpoint of a Thomist.

It is well known that, with respect to what he calls the *psychopathology of everyday life*, Freud's originality consists in asserting that lapses, forgetfulness, mistakes, and failures, convey a *meaning*—that they are both the results and the signs of hidden affective tendencies. His theory of dreams is also known. To explain all dreams as the disguised satisfaction of desires, is a pretension so evidently simplified, that Freud himself has been obliged to qualify it. In 1920, in his *Essays on Psychoanalysis*, he recognized the automatism of repetition (the repetition compulsion), and admitted "that there exists in psychic life an irresistible tendency toward reproduction or repetition—a tendency which asserts itself without taking pleasure into consideration, and placing itself above it."

Let us note here that in the theory of dreams, considered as the realization of desires, desire is not considered by Freud (as is too often thought) as being *always* of a sexual nature. He has explained himself very clearly on this matter.

Let us put this question aside. If the world of dreams seems to me something infinitely more complex and more mysterious than what Freud makes of it, and if he has not succeeded in explaining it, yet he has correctly surmised that here one must grant a preponderant part to tendential dynamism. But it is in the Freudian theory of neurosis that the part played by this dynamism most clearly appears. Indeed, I believe that we must admit the existence of neuroses of psychodynamic origin, and that the explanation of them given by Freud is well founded. In an extremely detailed discussion, Roland Dalbiez has shown that the famous studies of Pavloff, concerning conditioned reflexes, afford Freud the most remarkable confirmation in this matter. According to Freud, psychoneuroses "are due to an interior conflict. An instinctive pressure has been driven back into the unconscious, victoriously repressed during a more or less prolonged period; then the equilibrium is upset; the repression is made to yield, and what was repressed returns in the form of psychoneurotic symptoms." Now, Pavloff has produced experimental neuroses in dogs by effecting a conflict of instincts, in a manner exactly paralleling the Freudian scheme.

✦

There is another aspect of Freudian psychology, a nocturnal aspect, which naturally has attracted most attention from the general public.

I mean, in particular, the theory of the libido, concerning which Freud has expressed himself in rather contradictory terms; so much so, indeed, that the libido sometimes appears as a simple equivalent of what theologians call *concupiscence*, the unquenchable desire for everything that can satisfy the senses and the taste for pleasure; sometimes as a sort of metaphysical Eros, expressing the energies of *being* and its striving toward existence and life; and sometimes as a sexual desire. However, this last significance is manifestly preponderant, either because sexual psychology has been a privileged field of study for Freud, or because, as I shall point out further, he lacks all philosophical criteria of specification and therefore brings back every common notion to its most striking type of realization. The charge of pansexualism, with which Freudian psychology has been reproached, is justified therefore; and this psychology often appears as itself dominated by a kind of sexual obsession.

On the other hand, a general philosophy of a very inferior type hinders Freud from distinguishing the potential and the actual; he replaces potentialities by a summation of actualities opposing each other; for the indeterminate tendency, turned toward normal actuation, but capable of a number of abnormal actuations, he substitutes a constellation of contrary and conflicting actuations. What we call the normal appears (to him, therefore), only as a particular case of the abnormal—health as a particular case of illness. And from this follow all the exaggerations in his theories of infantile sexuality, of the Oedipus complex, etc., wherein he interprets pathological material of indubitable value, in a violently and aggressively degrading sense, allowing himself the most arbitrary generalizations, thus making the existence of the Oedipus complex a universal law, and considering the child as *polymorphous perverse* (the word "perverse" conveying, of course, no judgment of moral value).

Let us consider, nevertheless, that all the play of instincts, however numerous and powerful, remains open in man; it involves a relative indetermination, which finds its normal achievement and its normal regulation only in reason, so that the indifferentiation of instincts, at such and such a stage, leaves open the *possibility* of abnormal fixations. We must, therefore, understand that if certain perversions appear as a regression toward an infantile stage in the evolution of instincts, there is, however, an essential difference between "infantile *non-integration* and *disintegration*, always complicated by anachronic and discordant reintegration, which is the property of a pathological state."[3] And we shall then see the absurdity of the notion of polymorphous perversity, which Freud applies to the child. If we replace this notion of *polymorphous perversity* by that of *polymorphous pervertibility*, the error is corrected, but we shall have gone beyond Freud. "When someone has *become* grossly and manifestly perverse," writes Freud, "one might say with greater accuracy that he has *remained* as such; he represents a state of arrested development." This formula is typical of the central error of Freudian psychology, which I have just indicated.

Finally, this psychology seeks to be (and such a tendency is justifiable in itself) a psychology of purely empiriological type. But it is invaded and submerged on all sides by a pseudo-metaphysics of the most vulgar quality, which Freud is the less willing to eliminate, the more he imagines himself secure from philosophy and metaphysics. I have said pseudo-metaphysics

---

3.    Dalbiez, *La méthode psychoanalytique et la doctrine freudienne.*

of the most vulgar quality, because it combines all the prejudices of deterministic and materialistic *scientism* with all the prejudices of *irrationalism*.

The confusion between the schema of an entirely empiriological psychology and the analyses of a philosophical psychology finally engenders a sort of explanatory mythology, where the *instincts of life*, attached to the libido, and the *instincts of death*, attached to the instinct of individual self-preservation (that is, in Freud's opinion, of the return to the inorganic elements which are the materials of the living organism), have no more scientific value than the Eros and the Thanatos of old Heraclitus. Instead of discussing these matters further, I would rather say a few words concerning a concept which plays an essential part in Freudian psychology: the concept of sublimation.

The notion of the specification of tendencies by their *formal object* is entirely absent from Freud's thought; considering tendencies and instincts exclusively on the side of the subject, he cannot possibly discover in them a distinction in essence. How, then, could he help making them all flow back to the same fundamental instinct, of which they would be but transformations, or rather, different masks? On the other hand, his negation of the autonomy of the spiritual and his desire to humiliate the human person, could only lead him in the same direction. As a result, the so-called *superior* states—the inspiration of the poet, the love of the mystic, for instance—are, in Freud's opinion, only transformations and masks of animal instinct, the diverted path by which a sensuality, inhibited in its normal exercise, satisfies itself in an insidious and veiled manner: all human exhilaration is specifically sensual.

It is easy enough to observe that mixtures and collusions can occur by accident in the miserable mechanisms of human nature. But this observation only bears witness to the fact that the dynamic structures thus mixed are of distinct essence. Freudian interpretation is founded on no compelling reason, but on a simple and brutal negation *a priori* of an order of realities, whose rational certitude is established by philosophic means, and can be established only by such means.

Does this mean that the word "sublimation," whose Freudian meaning is unacceptable, must be rejected in itself? I do not think so. It seems, on the contrary, that it is capable, in quite a different sense, of naming a psychic process of the greatest importance.

The rapture of the lyrical or religious soul is in itself specifically spiritual, and, therefore, *specifically distinct* from the animal instinct. Does this mean that this rapture is *separated* from instinct? It is absurd to absorb the superior in the inferior, but it is unhuman to disjoin them.

There exist, as I have suggested, typical differences between the instincts of man and the instincts of animals devoid of reason. If, in man, they possess a relative indetermination far greater than in the animal, and demand from reason their final regulation, it is because in man they are related to the spirit; they are made for the spirit: "their real center, their supreme depth, resides above organic life." There is in them a secret aspiration to bathe "in those delicate vibrations which commune with the spirit." And this is true of the typical tonality due to the difference of sexes, as well as of the other tonalities of affective life. This typical tonality (and here we join Freud in the distinction between the *sexual* and the *genital*), this typical tonality in the human being far exceeds the instinct of procreation; it pervades the most beautiful creations of culture, and plays a most important part in the genesis of superior affective states.

Hence, we can define sublimation—real sublimation— in the words of the French psychologist Gustave Thibon, as "a sort of ascensional reflux of instinct toward the immaterial sources of being, as a *qualitative* integration of sensitive rhythms in the pure melody of interior life. Subjectively, it is accompanied by a feeling of equilibrium, of peace and of intimate plenitude, by an impression of liberation from the slavery and discordance of inferior appetites, and by a sort of spontaneous transparency of all the depths of nature to the rays of the spirit."[4] If moral progress requires from us an ascetic struggle of spirit against flesh, and passes through stages of non-sublimation, where inferior instincts are conquered, though becoming even more besetting—this moral progress also aspires to end in a phase of final integration, which corresponds to sublimation, such as we have defined it, and whose evangelical name is beatitude of peace.

## IV. *Freudian Philosophy*

I will take up very briefly the discussion of the third item, which I mentioned at the beginning of this chapter, namely, Freudian philosophy; and I must say that I do not regret this brevity. Nothing is more unpleasant than to speak of a philosophy which does not recognize itself as such.

The whole of Freudian philosophy is based upon a prejudice: the violent negation of spirituality and liberty. Experimental views, which are often correct, become philosophically hardened, and transform themselves into the worst errors. With great sagacity, Freud saw that even the most normal human nature implies a certain pluralism of more or less antagonistic forces. This pluralism becomes absolute, and the human person decomposes and decays under the very eyes of the psychologist. Freud invented a powerful instrument for exploring the unconscious, and beheld with deepest

---

4.    Gustave Thibon, in *Études Carmélitaines*, April, 1936.

insight this fearful world, the interior inferno, full of all the monsters repressed in the unconscious. But he mixed up the unconscious itself with this inferno, which is only a part of it. He separated it from the life of reason and of the spirit; he therefore considered as a pure bestiality hidden in man the whole of instinctivity, and not only that part which has effectively *separated* itself through repression, or through vice or wickedness. He thus ignored the central law, which I have mentioned, the law of the *essentially human* character of normal instinctivity in man. Repressed, active, bestial, infantile, alogical, sexual—these are the six terms which Jones uses to characterize the unconscious according to Freud.

We must admit that in Freud's error in itself, just as in Marx's, there is something grandiose, something which carries a fundamental truth to absurdity. Both have seen the importance of what the Thomist calls material causality. It is only unfortunate that they made it everything or, at least, the most important part.

It is difficult not to perceive in the work of Freud a punishment inflicted upon the pride of that conceited, pharisaic personality, which rationalism had built up as an end supreme in itself. The masks drop one after the other, and what was hidden in the white-washed sepulchers appears in broad daylight. Man had denied all the evil and the irrational, which he carried in him, in order to be able to enjoy the testimony of his conscience, and to be pleased with himself and justified through himself. Established in the illusion and the trickery of a false nominalist conscience, he made great use of moralism and of spiritualism, devoid, however, of their substance.

The achievement of Freud is to have denounced the lie of this false conscience. Truly speaking, the latter covers up and hides deep unconscious undercurrents—not only economic interests, class interests, as Marx proclaimed—but all the domain of concupiscence and of self-love, of the savage and of the demonic, which man had striven to deny. After Freud, a certain form of pharisaism has become impossible. Man will have to look for a new freshness, a new and deeper mode of being conscious of himself, in order to rediscover his unity and his personality.

On the other hand—and this is a good occasion for speaking of ambivalence—this stubborn will to lay bare human nature and to show it its own ugliness, is accompanied by a strange but indubitable pity: pity for the sick, pity for the child, whose first experiences are experiences of shame and pain, pity for man, who is the slave of so many wild forces, and who is lost and full of distress in the midst of himself. One might say that Freud conceives them all as the morbid and tortured victims of an inexorable fate.

Whatever be the value of these affective dispositions, they can only produce havoc and manias when they pass into the mind and command a philosophy. Freud's masked philosophy appears as a morbid symptom affecting intelligence, as a result of unsuccessful repression of the above-mentioned affective dispositions. It is but the disguise of a deep hatred of *reason's form*—that is, of the informing of being and life by rational norms. Let us be content to record here the failure of the effort, made by Freud and by his school, to explain by psychoanalysis and by an empiricism or a radical sensualism of a sexualist tendency, the superior activities of the human being: art, morality, religion. This failure has been disclosed by Jung in relation to art, by Malinowski in relation to the origin of morals and the extraordinary theory of primitive patricide which, as Dalbiez says, belongs to the realm of romantic anthropology. (You will remember Freud's story in *Totem and Taboo*, which he does not seem to intend as humorous. "One day, the brothers, who had been expelled, met and killed and devoured their father, and this put an end to the paternal horde." And this act of cannibalism is not only the origin of Totemic sacrifice and of exogamy—it gives the key to all religions. "I would be able," writes Freud, "to end and sum up this brief study by saying that one finds in the Oedipus complex the beginning of religion, of morals, of society and of art." Does not the father of the Oedipus complex display a somewhat exaggerated paternal pride?)

Finally, it seems to me that Freudian metaphysics contain in their very depths what Max Scheler calls resentment: the resentment of a soul wounded and humiliated from childhood, and which, as it seems, strikes at human nature itself; and especially resentment against all rational, moral, religious regulations, which pretend to conquer the world of instinct, and which in reality augment, in Freud's opinion, man's misfortune and lead to psychic disorders. *Acherunta movebo.* I have already observed that this bitter pessimism is not devoid of a certain grandeur. Indeed, a sort of desperate pity, which is also found in Luther, causes Freud—who considers everything from the angle of the clinical aspect of psychoneuroses— to make morals, with their restrictions which he finds arbitrary, and with the feeling of culpability which they develop, responsible for the innumerable ills and supplementary sufferings which men inflict upon themselves. And it is especially against cultural sexual morals that Freud rises in wrath. Here, it seems to me, we must note, first, that the human species is a species which can live and develop only in a state of culture; second, that the rules of cultural morals precisely tend to diminish the causes of the sufferings and ills to which the human species is exposed, and to augment its creative tension, but they cannot achieve this aim without imposing hardships on the individual. Hence, morals become for humanity a yoke as intolerable as it is indispensable if love does not lighten this burden, and if a regime of divine mercy does not help to *compensate* the regime of law, and place itself above it without abolishing it: thus creating for those for whom, through undeserved luck, the accomplishment of the law is less strenuous, very special duties of friendship and of fraternal respect toward the others.

This is not the moment to embark upon a discussion of this subject. I only want to observe, in order to conclude this chapter, that we find in Freud a striking example of the statistical law, according to which great discoveries, by reason of man's unhappy condition and of his weakness in bearing the truth, seem—especially when they concern themselves with the world of the senses—to need violent affective stimuli which, while giving an impulse to research and guiding it, at the same time incline the intelligence toward error. Yet, finally, it is truth that error will thus have served in spite of itself; and thanks to the process of purification and of reintegration which reason will be obliged to follow, it is truth which will have said the last word.

Thus, in the case of Freudianism, will vanish the attempts, made by an aberrant philosophy, to disintegrate and dissolve human personality and unity into a world of instincts, sex and dream, animality and matter. And it is to a spiritual purification, and to a better consciousness of its own world, that the human person will be led by a correct understanding of Freud's discoveries.

# CHAPTER VII

## *Action & Contemplation*

### I. *Greek Philosophy*

The debate between action and contemplation not only concerns each of us personally, but is also of vital importance to human culture and to the destiny of civilization. I hold it to be of special moment to this continent, as I shall try to suggest at the end of this chapter.

We know well enough how emphatic the East is about its calling to the contemplative life and how proud of it; while the West with no less pride—a pride which is beginning to suffer much—boasts that it has chosen action. Could this lead us to affirm without more ado that the East is contemplation and the West action? Such an affirmation would be all too simple. Things do not tell their secrets so easily. Occidental activism might be, in its misery and agony, a degenerated and pathetic form of what was once an incomparable sentiment of life and human values. The West, I believe, had once a habit of contemplation in harmony with the deepest postulations of spiritual reality.

✦

In philosophical language the problem of action and contemplation is that of *transitive* (or *productive*) and *immanent* activity (immanent activity in its most typical and purest function).

Transitive activity is that which one being exercises upon
another, the so-called *patient*, in order to act upon it, imparting
to it movement or energy. This activity, which is quite visible,
is characteristic of the world of bodies; through it all elements
of material nature inter-communicate, and through it we act
on matter, transforming it. It passes away in Time, and with
Time. Not only is it transitory, it is transition. The Greeks
were right in saying that in this activity, the action in which
the agent and the patient intercommunicate is accomplished
in the patient, *actio in passo*, and being common to both, makes
the agent (notwithstanding its being as such the nobler of the
two) dependent on the patient, in which alone it obtains perfection. The Agent is itself *in actu* and attains its perfection
only by acting on another than itself, and in the instant of this
action. Transitive action is a mendicant action, which achieves
itself in another being, and is essentially in need of another
being. On the other hand, while the agent's perfection is also,
in fact, that of the patient, the agent as such does not seek
the patient's good, but its own (this is a typical characteristic
of purely transitive action). Hence its "egotism." People who
exercise philanthropy as a transitive activity need the poor to
help if they want to be helpful, sinners to preach to if they
want to be preachers, victims whose wrongs they can redress.
They need *patients*.

Immanent activity is of quite a different order. It is the
characteristic activity of life and spirit. Here the agent has its
own perfection in itself; it elevates itself in being. Immanent
action is a self-perfecting quality. The acts of knowing and
of loving are not only within the soul, they are for the soul
an active superexistence, as it were, superior to the merely

physical act of existence. Thus the soul, when it knows, becomes thereby something that it is not, and when it loves, aspires toward what it is not, as to another self. This action, as such, is above time.

It speaks for Aristotle's greatness to have known and taught that immanent (or vital or interiorizing) action is nobler and more elevated than transitive (or non-vital or exteriorizing) action.

In their doctrine of immanent action, the Greeks held that the immanence of the intellectual act is, as such, more perfect than that of the act of will; that is why, according to a thesis which St. Thomas made classical, intelligence is nobler than will, from the sole point of view of the degrees of immanence and immateriality of the powers of the soul.

All this led the Greeks to a twofold conclusion, which, in its first part, formulated a most valuable truth; and, in its second part, transformed that truth into a great error.

The great truth which the Greeks discovered (and which their philosophers conceptualized in very divers spiritual ways) is the superiority of contemplation, as such, to action. As Aristotle puts it, life according to the intellect is better than a merely human life.

But the error follows. What did that assertion mean to them practically? It meant that mankind lives for the sake of a few intellectuals. There is a category of specialists—the philosophers—who lead a superhuman life; then in a lower category, destined to serve them, come those who lead the ordinary human life, the civil or political one; they in turn are served by those who lead a sub-human life, the life of work— that is, the slaves. The high truth of the superiority of contemplative life was bound up with the contempt of work and the plague of slavery. Even the work of freemen, of the artist or the artisan, was scorned. Plutarch wrote: "Who, having

the choice, would not prefer enjoying the contemplation of
Phidias' works, to being Phidias himself?" "All artisans have a
despicable occupation, because there can be nothing noble in
a workshop," said "the good Cicero." And farther to the East,
the Brahmin's contemplation reposes socially on the untouch-
ables' misery; wisdom, on offence and humiliation.

## II. *Christianity*

Christianity has transfigured everything.

What innovations did Christianity introduce on the subject with which we are dealing? I should say they are fourfold.

First, it teaches us that love is better than intelligence. St.
Thomas admits, like Aristotle, that considering the degrees of
immanence and immateriality of the powers of the soul in
themselves, intelligence is nobler than will, but he adds that
considering the *things* we know and love, these things exist in
us by knowledge according to the mode of existence and the
dignity of our own soul, but by love they attract us to them
according to their own mode of existence and their own
dignity, and therefore it must be said that to love things that
are superior to man is better than to know them. It is better
to love God than to know Him; it is also better to love our
brethren, in whom the mystery of God's likeness is concealed,
than to know them. And the love which is *caritas* is, not in the
moral order only, but in the ontological as well, that which is
most excellent and most perfect in the human soul and in the
Angel.

Second, Christianity has transfigured the notion of contemplation, and endowed it with a new meaning. Albert the
Great sums it up in his admirable treatise *de Adhaerendo Deo*:
"The contemplation of the philosophers," he writes, "is concerned with the perfection of the contemplator, and hence
does not go farther than the intellect, so that their end is

intellectual knowledge. But the contemplation of the saints is concerned with the love of the one who is contemplated—of God. And this is why, not content with the intellect, with knowledge as its ultimate end, it attains the heart through love, *transit ad affectum per amorem*." And love indeed is its own instrument, love's dark fire is its light. *Quia ubi amor, ibi oculus.* This leads to consequences, which we shall presently see, and which make the word "contemplation" rather unsatisfactory.

Third, Christianity has also transfigured the notion of action and has given it a new meaning. Christian wisdom has seen, better than the wisdom of philosophers, that the action which man exercises on matter or other men, though it is transitive, cannot be reduced to transitive action such as is found in the world of bodies. It is essentially human activity. It has not only been thought and willed before being exercised—being born in the heart before being made manifest in the external world; it not only necessarily proceeds from an immanent act, but, moreover, it goes beyond the work it serves, and by an instinct of communication which demands to be perfected in goodness, proceeds to the service of other men. You can give high wages to a workman for work manifestly useless—for instance, the task, which used to be imposed on convicts, of digging holes and then filling them up—and this workman will be driven to despair. It is essential to human work that it be useful to men.

As has often been remarked, Christ in assuming for Himself the work and condition of an artisan in a small village, rehabilitated labor, and manifested its natural dignity, a dignity which Antiquity had denied. The *hardship* of work is a consequence of the Fall and of the loss of privileges proper to the state of innocence, but not *work* in *itself*. Adam in the state of innocence worked—without any pain—and had the mission of cultivating and keeping the Garden.

Man's labor in its first and humblest stage is a co-operation with God the Creator, and Christianity's rehabilitation
of labor in the moral order is bound up with revelation, in
the dogmatic order, of creation *ex nihilo*. *Pater mens usque mod
operatur, et ego operor.* My Father worketh hitherto and I work
too. Here is the foundation of labor ethics, which the modern world is seeking and has not yet found. The work which
Antiquity most despised, manual work, imposes the forms
of reason on matter, and delivers man from the fatalities of
material nature (provided however he does not turn his industry into an idol which enslaves him even more); thus, work has
a value of natural redemption; it is like a remote prefiguration
of the communications of love. Man is both *homo faber* and
*homo sapiens*, and he is *homo faber* before being in truth and
actually *homo sapiens* and in order to become the latter.

Fourth, and this is a consequence of the preceding considerations, another innovation which Christianity has introduced,
relevant to our subject, is that contemplation (supernatural
contemplation, which would be better called *entrance into the very
states of God, of God Incarnate*) is not only the business of specialists or of the chosen few. This was an astounding revolution in
the spiritual order. Greeks and Jews, masters and slaves, men
and women, poor and rich (but the poor, first), souls who have
known evil and souls (if there be such) who have not, whatever
their condition, race and wounds—all are called to the feast of
divine Love and divine wisdom. That wisdom calls them all, it
clamors in the public places and in the roadways. All, without
exception, are called to perfection, which is the same as that of
the Father who is in heaven; in a manner either close or distant,
all are called to the contemplation of the saints, not the contemplation of the philosophers, but to loving and crucified contemplation. All without exception. The universality of such an
appeal is one of the essential features of Christianity's *catholicity*.

At the same time and symmetrically, all are bound by the
law of work. There are no more privileged by pain and labor.
Work is for everyone, as well as the sin of which everyone
must be cured. If any will not work, neither shall he eat. It is
St. Paul who said this, and the evolution of modern societies shows more clearly every day how universal that assertion
is. I know well that some people who have adopted it as a
motto, not knowing its author, perhaps, give it a wrong interpretation, believing that there is but one kind of work—that
which creates economic values. They fail to see the admirable
analogical variety of the notion of work. According to the
social conscience which the Christian leaven has awakened,
no one can be dispensed from activities directed to the good
of men, be it to clothe or feed their bodies, to teach them or
guide them, to bring them to truth and beauty or delights of
the spirit, to feed them with the words of God, or, like those
dedicated to contemplative life, to wear oneself out in praying
for them. All those varied activities are fraternal, and communicate analogically in that notion of work which the Christian
Spirit has renewed.[1]

I have just said that the notion of work is verified in a most
refined way, even in those dedicated to the contemplative life. It
is true that contemplation itself is in fact not work, not a thing
of utility. It is a fruit. It is not ordinary leisure; it is a leisure coin-
ciding with the very highest activity of the human substance.
According to the profound views of St. Thomas Aquinas, following Aristotle, those who go beyond the socio-temporal life

---

1.   I do not think that the word "work" and concept of work must be
     reserved only to manual work and to intellectual activities preparing for or
     regulating the latter. I consider the fact of some things, being *per se*, or by
     itself, related to the utility of the human community, as the true criterion
     of work in the ethico-social sense. And lawyers, statesmen, teachers, have
     an activity no less related to the usefulness of the community than the
     activity of farmers or miners.

achieve in themselves the supra-social good to which the social tends as to a transcendent term, and by that very act are free from the law of labor. There remains no more for them but Thee and I, Him whom they love, and themselves.

But in virtue of that generosity which is inherent in immanent activity at its highest degrees, loving contemplation overflows as a protection and a benediction to society. And though not itself a useful service or a work, even in the widest meaning of the word, that which is beyond usefulness super-abounds thus in a usefulness, in which the notion of work is still realized at the extreme limit of refinement.

Thus, it will be understood why I have said above that all activities, from manual labor to the gratuitously added util-ity of contemplative leisure, are fraternal activities, in which the notion of work can be found at very different degrees of analogy.

Christianity has not condemned slavery as a social and juridical form, save in its most extreme modes, which are absolutely incompatible with human dignity. It has done bet-ter by annihilating, from within, its functional necessity in human conscience. It has evacuated that necessity from con-science, and is evacuating it progressively from existence (for ancient slavery is not the only form of servitude), and it will require the entire history of mankind to have completely fin-ished with it. For Christian conscience, as I have just pointed out, there do not exist two categories in humanity, *homo faber* whose task is to work, and *homo sapiens* whose task is the con-templation of truth. The same man is both *faber* and *sapiens*, and wisdom calls us all to the freedom of the children of God.

## III. *Superabounding Contemplation*

The contemplation of which I have been speaking is Christian contemplation—what Albert the Great, in the text quoted above, called *contemplatio sanctorium*. The Christian doctors tell us that it is supernatural, that is to say, it is achieved by the gifts which Sanctifying Grace—formal participation in us of divine nature—brings to the soul; and not only by its object, but in its mode as well, it goes beyond anything that the energies of human nature, left to themselves, can achieve.

It can be called Christian in a historical sense, since for nearly two thousand years Christian contemplators have made it manifest to us. It can be called Christian in a different sense, ontological or metaphysical, since it lives by the grace of Christ. In that sense it can even be found—substantially the same, whatever the difference of mode, degree, purity, or human setting—in eras or lands where Christianity is not professed. It is the supernatural contemplation of the Old Testament and the New, of Moses and St. Paul, such as is exercised by the living faith and supernatural gifts. The existence of these divine gifts is taught us by Christian revelation, but they are alive in all who have the grace of Christ, even when not belonging visibly to His Church (for instance, some of the Jewish Hassidim whose story was told by Martin Buber, or that great Mohammedan mystic Al Hallaj, whom Louis Massignon has studied).

At the same time, supernatural contemplation achieves and fulfills a natural aspiration to contemplation which is consubstantial to man, and to which the sages of India and Greece bear witness. According to Albert the Great, this natural contemplation, as such, has its term in intellect and knowledge. No doubt, love can crown *gnosis*, but here it remains an effect; it does not constitute the proper end of the contemplative act itself, nor the proper mean of it.[2]

---

2.   For a more detailed analysis of these questions, see our essay on "L'expérience mystique naturelle et le vide," in *Études Carmélitaines*, October, 1938.

✦

It must be remarked that there are in the spirit many activities, discursive activity and activity of desire, which are neither repose nor contemplation. But while being a labor, this labor of the intelligence and of the heart tends toward contemplation and prepares for it, and in this measure participates in the end to which it is directed. It follows that there is a vast region of life of the spirit, where contemplation is prepared, even outlined, not being, for all that, disengaged from active life and laborious activity. In this wider sense, the philosopher and the poet can be said to be already contemplative on the plane of natural activities.

This should help us to resolve a rather difficult problem. In the order of the Kingdom of God and eternal life, many are surprised by the theological teaching that action is directed to contemplation. In the order of temporal life and terrestrial civilization, the philosopher has to acknowledge that same law of work being directed in the end to contemplation and to the activities of repose. But what activity of repose and what contemplation? The contemplation of the saints is not a proper and direct end of the political life. It would be more than a paradox to give as a direct end to the life of men, as members of a terrestrial community and as part of the temporal universe of civilization, the transcendent and super-terrestrial end which is their absolutely ultimate end as consorts with the saints, and souls redeemed at a great price; in other words, to solve the question of the workmen's leisure by saying that work has for its end, on the ethico-social plane, mystical union, preluding the ultimate end. And yet, even in the ethico-social order, work is not its own end; its end is rest. Is it then directed to leisure and holidays, understood as a mere cessation of work, a pleasure, or honest pastime, a family party, winter sports, or the movies? If so, it would then be

directed to something less noble and less generous than itself.
We are far from looking with scorn on rest and relaxation
which recreates the worn out human substance. But that rest
is but a preparation to a renewed labor, just as sleep prepares
for the toils of the day.

In reality, human work, even on the plane of social terrestrial life, must be accomplished with a view to an active
and self-sufficient rest, to a terminal activity of an immanent
and spiritual order, already participating in some measure in
contemplation's supertemporality and generosity. For all that,
such active rest is not yet the rest of contemplation properly
speaking; it has not yet attained to contemplation. Let us say
it is the active rest of the culture of the mind and the heart,
the joy of knowing, the spiritual delectations which art and
beauty offer us, the generous enthusiasm supplied by disinterested love, compassion and communion, zeal for justice,
devotion to the commonwealth and to mankind. The very
law of work to which every member of the commonwealth
has to submit, demands that all should have access to that
leisure. There is nothing here that is contemplation, properly
speaking. But if in this kind of leisure, instead of shutting up
human concerns in themselves, man remains open to what is
higher than himself, and is borne by the natural movement
which draws the human soul to the infinite, all this would be
contemplation in an inchoate state or in preparation.

But enough of this. Let us ask St. Thomas and the
theologians what they think of supernatural *contemplation*.[3]
In a famous passage, St. Thomas says first that, absolutely

---

3.    Cf. Jacques and Raissa Maritain, *Prayer and Intelligence* (New York: Sheed &
      Ward, 1928).

speaking and in itself, contemplative life is better than active life. This is a thesis characteristic of any conception of life worthy of the human person's dignity—the fundamental thesis of the intrinsic superiority of contemplation. St. Thomas proves it by eight reasons drawn from Aristotle and illuminated by eight texts from Scripture. And there is, he says, a ninth reason, added by the Lord when He says: "Mary has chosen the better part."

After this, there is a second point of doctrine to be considered: contemplation, being the highest degree of the life of the soul, cannot be an instrument of the moral virtues and the operations of active life, but the end to which those things have to be directed as means and dispositions.

A third point, made manifest by the example of Christian contemplatives and by the teaching of theologians, is that the contemplation of the saints does not merely attain to the heart through love. Not being confined to the intellect, being the fruit of love in act through which faith becomes as it were a thing of experience, this contemplation also enters the sphere of action, in virtue of the generosity and abundance of love, which consists in giving oneself. Action then springs from the superabundance of contemplation, *ex superabundantia contemplationis*, be it by the very reason of the *nature* of the work it produces (thus preaching things divine must overflow from a heart united to God or be vain), or by reason of the *mode* of the production, which makes a work, whatever it is, an instrument employed by sovereign Love to touch and vivify the heart.

It is by virtue of such a superabundance, which comes from the supernatural ordination of human life to the fruition of God, that Christian wisdom, unlike that of the philosophers, is not merely speculative, but practical as well, and directive of human life, for this life is not regulated by human measures only, but by divine as well, and thus becomes the object of that very knowledge which contemplates God. More excellent than any purely intellectual wisdom, because it attains closer to God, being a wisdom of love and union, the act of the gift of wisdom is not a self-sufficing contemplation, but one which, as St. Paul puts it, walks toward them that are without, redeeming time.

When explaining the words of Jesus: "Know ye not that I must be about my Father's business?" St. John of the Cross, the great doctor of contemplation, liked to recall Dionysius's sentence: the divinest of all things divine is to co-operate with God in the salvation of souls; which means, St. John of the Cross tells us, "that the supreme perfection of every creature, in its own hierarchy and degree, is to ascend and grow according to its talent and resources in the imitation of God; and it is most admirable and most divine to co-operate with Him in the conversion and salvation of souls. God's own works are resplendent in that."

We have arrived here at a fundamental truth: Christian philosophy is a philosophy of being; more than that, a philosophy of the superabundance of being; and in this it stands incomparably higher than other great philosophies of being, such as Hindu metaphysics, where being does not give being and can but absorb in itself—*maya* and soul itself. Christian philosophy, better than the Greek, has seen that it is natural that immanent activity should superabound, since it is super-existing. Purely transitive activity is egoistic, as I have said at the beginning of this chapter. Immanent activity is "generous," because, striving to be achieved in love, it strives to achieve the good of other men, disinterestedly, gratuitously, as a gift. Christian theology is a theology of divine generosity, of that superabundance of divine being which is manifested in God Himself, as only revelation can tell us, in the plurality of Persons, and which is also manifested, as we could have discovered by reason alone, by the fact that God is Love, and that He is the Creator. And God, whose essence is His own beatitude and His own eternal contemplation, God who creates, gives, has never ceased to give, He gives Himself through Incarnation, He gives Himself through the Holy Spirit's mission. It is not for Himself, St. Thomas says, it is for us that God has made everything to His glory. When contemplation superabounds in efficacious love and in action, it corresponds within us to that divine superabundance communicative of its own good.

## IV. *The Call to Contemplation*

That is what philosophers can be taught about supernatural contemplation both by theology and by the experience of the saints. Properly speaking, such a contemplation is a participation in the divine life and perfection itself—an entrance, as I said above, into the very states of the Word Incarnate. It is that purely and simply terminal freedom of exaltation and of autonomy, mentioned in a preceding chapter.

But have I not said that Christianity's great novelty is its universalism, which calls all men to what is most difficult, to perfect life, a life of union and contemplation? Let us consider this more closely. It was much discussed, some years ago, whether contemplative graces are exceptional not only *de facto* but also *de jure*, whether it is temerarious to desire or hope for them, or whether they are the normal flower within us of the living grace of virtues and gifts. This discussion, momentous to all who are anxious to know man, has been complicated by many extraneous considerations springing either from inadequate vocabulary, or practical preoccupations. I shall say a word about it before finishing.

The anti-mystical tendencies, which have developed since the sixteenth and seventeenth centuries, were generated by an all too legitimate fear, that of shame and quietism; the wine of the Holy Spirit is apt to go to one's head when mingled with the alcohols of imagination. Books of spirituality, not those only which make commonplace literature out of the saints' experiences, but even those of authentic spirituality, are apt, when falling into impatient and weak hands, to cause many a victim which psychiatry claims as its own. It is terrible to throw anything divine to men, who make use of everything to feed their chimeras.

And yet God, who is wise, has dared to do that terrible thing; and at what risk, when giving us His Truth. If books were judged by the bad uses man can put them to, what book has been more misused than the Bible? Let us live danger-ously, says Nietzsche; that is a pleonasm. One is out of dan-ger only when dead. To turn souls away from aspiring to the graces of contemplative union, to deprive them of the teach-ing and-advices of a St. Thérèse or a St. John of the Cross, is to deprive them of the channels of life, to condemn them to a parching thirst. If anti-mystical tendencies were completely systematized, they would turn Christianity into a mere moral system, while it is, first of all, a theological communion.

And this is why in the discussion to which I referred, theo-logians are coming to an agreement (though with many differ-ences of nuance) on the point that all souls are called, if not in a proximate manner, at least in a remote one, to mystical contemplation as being the normal blossoming of grace's vir-tues and gifts.

For if we define mystical life (or life according to the spirit) as a coming of the soul under the regimen in which the gifts of Grace, called in sacred terminology gifts of the Holy Spirit, predominate (so that henceforth the soul is docile to the spirit of God, who disappropriating it of itself, takes it into His own charge), then it is clear that every soul is called—at least in a remote manner—to mystical life *thus defined*. Why is that so? Because all are called to the perfection of love. And that perfection cannot be attained without the radical purifications and substantial remoldings which are the mystical life's sacrificial privilege. St. Thomas teaches us that the gifts of the Holy Spirit are necessary to *salvation*, because we are so foolish that we could not, on certain difficult occasions to which we are all exposed, make by ourselves the proper use of theological and moral virtues to avoid *mortal sins*; then it must be said with still more reason that we are too foolish and too miserable to make by ourselves the proper use of those virtues to *attain perfection*, and hence it is necessary for this aim that the gifts of the Holy Spirit should govern our life as directive habits.

We must now observe that among the inspiring gifts which Catholic theology has learned to enumerate from Isaiah, some, like those of Counsel, Force, Fear, mainly concern action, while others, like those of Intelligence and Wisdom, are mainly related to contemplation.

It follows that souls which have entered upon the ways of spiritual life will behave in very different manners, each according to its calling. Some will be favored in a pre-eminent manner with the highest gifts, those of Wisdom and Intelligence; these souls will represent mystical life in its normal plenitude, and will have the grace of contemplation in its typical forms, be they arid or comforting. In the case of other souls it will be primarily the other gifts of inspired freedom; their life will be indeed a mystical and dispropriated life; but it will be such pre-eminently in relation to their activities and works, and they will not have the typical and normal forms of contemplation.

They will not be, for all that, deprived of contemplation, of participating and experiencing lovingly the divine states.

For St. Thomas teaches us that all the gifts of the Holy Spirit
are connected and therefore cannot be present in the soul
without the gift of Wisdom; though in the case we are dealing with, it will be exercised in a less apparent way, and in
an atypical, attenuated, or discontinuous mode. The contemplation of the "active" souls will be *masked* and inapparent,
but they will have contemplative graces; perhaps they will be
capable only of saying rosaries, and mental prayer will bring
them only headache or sleep. Mysterious contemplation will
not be in their way of praying but in the grace of their behavior, in their sweet-minded hands, perhaps, or in their way of
walking perhaps, or in their way of looking at a poor man or
at suffering.

It should perhaps be added that contemplative life is
superhuman, whereas the active life is connatural to man and
better adapted to the equilibrium of his natural energies. It
appears that the forms of contemplation to which souls faithful to grace will actually attain most often, will not be the typical one, where the supernatural sweeps away everything, at
the risk of breaking everything, but rather the atypical and
masked forms which I have just mentioned, where the superhuman condescends in some measure to the human and consorts with it.

We see now with what nuances and distinctions we should
understand the theological doctrine, which we have been
reviewing, of every single soul being called to contemplative
graces. Each is called, if only in a remote manner, to contemplation, *typical or atypical*, apparent or masked, which is the
multiform exercise of the gift of Wisdom, free and unseizable,
and transcending all our categories, and capable of all disguises, all surprises.

In this sense, if all this is kept in mind, the Thomist the-
ses about contemplation—its necessity for the perfection of

Christian life and its intrinsic superiority over action—appear
in their manifest truth.

The doctrine I have stated summarily means that
Christian contemplation springs forth from that Spirit which
bloweth where it listeth, and one hears His voice and no one
knows whence He comes or whither He goes. It means that
Christian contemplation is not the affair of *specialists* or *techni-
cians*. The active ways through which the soul disposes itself to
it are not techniques, but only fallible preparations to receive
a free gift, fallible preparations which this gift always transcends.

Natural spirituality has techniques which are well determined and are, moreover, good and useful. This apparatus of
techniques strikes everybody who begins to study comparative Mysticism. Now, the most obvious difference between the
Christian and the other mystics is the freedom of the former
from any techniques, recipes or formulas. It is, essentially, not
esoteric or *reserved to specialists*.

We meet here with two difficulties which I should like to
mention, and which are due, the one to vocabulary, the other
to the masters.

There is a difficulty which comes from vocabulary. It is
that words are *specialists*. They cannot have the amplitude of
transcendentals. They particularize what they denote, in virtue of their past, and of the associations, sometimes extremely
heavy, which they drag along with them. That word "mystic,"
for instance, which I have used all through this essay because
I had to, is not satisfactory. It evokes a procession of phenomena, ecstasies, and extraordinary gifts belonging, when
they are genuine, to what theologians call *charisms* or gratuitous graces—which has nothing to do with the essence of the
mystical or disappropriated life, as we understand that word:
since we have (following the theologians) defined mystical life

by the dominating regimen of the Holy Spirit's gifts—the *habitus* of inspired freedom—which are quite different from charisms. The word "contemplation" is hardly better. I have already said it is quite unsatisfactory. It leads a good many people into error, making them believe that it pertains to some spectacular curiosity. It carries with it a Greek past, the Greek notion of theoretical life. We have seen, at the beginning of this essay, with what care we ought to strip the great truths of Antiquity of the errors which grow parasitically on them. Shall we then try to find other words? That would be vain. The new words would soon become clichés as misleading as the old ones. We must accept the fact, and particularly in this matter, that words cannot relieve us of the effort of thinking.

Nor can the masters! This is the second difficulty I wish to note. The masters, too, are inevitably specialists, specialists of what they teach. St. John of the Cross is a specialist of contemplation and heroism. He teaches a common way, a way open to all (to "all those who have heard" in a proximate manner the call of God); but he teaches this common way according to the purest and *most typical* paradigm of the states through which it leads. In brief, he speaks to all, to all those who have entered on the road, by addressing himself to a few Carmelite nuns of the noblest trend. Through them, he speaks to all. This means that we who read him are expected to hear him according to a whole keyboard of analogical values, to hear with *universal resonances*, and in a non-specialized sense, what he says as a specialist of genius. To understand him differently would be to betray him. Thus, for instance, concerning the nights and the passive purifications which he describes, one must grasp the fact that in other circumstances and in other states of life, these typical forms can be supplemented by other ordeals originating in events or in men, and which play an analogous purifying role. By pursuing this line

of reflections one would see many things become more plain.
One would also begin to see what is the role of a St. Thérèse
of Lisieux, teaching in truth the *same doctrine* as St. John of the
Cross, and the same heroism, but in the simplicity, entirely
denuded and *common*, of the "small way."

## V. *Orient and Occident*

To come back to where we started, to the debate of East
and West, we see, if what we have said be true, that activism and pragmatism, the rejection of contemplative values,
the dethronement of Wisdom, are the West's greatest woe.
It seems as if today the West sought a remedy in the frantic
exaggeration of this evil. The attempts to create new civilizations which are taking form before our eyes—where the civil
community becomes the soul of a dynamism which is purely
activistic, industrial, and warlike, and mobilizes for that active
end both science and thought—do not make our prognos-
tications optimistic. The West has here much to learn from
the East and from its fidelity to the primacy of contemplative
values.

But, at the same time, what I want to point out is that,
while denouncing the errors and shortcomings of our unhappy
West, the Christian feels for it a piety that is filial, and can
plead its cause in the face of the East. For this activism and
pragmatism are the catastrophe of a truly great thing which
the spirit of separation from God has led astray. I mean the
generosity, the propensity to give and communicate, the sense
of ontological superabundance springing from Evangelical
Love, and of holy contemplation superabounding in activity.

And the impassible contemplation of which the East
boasts—which proceeds from the energies of the soul striving
toward liberation by techniques and formulas, by the athletic
efforts of ascetics, and of active concentration—manifests,

on its part, in the very order of spiritual things, a pragmatism that is infinitely more subtle, but which no less withdraws
from the testimony that God expects from mankind.

Let us remember the great words which St. Thomas
wrote about the Incarnation, and which to my mind throw
the deepest light upon those problems: "In the Mystery of
Incarnation," he says, "the movement of *descent* of divine
plenitude into the depths of human nature is more important
than the movement of ascent of human nature toward God."
This is a truth that holds good, not only for the Head but
for the whole of the Body. It explains to us how supernatural
contemplation, proceeding thus from the descent within us of
divine plenitude, superabounds within us in love and activity.

We hold that the West will not surmount the crises in
which it is engaged, unless it reconquers that vital truth,
and understands that external activity must overflow from
a superabundance of internal activity, by which man is
united to truth and to the source of being. If the East, perhaps because its efforts toward contemplation aspired above
all toward philosophical forms of contemplation, has given
great importance to natural contemplation and spirituality,
even in things that belonged to the secular and temporal
order; one might ask if in the West, by a sort of division
of labor, spirituality and contemplation—not philosophical
but supernatural contemplation—have not been too much
the exclusive preoccupation of souls consecrated to God and
to the things of His Kingdom; while the rest of mankind
was abandoned to the law of immediate, practical success
and the will to power. If a new age of Christian civilization
should dawn, it is probable that the law of contemplation
superabounding in action would overflow in some way into
the secular and temporal order. It will thus be an age of the
sanctification of the profane.

✦

As I have said at the beginning of this chapter, the debate between action and contemplation is particularly important to this continent. Is it not a universally repeated commonplace that America is the land par excellence of pragmatism and of the great undertakings of human activity? There is truth in this, as in most commonplaces. Whitman celebrates the pioneers in a manner which is certainly characteristic of the American soul. But, in my opinion, there are in America great reserves and possibilities for contemplation. The activism which is manifested here assumes in many cases the aspect of a remedy against despair. I think that this activism itself masks a certain hidden aspiration to contemplation. To my mind, if in American civilization certain elements are causing complaints or criticisms, those elements proceed definitely from a repression of the desire, natural in mankind, for the active repose of the soul breathing what is eternal. In many unhappy creatures, good but wrongly directed, nervous breakdown is the price of such repression. On the other hand, the tendency, natural in this country, to undertake great things, to have confidence, to be moved by large idealistic feelings, may be considered, without great risk of error, as disguising that desire and aspiration of which I spoke.

To wish paradise on earth is stark naïveté. But it is surely better than not to wish any paradise at all. To aspire to paradise is man's grandeur; and how should I aspire to paradise except by beginning to realize paradise here below? The question is to know what paradise is. Paradise consists, as St. Augustine says, in the joy of the Truth. Contemplation is paradise on earth, a crucified paradise.

The cult of action is not specifically American. It is a European idea, an idea of post-Renaissance and post-Reformation Europe. What may mislead us in this matter, so it seems to me, is that the New Continent, with terrible loyalty, has taken some of the Old World's ideas, transplanted in virgin soil, and carried them to their limits. When in America some few come to realize better the value of contemplative activity, its superiority and fecundity, I believe that the possibilities I have spoken of will manifest themselves, at least in a small way, but forcefully enough gradually to modify the general scheme of values. Then this country will give some of its generosity, good will, confidence in the future and courage, to things contemplative, to contemplation overflowing in action. And this is one of the reasons why even if a moment of general catastrophe should befall civilization, I would still not despair of civilization.

# Chapter VIII

## *Catholic Action & Political Action*

### I. *The Three Levels of Christian Activity*

The Catholic conscience today is intensely preoccupied with problems concerning what we may call the "structure of action," something which cannot be treated unless we make distinctions as unpleasant and as necessary, as the realities to which they refer are complex and fluid. The Middle Ages were filled with discussions on two powers, on spiritual and temporal authority. The historian wears himself out following the detours of these controversies. Today, under very different conditions and relative to problems completely transformed, analogous discussions impose themselves on us. These are more acute in Europe than in the United States and everybody knows what violent and insidious attacks are made on Catholic Action in the totalitarian countries. But the principles and distinctions involved in the debate are as important in the New as in the Old World. For if we neglect the essential differences of finality and of object, we expose ourselves to immeasurable ruin.

What we must keep in mind here is the diversity of orders or of levels which the action of the Christian must necessarily admit, once he is given the Gospel distinction between the things which are Caesar's and the things which are God's. For one who considers things with attention, the activities of the Christian distribute themselves on three levels: the level of the spiritual, that of the temporal, and an intermediate level where the spiritual joins the temporal by relating it to spiritual objects and spiritual values. Because there is a link between spiritual and temporal and because the former is of greater worth, there is point to giving separate mention to this third level. But, in fact, it is merely the level of the spiritual itself, considered in a number of its attributes and in the fullness of its extension.

On the first level of activity—that of the spiritual—man acts as a member of the Mystical Body of Christ and as occupied with the things of God; on the second level—that of the temporal—he acts as a member of the earthly city and as occupied with the business of earthly life.

These two orders are distinct, but they are not separate. If grace captures us and recreates us in the depth of our being, it is in order that the whole of our action may be affected by it and illuminated with it. But on the temporal level, although our action—if it is what it ought to be—will be an action proceeding from Christian inspiration, yet it will not present itself as specifically Christian; it will present itself as formally determined by such and such temporal object, such and such temporal specification (political action, national, cultural action, etc., under Christian inspiration).

On the other hand, on the spiritual level, it will be not only under Christian inspiration, but it will also present itself, in the very measure in which it will have as its object the expansion of the Kingdom of God in souls, as specifically Christian (the Christian apostolate).

And it will be the same on the third level, that of the spiritual considered as joined to the temporal, so far as the action of the Christian belongs here also to the apostolate, but to the apostolate as touching things of earth; I mean so far as it has for its purpose to infuse evangelical vitality into the temporal life, or as it intervenes in politics in the very name of Christianity when politics touches the altar.

The work of Catholic action is fully accomplished on the first and third level; that of political action is accomplished on the second.

## II. *What Is Catholic Action?*

Some excellent works, consecrated to Catholic Action, explain its nature according to the papal documents. In this essay, I do not speak of *Catholic Action* as a proper noun designating an official institution of the Church, but rather of *Catholic action* as a common noun designating a certain task and work which it is the object of Catholic Action (with a capital A) to organize; and this task, this work (Catholic action with a small a), is not a new thing in the Church, it has always existed; and neither is the word new. What is new is the use made of it in the papal documents, first by Pius X,[1] and especially by Pius XI, who consecrated it. What is new is the insistence with which Pius XI has clarified the nature of Catholic action, precisely stated its meaning and made its applications explicit—the central, essential importance which he attaches to Catholic action, his affirmed will to develop it everywhere, the solicitude with which he watches over it. Has he not said that it is as dear to him as the apple of his eye?[2] Has he not written of Catholic action that it is that which the "supreme Head of religion is known to prize and cherish most"?[3] And recently

---

1. Letter to Count Giovanni Grosoli, November 6, 1903; *Motu Proprio* on Popular Christian Action, December 18, 1903; Encyclical *Il Fermo Proposito*, June 11, 1905.

2. Discourse to the Committee on Italian Catholic Action, March 9, 1924.

3. Encyclical *Non Abbiamo Bisogno*. June 29, 1931.

he said yet again: "Whoever strikes Catholic action, strikes the Pope." (And he added: "Whoever strikes the Pope, dies.")

He himself has given and with especial solemnity, the definition, which has now become classic, of Catholic action: *participation by the laity in the hierarchical apostolate.*[4] And again: "Catholic action in sum is nothing other than the apostolate of the faithful, who, under the guidance of their bishops, put themselves at the service of the Church and assist her in the integral fulfillment of her pastoral ministry."[5]

These words, which should be retained and carefully weighed, show how far, in the thought of the Pope, Catholic action is a thing of the Church and has the same finalities as the Church's pastoral ministry itself: laymen are called to assist the Church in *the integral fulfillment of her pastoral office*; they are called to the apostolate, to that same apostolate with which Christ has charged the Twelve and their successors; and they receive for this an explicit mission.

In the preceding chapter, on action and contemplation, I insisted that all souls are called in some degree to the contemplation of the saints, which, because it is a contemplation of love, abounds in action. But now, and as corresponding to this call of God deep in our hearts, we are to meditate on another call, the call to action, apostolic action, which the Church addresses in some degree to all the faithful. For the latter, the problem is that the *spirit* responds to the *mission*.

Catholic action, participation by laymen in the apostolate of the Church: One sees two things here immediately. In the first place, where there is no *action*, action on the world, there is no *Catholic action*. That is why, no matter how great their role

---

4.    Letters to Mme. Steenberghe, July 30, 1928; to Cardinal Bertram, November 13, 1928; to Cardinal Segura, November 6, 1929; Encyclical *Non Abbiamo Bisogno*.

5.    Letter to Cardinal Van Roey, August 15, 1928.

be in the life of the Church. neither those states of life exclusively contemplative, nor the works of pure piety or of pure personal edification, or of purely scientific culture, enter into the concept of Catholic action. In the second place, where this action on the world is not itself directed to apostolic ends concerned with the "pastoral ministry of the Church" in its integrity, in short where it has not as its direct end the *expansion of the Kingdom of God*, there is no *Catholic action*. There is, of course, *action by Catholics*, but there is no *Catholic action* as such. That is why economic and professional works—co-operatives, social insurance, trade unions, and the like—no matter how Christian their inspiration may be, do not enter into the concept of Catholic action; nor do works of social relief and assistance, nor Catholic youth sport programmes, even when their initiative and inspiration are Catholic[6]; nor do political works, though under Christian inspiration. (If there are any of these last, they are at present very few. There are many political publications under Catholic banners and with Catholic customers, but they have political, or even less than political, inspiration. One can count on the fingers of one hand the political publications under political banners, which spring forth from Catholic inspiration.)

On the contrary, as large and ample as is the concept of the apostolate, of the pastoral ministry of the Church, of activity turned of itself to the expansion of the Kingdom of God, just so large and ample is the concept of Catholic action. A mother who teaches the catechism to her children performs Catholic action, and very good Catholic action, too. Men who devote themselves to the work of education and of doctrinal formation, perform Catholic action. Works whose

6.    One classes as "auxiliary to Catholic action" the various works of which we have just spoken.

object is to make the Christian life and spirit penetrate into
the profane and secular, into social life and into particular
social activities, are works of Catholic action, and with so
eminent a title that today they appear as works of Catholic
action par excellence.

As I said a moment ago, it is on the *first* and on the *third*
level of the Christian's action—on the level of the purely spiritual and on that of the spiritual uniting with the temporal in
the name of spiritual values—and only on these two levels,
that Catholic action is accomplished, because this is, by definition, an apostolic action.

## III. *The Internal Dynamism of Catholic Action*

Let us consider now what we may call the internal dynamism of Catholic action.

1. The first remark is concerned with the relation between
Catholic action and the spiritual life. What does St. Thomas
say of the apostolate, of the preaching of the Gospel? That
these are works which *by their nature* have to proceed from a
superabundance of contemplation. And what is Catholic
action, if not, by definition, an apostolic action? The conclusion is evident. To participate in the apostolate of the Church
is to participate first in her contemplation. Christians would
be traitors to Catholic action, if they did not fit themselves for
it by prayer, and if they did not ask of Him without whom
we can do nothing to cause it to flow into them from contemplation; I do not say from contemplation in its typical and
sublime forms, but at least from that *masked* contemplation
which was dealt with in the preceding chapter, and which is
often encountered, though they themselves know it not, in
souls faithful to grace. Can a man in fact give without having
first received? What pretension it would be to give when one
is oneself destitute!

Concerning the call to Catholic action addressed by the Church to laymen, we noted just now that the great problem, as always in such cases, is that the spirit respond to the mission. When they meditate on this, how should laymen not envisage with some fear the responsibility with which they are thus charged? When the mission is an apostolic one, is not the spirit of the mission the Spirit Himself who since Pentecost assists the Church of Christ in a special way? Behold of what spirit they are, who enter the lists for Catholic action. This spirit requires them to turn first toward wisdom and contemplation. This spirit is by definition an evangelical spirit. It does not ask us to train troops so as to execute orders at beck and call, disregarding or denying the "interior man" and his conscience in order to act, to speak, to write or vote as the journal of a party prescribes; it asks us to prepare human persons to understand in the depths of their conscience the word of the Church herself and to discern the meaning of it. This spirit does not require that the "good" call down fire from Heaven upon the "wicked," nor that they hold that the true proof of the love of God is, not to be ready to die for Him, but to kill for Him. It demands that useless servants remember their Master, who having taught that the greatest love is to give one's life for one's friends, willed to die for His enemies also, so that they might be His friends, because He loved them.

2. My second remark is the following: it seems to me that the coming of Catholic action marks the end of the *separatism* and *dualism* which have reigned too long in the Christian world. This process of disassociation has been already mentioned in the first chapter. Too long, in modern times, "has the Christian world obeyed two opposed rhythms, a Christian rhythm in matters of worship and religion, and, at least among better men, in things of the interior life; and a naturalistic rhythm in things of the profane life, the social, economic,

and political life, things too long abandoned to their proper carnal law."

Today, at least for Christians who have ears to hear, this dualism is past. An age now appears in which the organic and vital unity of all that has been inhumanly dissociated will be restored. And Catholic action is a precious sign of this, and is itself efficacious of it. If laymen are henceforth mobilized for the apostolate, this surely is the proof that the world and profane existence ought to be penetrated and vivified to their depths by Christian energies, and that the things of God ought to reach man in all his reality, temporal as well as spiritual, social as well as individual.

And precisely because, by his kind of life and his work, the real man is normally pledged to certain definite communities and certain friendships, the Christian apostolate ought to reach him at the heart of these communities and of these friendships, in order to aid him to transform his life. That is why Catholic action, without thereby limiting itself to this kind of apostolate, has, in many countries, preferred—and it seems that this is its most typical way—a form which we may call communal and which answers to what people also call, in a somewhat official term, *specialized movements*: the trade, the kind of work, the class, constitute the milieu within which man can act on man. "The first apostles, the immediate apostles of the workers," writes Pius XI, "will be workers; the apostles of the industrial and business world will be industrialists and business men."[7]

The most significant example of such a movement is the vast movement, begun in Belgium and expanded from there into France and other countries, of the Jeunesse Ouvrière Chrétienne. The Abbé Cardijn, founder of it, is himself

---

7.    Encyclical *Quadragesimo Anno*, May 15, 1931.

the son of a workman. In his own family, he was witness of the tragic conditions imposed on the industrial proletariat; he made a promise to God to devote his life to the working class, and he kept his word. Everyone knows that Jocisme now brings together hundreds of thousands of young workers who carry the testimony of Christ into the factory and workshop, by their personal life and their example, as well as by their effort to obtain more respect for human dignity in work, more respect for woman and the young apprentice, more humanity and justice in working conditions.

3. Thus—and this is my third remark—Catholic action does not remain on the purely spiritual level; of itself, it demands passage to the social level. In all countries where it does not suffer constraint, Christian social action is par excellence its mode of action.

In what sense is this so? In a quite precise sense: in the sense in which social action concerns *the third level* of action indicated at the outset, the level of the spiritual joined to the temporal, in the sense in which social action concerns the apostolate and the integrity of the pastoral ministry of the Church, and brings into social life the testimony of Christ and of the Kingdom of God; in other words, by reason of the spiritual and apostolic values invested in social action, values to which only Catholic action is directly orientated. Let us not forget that the social, the economic, and the political, are intrinsically dependent on ethics, and that, *by this title*, for this formal reason, the social, the political, and the economic, are concerned with eternal life, and therefore with the pastoral ministry of the Church. The problem of destitution, for example, of misery, is certainly a temporal problem: but it is also a problem of eternal life. St. Thomas teaches, and it is evident, that a certain minimum of well-being is *necessary* for the development of the properly human life and of

virtue. Destitution, or misery, Léon Bloy and Charles Péguy
have adequately said, is quite different from poverty, it is a
hell on earth, it cuts man off from the communion of the
living, it drives him to despair. The problem of destitution
is a problem of eternal life for him who suffers it and who,
being treated like one damned, breathes the air of damnation
and runs the greatest risk of turning against God (and God
is merciful enough to be willing to save him even then); and
it is a problem of eternal life for him who contemplates the
destitution of others with an indifferent heart, sometimes in
order to make a profit out of it (and for this man to be saved,
mercy ten times greater is needed, and repentance). As long
as modern societies will secrete destitution as an ordinary
product of their functioning, there cannot be any repose for
the Christian.

The Church, then, has established in the speculative order
a doctrinal firmament of principles and truths dominating
every social and economic subject. Practically, she gave her
faithful mission to enter her own pastoral ministry in order
to bring into the social life and the treatment of social problems, through Catholic action, the testimony of Christ and an
apostolic zeal for the salvation of souls and the expansion of
the Kingdom of God. It is not the direct and proper function
of Catholic action to solve the social problem, but to make
the vivifying inspiration of the Kingdom of God and His
justice penetrate the social matters themselves; and—I mean
in respect of Catholic action, and without prejudice to other
kinds of action, of themselves directed to earthly things—it
is an *additional* matter that the solution of the social problem
occurs—if it *does* occur.

Too long have people been obliged to observe, as I said
several years ago, the terrifying lack of attention on the part
of Catholics to the teachings and exhortations of Leo XIII

and his successors. The mission of Catholic action is to put a stop to this inattention. Catholic action will, in this measure, help to put a stop to what Pius XI, in an interview with Abbe Cardijn, called *the great scandal of the nineteenth century*, the fact that the working class has gone, seeking its way, far from the crib of Christ, the fact that the poor have believed that they are not at home at that crib. These matters are not mended in a day. This scandal has a historical importance surely greater than all the questions of political regimes, of parliamentarism, or of dictatorship, which today preoccupy so many minds. We ought not to lose sight of it for a single instant.

It is natural for the poor to hope in God, because they have hardly anyone else in whom to hope. And from whom, if not from Him and from those who believe in Him, should the offended and the humiliated think they can obtain that of which man stands so greatly in need in order to exist: the feeling that he himself is respected as a human being? Who most respects the creature, if not the Creator? The poor look for this respect from those especially who call themselves the friends of God. When we see hatred of God in certain hearts, let us ask ourselves what resentment and what bitterness, what accumulated humiliations, lasting perhaps for generations, have dug in the soul such a wound, and let us ask ourselves, we who believe in the Communion of Saints, and in mutual responsibility, whether we are sure that for our own part we are innocent of this wound. And first and foremost, let us act in such a way that we will not aggravate it.

4. My fourth remark is the following: By the fact that it marks the end of separatism and dualism, Catholic action marks the end of that sort of effectual life which makes so many people, and sometimes some Christians themselves, believe that Christianity is a party to social conduct which is anything but Christian. This is what I mean: When separatism

and dualism reign among Christians, there is a whole por-
tion of their life and activity, and especially perhaps in the
social domain, which does not arise from Christianity and is
not animated by it; and from what does it arise then, if not
(sometimes even among souls who are individually good) from
sociological reflexes and prejudices that are unconscious and
uncontrolled, from pride and egoism of race, of class, of family, or from that simple hardness and natural harshness which
only a vigilant charity can soften? But as this conduct is in fact
met with among Christians, especially those who are more
taken up with the externals of Christianity in proportion as
it penetrates less into their existence, why would the world
not hold Christianity responsible for it, and why would it not
believe Christianity federated with a whole order of injus-
tices and evils to which it sees so many Christians attached?
Separatism thus engenders the greatest confusion.

In putting a stop to separatism, Catholic action puts a
stop to the confusion. From the single fact that it tends to vivify with a Christian and apostolic energy, the whole life and
action, and especially the social action, of the Christian, it will
make impossible the conduct of which I speak. It will make
impossible, indeed it will end by making impossible among
Christians, hatred and contempt of race and hatred and contempt of class. It will make impossible, it will end in making
impossible in us, belief in the efficacy of hate, the cult of violence, the despising of everything which in any way resembles
hope in the force of good will, and love and truth.

However, generous sentiments are not enough. In human
matters (that is, on the level of the concrete action), it is
impossible to see truth, if one does not already also "make
it"[8]; in other words, if one does not love. But, on the other

---

8.    "Qui facit veritatem, venit ad lucem" (John 3:21).

hand, the most sincere love risks not performing any good, or even performing a great deal of evil, unless it passes through the Word and through Truth. An immense and difficult task here imposes itself upon Christian intelligence. I believe that the modern centuries have sought many good things but by bad means; one must neither deny these good ends, because the means were worthless, nor be indulgent to the bad means, because the ends were good toward which one thought these means were leading. The effort toward social justice, toward international peace, toward political and economic realizations of that freedom to which the person aspires, has been linked in fact to the errors of individualistic liberalism, to the belief in the original goodness of human nature and in necessary Progress, to the idea that Number is the source of authority and of right to the Rousseauist myths and to the socialist myths. It must be freed from these myths and these errors. It is only too true that Christians face today, in the social-temporal order, problems very much like those which their fathers encountered in the sixteenth and seventeenth centuries, in the order of the philosophy of nature. In those days physics and modern astronomy, which were being born, were closely bound to erroneous philosophies, and turned against tradition. The defenders of tradition were unable to make the necessary discriminations; they chose to be, at one and the same time, against that which was to become modern science, and against the philosophic errors which grew like a parasite upon this science in its origin. Three centuries were required to get over this misunderstanding, if one can say that the world has really gotten over it. We are not required today to repeat all over again the same sort of mistakes in the realm of practical and social philosophy. For my part I believe that the criticism of liberalism must lead to a doctrine of the pluralistic state, the criticism of anarchic democracy to a doctrine of an organic and personalist democracy, the criticism of anthropocentric humanism to a doctrine of integral humanism.

I do not think that such a philosophical and cultural work must be placed in the category of Catholic action, as that is defined by Pius XI; it is, indeed, to be achieved in the bosom of the historical particularities of the profane and temporal order, and as determined by profane awareness. It concerns what I have called the second level of the Christian's activities. But I believe that, through the theological wisdom on which it depends, and through its highest principles, it is connected with one of the typical functions of Catholic action, illuminating the mind with that doctrinal firmament of which I have spoken above.

5. And finally my fifth remark. I have said that Catholic action of its nature demands translation into social action, in the precise sense in which social action concerns the apostolate, and the integrity of the pastoral ministry of the Church, and bears witness to Christ and to the Kingdom of God in the social life; in other words, because of the *spiritual and apostolic* values invested in social action and to which alone Catholic action is directly ordained.

It is of essential importance to understand that this is a *certain* social action, a certain higher zone of social activity: to use a more explicit and precise word, let us say that this is *Christian or apostolic social action.* But the whole domain of social activity is not thereby covered. The social is attained only so far as it concerns the third level of action mentioned at the outset of this study, the level of the spiritual linked to the temporal, a level on which we act insofar as we are Christians, and as sent by the Church.

Taken in the ordinary sense of the word, and so far as it concerns the common good of the earthly city and of

civilization—in other words, because of the *temporal* values
which are within its jurisdiction—the social is by its nature
concerned with the second level, the level of the temporal, on
which we act as members of the earthly city, and on which
we ought to act *in a Christian manner*, on our own responsibility
and on our personal initiative, at our risk and peril, but not
*professedly* as Christians and sent by the Church. In this case, it
is no longer a question of the apostolate, nor of the pastoral
ministry of the Church; it is a question of the earthly life of
men, considered from the point of view of the proper laws of
this life and of the earthly good to which it is directed; it is a
question of the modes of realization according to which the
principles and higher truths contained on this subject in the
doctrine of the Church must pass into concrete existence, and
which depend on the philosophy of culture, of society and
history, which we believe to be true, and also on the particular
circumstances of the historical matter on which we are working. What position shall we take in the debates concerned
with trade unions, co-operatives, distributism, etc.? On the
problems of inflation, deflation, reflation, or monetary deval-
uation? On the concrete problems regarding the evolution of
modern economy, the historical link between the conflict of
classes and the capitalistic regime, and the rise of the working
class to property? The connotations most formally temporal
of the word *social* almost correspond, in modern tongues, to
what Aristotle called *political*. In order, then, to characterize, in
a more explicit and precise manner, social action understood
in this sense, let us say socio-*temporal* or socio-*political* action.
Such action tends directly and of itself, as to a proper and
proportionate effect, to the solution of social problems.

    This socio-temporal or socio-political action is not within
the province of Catholic action. At this frontier, Catholic
action stops. Its competence goes no farther, because its direct

and proper end is *apostolic*, not *profane* and *temporal*. It has formed, enlightened, prepared (and in doing this it is in vital relation with the action of which we speak). It hands the task over to this other kind of action.

So, by the spiritual and doctrinal formation which it gives them, Catholic action prepares Christians—at least those who feel called to it—to approach as they should the studies of political science and philosophy and the problems of political action, and themselves to enter into political action. It itself does not take the place of these studies, or of this action.

As I wrote in a previous work, "if by the teaching it dispenses and the spiritual formation it procures, Catholic action *prepares* laymen to act *as* Christians, to participate in struggles of the temporal and to participate in them as Christians, to assume social and political tasks to which they consider themselves called, and to assume it *as* Christians, Catholic action, however, restrains itself most carefully from laying the shadow of a finger on this second level. And this not only because the Church does not want to find itself, at any price, enslaved to temporal things. It is also because, as regards the work proper to the second level, as regards the task which must descend to the ultimate contingent realizations demanded by the service of the temporal common good, the competence of an activity belonging to an entirely spiritual order, soon finds its limits."[9] There exists a judgment of *Catholicism* about the connections which art and literature have to ethics and to the moral capacities of the average of men; but this judgment does not suffice to tell me what I must think of a book by Joyce or of a poem by Rimbaud, as works of art. There exists a judgment of *Catholicism* about the duty to work on behalf of international peace and of the principles of social justice; but this judgment

---

9.    *True Humanism.*

does not suffice to tell me what I should think of the law of the forty-hour week and of the statute of the League of Nations. It is my business to judge these problems as a Catholic (as far as possible with Catholic intelligence rather than with Catholic prejudices), but without pretending to speak in the name of Catholicism, nor to draw in my wake Catholics as such.

The extreme care which the Church exercises not to let Catholic action be contaminated, even the least bit, by political action, corresponds to the nature of things. It would be the ruin of a fundamental truth of the Gospels, the ruin of the distinction of the things which are Caesar's and those which are God's, and as a consequence it would inevitably be a catastrophe, as a matter of fact, if Catholic action were itself to become engaged in the affairs of the day and in political struggles (except when it is a question of defending, on certain precise points, quite superior to the conflicts of parties and of political forces, interests specifically moral and religious).

The exception which I have just indicated concerns what one might call, in the strict sense of the word, Catholic *civic* action. It is here necessary to point out that to interfere in political matters in order to defend spiritual interests and in the exact measure required by this defense, "is not at all the same thing as to work toward an object properly political, directed by a certain conception of the temporal common good to be procured. In order fitly to practice politics, it is necessary to discern political realities, to have a concrete idea of the means capable of assuring the common good of the earthly city. In order to defend the religious values engaged in the temporal, it suffices to discern these religious values."[10]

In consequence, normally speaking, it is not by taking sides for a certain political idea of the political common good,

---

10. Ibid.

judged more favorable to religion, nor by making Catholics, as such, enter upon the service of historical forces and temporal interests linked to this idea, that one will best defend religious rights and values; in brief, it is not by trying to find *in one particular political camp* an instrument for religion, that the action we spoke of (and which, entering the political realm but from the outside, has no particular guarantee of properly political competence) will be achieved in the best and most efficient manner; it is rather by laying *every political camp whatsoever* under the necessity of respecting these rights and values, if it does not wish to be fought by the Catholic masses. Such procedure raises above the diversity of political ideas concerning the political common good—political ideas to which a Christian may legitimately adhere—the idea of religious and spiritual values to be served, and thus maintains under the only ascendant of the things of God, even in political matters, the effort of Catholics insofar as they are Catholics.

By following this line of reflection, one would, no doubt, be able to grasp the specific difference between a "clerical" conception and a conception truly "ecclesiastical," of the political defense of the rights and liberties of religion.

In fact, nothing demands clearer understanding, under penalty of being distorted, than the great practical verities on which we are trying to meditate. The teachings of the Church proceed from a superior intelligence, an intelligence assisted by the Holy Spirit, and admirably trained to anatomize reality, as with a scalpel, along the lines of its jointures and essential distinctions. On the other hand, the mass of men who hear these truths more or less exactly reported, and also sometimes those who apply them, are not always sufficiently trained "to distinguish in order to unite." Every great idea is a powerful explosive, which requires intelligent handling. The idea of Catholic action, the idea of Christ the King, are ideas of this kind. The spirit of the world, which hates them, as it hates the Gospel, is quite willing to imagine, in a sort of bad dream, that Catholic action has a mission to do, or at least to command a political work, or to advance what is called today a "front," whatever that may be, of social and "ideological," imperial or military struggle; or to imagine that the Kingdom of Christ is not that of a King of Grace and Charity but a leader of war imposing his will by constraint. If, in spite of the reiterated teaching and the exact prescriptions and the exhortations of the Popes,[11] there should be found somewhere imprudent men who give by their conduct even the shadow of plausibility to such nonsense, the havoc to the Church and to civilization would be enormous. That is why the Church never ceases to insist on the distinctions which I have repeated here.

## IV. *Political Action*

In one sense Catholic action, becoming more explicitly aware of itself, will thus "liberate" political action; I mean that in the historical age which we are entering, people will understand better and better, it seems to me, that once the realm of strictly temporal and political realities is entered, then the action of Christians, which on this plane is an action properly political, emanates solely, so far as politics does not touch on holy things, from their initiative as citizens.[12] Assuredly,

---

11. Cf. Pius XI, Letter to Cardinal Hlond, April 16, 1929; to the Archbishop of Toledo, November 6, 1929; Letters to the Mexican Bishops, February 2, 1926, and March 8, 1937; Letter of Cardinal Pacelli to the Bishop of Prague, etc.

12. The initiative of which I speak must itself—this is clear—take into account the rules of conscience furnished by the Church. It is known that the encyclical *Pascendi* condemns the error according to which "every Catholic, being at the same time a citizen, has the right and the duty—without concerning himself with the Church's authority, without taking into

this initiative itself remains subject to the general and special rules on which the morality of human conduct depends
and regarding which the Church has the office of instructing
the faithful; assuredly, it ought to be internally enlightened
and vivified by the principles of the Faith and of Christian
wisdom. But the impelling decisions, the initiatives on which
action depends—so far as politics does not motivate a special
intervention of spiritual authority because it challenges the
supreme values of our life—are only those of the conscience
of men who devote themselves at their own risk and peril to
the service of the State, and on which no constraining motion
comes down from any other sphere. Thus, in its domain,
political action is free, and not an instrument of the Church.

Let us not forget that the three kinds of activity which
we recognized at the outset of this study cannot take each

---

account its desires, its advances, its commandments, and even disdaining its
reprimands—to pursue the public good in the manner he considers best."
The right of the Church, thus being recalled by Pius X, can be applied
in two different senses: either in the special sense of the defense of the
altar and spiritual values when politics touch the altar (one is then in the
perspective of the *potestas indirecta in temporalibus*, and the Church has then
herself the initiative of the political act—or of the political refusal—of
the Christian); or only in the sense of the moral formation of the citizens'
conscience, whom the religious authority reminds of the rules of conduct
to which they must be attentive: in this case we have to do with an action
of religious authority which of itself concerns only the spiritual, and
which leaves to the citizens' conscience, thus instructed, the initiative and
the motive decision, the *judicium practicum* (practical judgment) concerning
the political act to be undertaken. It is in this category that many pastoral
instructions issued on the occasion of a particular event must be placed—
concerning an electoral consultation, for instance, where religious authority
enlightens and directs the conscience of Catholic citizens by reminding
them of their duty to insure the safeguard of religious liberties and of
spiritual goods, the maintenance of the rights and of the natural structure
of the family, the respect for established power, civil peace and international
peace, the sanctity of treaties, social justice, the rights of the human person,
the rejection of means of violence, the loyal preparation of a new order, the
patriotic obligations concerning national defense, public finances, etc.

other's places. They are all three necessary, each on its own level. In short, political action has its own proper function on its own proper level. It is as necessary as political life itself. It is of itself something "lawful and important."[13] It has, as its specific end, the common good of the earthly city. Pius XI has said that after Catholic action the most noble work is that of political action; by an interior education and formation in the order properly called theological, an order concerned at once with speculative theology and moral and social theology, Catholic action begins to prepare minds for that action which it cannot supply or command or suggest, and which cannot be accomplished in its name.

What I would remark here, above all, is the essential difference of rhythm and modality which distinguishes, because of difference of finalities, *political* action and *Catholic* action. Catholic action demands, on its level, the *union* of all Catholics; on its own level, political action implies, on the contrary, a normal *diversity* among them. *Catholic* action seeks, on its level, to develop itself in an *exclusively* Catholic framework; in a civilization religiously divided, *political* action, on its own level, normally implies the *co-operation* of Catholics and non-Catholics.

It must here be observed, in fact, that the more a population lacks ethico-political education, the more often religious authority will have to interfere in particular cases, and in political contingencies, in order to enlighten consciences, and to supplement their lack of ethico-political education. The more perfect the ethico-political education of a country's population (education, in which Catholic action is precisely called upon to play an important part)—in other words, the more a country's Catholic citizens are capable of acting as persons politically come of age—the more religious authority will be dispensed from interfering by its moral admonitions in the political contingencies, and be able to concentrate its efforts on its essential task, which is to conduct souls toward eternal life and to help them continue the work of the redeeming Incarnation.

13. Leo XIII, Encyclical *Cum multa*, December 8, 1882.

Let us return to the three levels of activity. On the first
and third levels (the level of the purely spiritual and that of
the spiritual joined to the temporal), on the level of *Catholic
action*, union must evidently be the watchword. It is clear that
only the union of Catholics can give enough strength to make
the participation of laymen in the apostolate effective. Union
is here the first necessity. And *all* Catholics are, as such, to
take part in Catholic action, *all* are required especially to take
part in some degree—at least, in countries where the thing is
not made practically impossible or very difficult, as a consequence of a political regime with totalitarian tendencies, all
are required to take part in that eminent form of Catholic
action which is *Christian-social* action.

The same must be said about that which concerns what
we have called Catholic *"civic"* action, which is a prolonga-
tion of Catholic action and whose object is the defense of
the proper values of God's city as it is engaged in temporal affairs: the union of Catholics is indispensable in order
efficaciously to compel the respect for religious interests by
civil legislation, "it being well understood that this concerns
purely the incidences of the spiritual in the temporal, and the
genuinely religious interests, such as are determined *hic et nunc*
by the Holy See and by the Episcopate, not by the particular judgment of no matter what personality or of no matter
what party usurping the mission of speaking in the name of
the Church and believing at times that they understand the
Church's interests better than the Church herself. One cannot
hide from oneself that fact that, as long as the education of
Catholic masses is not further advanced in this realm, as long
as they will not have learned more clearly to distinguish what
belongs to religion from what belongs to the socio-temporal
domain—the interests, prejudices and passions of a sociological order—the union of Catholics on the level of civic

action, however necessary in itself, will raise most intricate problems."[14]

But, on the second level, the level of the temporal, the level of *political* action, it is *diversity* which is the rule. "When the objective is the earthly life of man, when it concerns earthly interests, earthly goods, this or that ideal of the common earthly good, and the ways and means of realizing it, the normal thing is for the unanimity whose focus is of the supra-temporal order, to be broken, and for Christians who communicate at the same table to find themselves divided in politics. It would be contrary to the nature of things, and therefore quite perilous, to demand of Catholics on this level a unity which could only be artificial, and obtained either by a political materialization of religious energies (as is too often seen in "Catholic parties" such as the German Center Party), or by an enfeebling of the social and political energies of the Christian, and a sort of flight into general principles."[15]

Besides, on this second level, the level of political action, not all Catholics are required as such to participate. All, of course, are bound, as other members of the political community, to perform their duties as citizens (which demand, normally, and especially in countries with democratic constitutions, the development among them, along with the other citizens, of a personal consciousness of political realities, in their proper order). But the political action, about which there is a question here, is something much wider and much more complex than the simple act of voting, and demands a certain "specialization": it is an action which tends to make triumphant in

14. *True Humanism.*
15. Ibid.

existence a political ideal and the historical forces which represent it, to transform society, and so on. If it is good, then, if it is necessary that certain men consecrate themselves to political studies and to political action thus understood, this evidently concerns only those who feel called to such a task and who think themselves competent with regard to it, but it creates no obligation for others to follow the same path.

The diversity of which I have just spoken, which answers to a proper law of political activity, nevertheless remains, it is important to understand, a relative diversity. The existence of the common "doctrinal firmament" mentioned a moment ago, and the fact that all Christians as such receive their life from the same Redeemer's Blood and from the same spirit, which is the Spirit of Christ—this twofold fact shows us that a higher unity ought normally to rule all diversity among them, and to manifest itself even in the midst of this diversity. When Christians hate other Christians, when Catholics turn on other Catholics those looks of scorn and detestation which people have for traitors, for hopeless madmen and outcast dogs, they have already begun to wound the Christ within them.

However different be their ideas in temporal matters, if Catholics of diverse historical, social, and political formation all had a like respect for and a like knowledge of the common doctrine of the Church and of the papal encyclicals, if in their conscience there grew up at the same time an evangelical understanding of life, and a practical knowledge of the spirit of which they are, and of that absolute primacy of charity taught by St. Paul, it is clear that many unhealthy excesses and much blindness would cease. Diversity would remain, but it would be deeply penetrated by union.

Regimentation (*caporalisme*) may represent, perhaps, the ideal of certain political States, but it has never reigned and will never reign in the Church; that would be an absolute impossibility. If the Christian aspired and consented to this sort of unity, he would betray the very transcendence of the truth to which he has adhered. When a man leaves all in order to be converted to Jesus Christ, and understands that it would serve him nothing to gain the whole world if he lose his own soul, it is not to enter upon the service of a world, no matter which, nor of any kind of utilization of religion. It is certain that this man will submit with difficulty to orders given by partisans, even if they invoke divine wrath, with that zeal which generally characterizes personalities without a mandate.

If, in particular, one reflects upon the proper condition of temporal things, if one remembers that Christianity has vanquished ancient slavery, not with the help of decrees and regulations, but through the virtue of the evangelical leaven working inside consciences—one will understand that in the temporal realm, much progress which, in reality, depends upon Christianity, is achieved, less through the effect of rules and of discipline imposed from above, than through a kind of growth and maturing within the conscience, which is produced with the spontaneity of life, at first in a few, and sooner or later more generally.

What is the result of all this if it is not that in those matters, whereon the Church herself, and *as such*, has not made pronouncement and where her common doctrine is not questioned, the union so desirable between Catholics is and must be primarily a union of charity, of mutual respect and common inspiration in the diversity of positions which seem true and just to each? Such a union is not accomplished by means of suppression and excommunication; and it can, and must, be more real and go further than one generally supposes.

Let us consider now the second difference of rhythm and modality (mentioned earlier) between Catholic and political action.

*Catholic action*, by virtue of its definition as participation by laymen in the hierarchical apostolate, ought to be developed in an *exclusively Catholic* framework. The appropriate movement here—not in what concerns the apostolate itself, for this is essentially diffusive and radiating, but in what concerns the formation and constitution of active groups—is a movement of concentration of the Catholic community upon itself, thanks to which there will be accomplished, without admixture of error, the right awareness of the truths proper to Catholicism.

But it is no less clear that *political action*, by virtue of its definition as activity directed to the temporal good of the earthly city, aims at a common good and a common undertaking which ought to bring together in the same civil life and the same civil peace, in a *convivium* of temporal activities as harmonious as possible, all the members of the temporal city, members who in fact belong to different spiritual families. This action of itself, then, demands co-operation on the temporal level between believers and non-believers, and it involves a law of movement other than that of Catholic action: that is, a law of concentration on itself, not of the Catholic community as such, but of the community formed by men who are animated by the same social or political concrete ideal; who share in common the same vision of the socio-temporal *convivium*; and who, as members of the city as a whole, can belong to different spiritual families. We know that once fidelity is assured to the higher principles established in this matter by the common teaching of the Church, Catholics are free to adhere to quite diverse political conceptions, and that, as they say, a "Catholic of the left" can be as good a Catholic as a "Catholic of the right," and conversely.

From the fact that politics and economics depend intrinsically on ethics and on the ideas that one should have of man and his ends, the Christian's temporal ideal and his temporal means of action will, of course, differ from those of the pagan. Hence it follows that the dynamism of a party or of a political community under Christian inspiration will come chiefly from Christians, and will normally suppose Christian initiative and Christian direction. Nevertheless, what I mean is that non-Christians will have their place there also, and can play an important role there, and all the more so because the temporal ideal of this party or community will rest on a more just and more comprehensive notion of the natural structure of civilization and of the common earthly good and the natural *convivium* which it implies.

If these distinctions were well understood, many misunderstandings would be avoided. People would not ask Catholics to form a single bloc on the level of *political action*; and political divisions would not enter to annihilate and sterilize the best efforts on the level of *Catholic action*. Because of their union in *Catholic action*, Catholics would learn to esteem, to understand, and to love one another, no matter to which parties they belonged; and because of the work of *political action*, and the humble earthly realities it is obliged to consider, they would learn to esteem, to understand, and to love men of good will who do not share their faith; and they would be free of those many chimeras which disappear as soon as people are aware of them, but which dwell unnoticed in the imagination of many men. When one acts, usually without avowing it to oneself, *as if* the political community could not be served profitably except by Catholics, the only course open is either to suppress all other people, and probably no one relishes the thought of this solution, or to be made victims of journalistic or political adventurers, often not Christians themselves, who exploit these illusions for their profit.

My personal conviction, as I have said repeatedly for some years, is that the world suffers cruelly from the lack of political groupings—I may say specifically political, acting on the temporal level, finalized by a work of social renovation and transformation to be accomplished—and whose inspiration should be a vitally Christian one.

I am afraid I shall be tedious in insisting once more on this. I will say only that in my judgment a politics of Christian inspiration proceeds in the human soul from an activity natural in itself and elevated by its connection with the infused virtues; it pursues a concrete historical ideal, the specification of which is of a political and social, not of a religious, order, an ideal which Christian inspiration animates and vivifies from within. To ask Catholicism to specify a political or national ideal, and itself to replace, as a principle of temporal unification and temporal activity, the objects, the values, the impelling ideas, and the instincts, of the temporal order, would be contrary to the nature of things, precisely because Catholicism is by nature transcendent. One would risk, then, either having in the temporal order only a Christian embellishment placed at the service of earthly groups of forces and earthly interests, or achieving (as in Austria in the years preceding the *Anschluss*) an artificial construction and an ingenious political understanding deprived of historical roots and collective dynamism. To vivify and animate from within, to help organic forms to germinate—it is for this that Christian influences are called upon, in the present age more than in the past, to act on political realities; and it is thus that a new Christendom will perhaps someday be born.

Finally, as to the means of a Christian politics, summing up what I have said at length elsewhere, I would say: first, that these means should always be just, not excluding force but subordinating it; second, that a hyper-moralism demanding

that these means be not only good in themselves but phari-
saically pure—I mean free of contact with the impurities of
human history which would stain them from without—this
hyper-moralism is as contrary to a true political ethics as is
a Machiavellian cynicism; third, that the seemingly irresistible power of the weapons of violence, of deceit and infamy,
employed today by men who have discovered that the absolute rejection of all moral rule opens the way to a kind of
omnipotence and a paradise of force, obliges Christians more
than ever to fix their attention on the question of the hierarchy of means. If it is true, as Leo XIII says, that religion is
"the highest of the common goods, to which all others should
be referred,"[16] and that the chief thing in the New Law, "that
in which *all its strength (virtus)* consists," is, as St. Thomas says,[17]
"the grace of the Holy Spirit, given to those who believe in
Christ," it follows that the greatest evil with regard to the
common temporal good would be for Christians to cease to
bring into the life of the political community the testimony
and influence of the Gospel truths, of the Christian virtues
and the grace of the Holy Spirit. Aggression and co-action
are the only means known to men of blood. The Christian
knows a world of other means, and among these he ought to
attach particular importance to those I have called the means
of organic edification and the spiritual weapons of war; the
weapons of patience and of voluntary suffering which are par
excellence the weapons of love and truth. It is only by using
all these other weapons that "weakness can perhaps be com-
pensated for and even *turned* to victory, a weakness which, in
the order of the weapons of force or violence, arises from
the fact that the Christian is obliged to rule such means by

---

16. Leo XIII, Encyclical *Sapientiæ Christianæ,* January 10, 1890.

17. *ST,* I-II, q. 106, a. 1.

justice, and that they offend him in his spiritual sensitiveness. The state of a world, where all violence is let loose, would at once reduce to impotence or to self-surrender Christians who, wishing to act on the temporal level would not put the folly of love at the head of their means of action."[18]

At this moment of history and before certain disasters overtake us, it is already too late, perhaps, to hope for the emergence of Christian-minded social political groupings, and for political action properly undertaken by Christians. Perhaps there is starting, for the world, an hour of violence and darkness which will end in a catastrophe of the political sphere. But even in the midst of such an eclipse of all sound political activity, a field of activities remains open for the Christian on the temporal level: I mean the evangelical activities, the works of mercy and brotherly love, the testimony to the truth, thanks to which the Christian, existing with his people, and with the people in the depths of time and history, is able to act on time and history, not by historical or political, but by divine and sacrificial means.

---

18.  *True Humanism.*

# CHAPTER IX

## *Christianity & Earthly Civilizations*

### I. *The Church and the World*

The contact or meeting of the Church and earthly civilizations is the meeting of the Kingdom of God with the world. It is a question of two heterogeneous universes which enter into closest relations on one "common ground," namely man. The unity of the Church is supernatural. Civilizations, on the other hand, spring from the natural order.

To understand this more exactly, we must recall certain points of doctrine concerning, on the one hand, the common good of the Church and that of civilization, or, as St. Thomas says, of the *civil life*; and concerning, on the other hand, the natural virtues and the supernatural virtues.

The common good of the Church lies in eternal life and in union with the divine Persons; the common good of a civilization is the right life (the earthly and human right life) of a people or group of peoples. These are two specific ends, clearly distinct; they differ as heaven differs from earth. And it is clear that the earthly end is not ultimate, or is ultimate as St. Thomas says, only in a certain sense and in a given order. The last end, pure and simple, is eternal life, and that is why any order of civilization or culture is indirectly related or subordinated to the spiritual order.

On the other hand, the life of civilization, even when responding to natural inclination and primordial instinct, is not a simple physical fact: it is a work of reason and of virtue. And what are the virtues directly concerned with this life? They are the natural virtues which are grouped around the four cardinal virtues of prudence, justice, fortitude, and temperance. A social and political life which truly merits the name, and is worthy of man, is centered in natural justice and tends to develop the natural virtue of brotherly friendship between the members of the same society. Whereas the virtues by which we are fellow citizens with the saints and members of the Kingdom of God are not only the three theological virtues, but also the supernatural moral virtues which follow in their wake and correspond to the natural moral virtues of the same name.

We perceive here the great cultural importance of the doctrine of St. Thomas on the natural moral virtues and on the infused moral virtues. The first are in their nature connected with civil life; the second with the divine life begun here below, and, if I may put it in this way, for the heaven of the soul. "Man," says St. Thomas, "is not only a citizen of the terrestrial city, he is also a member of the celestial one; he belongs to that Jerusalem whose prince is God, and whose citizens are the angels and all the saints, whether they are reigning in glory and at rest in their homeland or whether they are still pilgrims on earth, according to the words of the apostle: 'You are fellow-citizens with the saints; and of the household of God.' But in order for a man to be a member of this city, his nature does not suffice; he must be raised up by the grace of God. For it is manifest that the virtues which are in man insofar as he is a member of this society cannot be acquired by his natural powers; that is the reason why they are not caused in us by our actions, but are infused in us by divine gift."[1] So much for the moral virtues which are infused and which fit us for the morality and the common life which are in keeping with the Kingdom of God, which is already here, teaching, struggling and suffering on earth: the Church, the wandering and crucified Kingdom.

If we are dealing with moral virtues which are acquired, "these," says St. Thomas, "are the directives in civil life; that is the reason their object is the civil good, the good of civilization."[2] Here our actions refer directly to goods "proportioned to human nature."[3] This is the reason why there is no infused political prudence in the earthly life of society; a supernatural virtue of political prudence would have to do only with the government of the Church of Christ.

Here, nevertheless, we find the organic union and the subordination mentioned above. There is no separation or breaking off; there is a vital cohesion between the natural virtues and the supernatural virtues. We know in fact that there is no perfect virtue without the love of charity. To arrive at their full state of virtue, the natural moral virtues must be united to charity and the infused moral virtues, which elevate them by attaching them to the supra-temporal aims of the human person. I have just said that there is no infused political prudence for the life of earthly society; it should be added immediately that there is no perfect natural virtue of political prudence except it be united in the human soul to the supernatural organism of infused gifts and virtues. The political prudence of a St. Louis was an acquired virtue; it was a virtue

---

1.   *De virtutibus in communi*, a. 9.

2.   "Virtutes morales acquisitae dirigunt in vita civili, unde habent bonum civile pro fine." St. Thomas *III Sent.*, dist. 33, q. 1, a. 4, resp.

3.   Cf. *De virtutibus in communi*, a. 10.

in the full and perfect sense of the word only because it was
elevated by the supernatural virtues.

This digression will perhaps aid us to understand why St.
Thomas teaches that he who has the care of the common
well-being of the multitude must be a *bonus vir*, pure and simple, a virtuous man in every respect. And thus we also understand why civilizations, themselves belonging to the natural
order, cannot arrive at their full state and dignity as civilizations, except insofar as they are elevated in their own order by
the influence of those virtues which arise in them, not from
what is Caesar's, but from what is God's.

It is possible to conceive in the abstract a civilization which
unites all men in the purely natural unity of a temporal life,
conducted in accordance with pure reason. This, however, is a
fiction because humanity is not in a state of pure nature; it is in
the state of a nature which has fallen and been redeemed. As a
matter of fact, civilizations vary as much as languages, and are
often opposed to each other. Can we hope that one day there
will exist here below a civilization which is really universal?
By this I certainly do not mean a uniform civilization, but one
which would allow for inward variety and internal dissimilar-
ities in accord with the historical, national, and cultural heritage, and the vocations proper to different human groups; for
such a variety responds to the natural necessity of exchange
and metabolism and also of the activating tension between
these groups. If one day there is to exist here below a truly universal civilization, that is to say, one founded—no matter how
strong its internal differences—on first common principles,
and recognizing in an organic and actual manner the same
common good, it will have risen higher, in its own order, by the
influence of the energies whose source is the grace of Christ.

May I add that this very possibility of a truly universal
civilization appears problematic, at least before the time of

the great reintegration foretold by St. Paul, and the sign of which he gave as being the conversion of Israel.

In the meanwhile, the Church, the Mystical Body of Christ, appears as a high unity of supra-temporal order spread in the midst of social formations opposed to each other. From this superior unity—one which actually exists—it follows that Catholicism is par excellence an agent of co-operation between civilizations. Nevertheless, it can only be so with the help of a very high tension of human energy, natural and supernatural, because the unity in question is of a transcendent order.

Let us make every effort to understand this paradox, which is united to the mysterious drama in which the history of humanity is enveloped, and to the mission assigned the Church of continuing here below the work of the Redemption by supplying what is lacking (in application, not in merit) to the sufferings of Christ. A mystical body, through which runs a life that is properly divine, and in which the prince of this world has no part, calls all men to itself, in a unity of supernatural faith and spiritual activity, as fellow citizens of the saints and intimates of God. This mystical body carries on its work in the very midst of natural bodies of society which live the life of this world and in which the devil plays his part; and which divide these same men, fellow citizens together in the pain and labor of temporal existence, into earthly groups which their own fleshly law, if it is not checked by a superior law, leads to opposition and conflict.

At one and the same time—our own time—co-exist civilizations of different origins and ages. In his *Outline of History*, Professor Arnold Toynbee, having eliminated some six hundred primitive societies, enumerates twenty-seven distinct civilizations in historical times, of which five survive today. I will return to this in an instant. Taking as a point of chronological departure the centuries in which the Christian Middle Ages reached their highest cultural level, that is to say in the twelfth and thirteenth centuries, we can summarily characterize the civilizations which we are dealing with here as: of *pre-mediaeval* origin (civilizations of China and the Far East, Hindu, and Islamic), civilizations of *mediaeval origin* (our Western civilizations), and forms which have but recently arisen in history, which aspire to establish *new* civilizations (soviet, fascist, national-socialist, etc.).

The five civilizations described by Mr. Toynbee are the civilization of China and the Far East; Hindu civilization; Islamic civilization; Western civilization which, as he says, comprises not only Europe and the New World, but all the navigable seas and their ports; and a fifth civilization which is that of Orthodox or Greco-Russian Christendom. It is this last civilization which is at present in a state of profound upheaval, caused by Soviet communism which rejects its fundamental beliefs and ethic. It will thus be seen that the new civilization which Soviet communism claims to establish is to be placed in the historical framework of a determined area of culture—in that of the fifth civilization described by Mr. Toynbee, with which it is very necessary to study its particular connections. On the other hand, the new civilizations which Fascism and National-Socialism claim to establish are to be placed in the historical framework of another area of culture, namely of Western civilization, and should be judged according to the good and evil which fructified in this civilization and according to its calling—which it has for the most part largely betrayed.

One might speak of still other new forms of civilization, those developing in China and Japan and placed within the historical framework of Far Eastern civilization. But this newness seems to be especially of a technical and morphological order, and it would seem that the spirit which animates Japanese imperialism, for example, continues to be in its innermost depths that same spirit which, as Okakura Kakuzo says, for centuries has made Asia one, that Asia "which is nothing, if it is not spiritual."

At first glance it might seem from the fact alone that Christians living under the different civilizations of which I have spoken are participating in the supra-temporal unity of the Church and are endeavoring to merit heaven in living their private lives as Christians, that they exercise in a sufficiently efficacious manner their office as agents of co-operation and vivification in the temporal world. But I do not think that this is so. It is necessary to introduce at this point a more precise notion, founded on the philosophical distinction between common causality and proper causality. I do not say that by the fact alone that they live truly Christian lives, Christians do not exert an effective action on the different civilizations to which they belong. From the fact alone that they lead truly Christian lives, they exercise an effective action on the world, even the first and primordial action which they are expected to exercise. What is it, as a matter of fact, to live a truly Christian life, if not to strive, each according to his condition, for Christian perfection, that is to say, for the perfection of charity? The first thing needed by the world is the contemplation of the saints and their love, because it causes the gifts of divine life and of substantial Love to abound on the earth. And if Christians really strive with all their hearts for a life of union with God, and if each Christian, in his private acts and judgments, tries to give testimony to justice, to fraternal love, and to the truth, so often betrayed by men; to resist the influences of hate, calumny, resentment and panic, the collective nervous storms to which nations are exposed in the troubled eras of their history—then centers of interior vigilance and peace will be multiplied, and their influence will modify imperceptibly but really and effectively the atmosphere in which world history is unrolled.

Nevertheless, the causality thus exercised on the social and political order, on the flow of civilization, is a higher causality, and in the philosophical sense of the word, common. And such causality, however necessary, however primordial, does not *suffice* for the development of social life required by nature and by Providence. For their reciprocal communication of energy and movement, beings demand prompt and direct causes in proportion to their nature. Such is the causality that Christians should exert in the temporal social order. *Haec oportebat facere*, says the Gospel, *et illa non omittere*: "These things you should have done, and those not left undone." In the sphere of private life we are called upon to exercise the natural and the supernatural virtues of Christian life. But in the sphere of social and political life, we are also called upon to exercise the natural virtues (guided and elevated by the supernatural ones) which properly have to do with that sphere, and by means of which the rules of Christian justice and charity may be introduced into it.

It is in this sense, that I have said above that by the fact alone that they participate in the supra-temporal unity of the Church and endeavor to merit heaven in living their private lives in a Christian manner, the Christians involved in the different civilizations do not yet exercise in a *sufficiently* effective manner their office as agents of co-operation and vivification.

For the action we speak of to be sufficiently effective, Christianity must penetrate into the social and cultural life itself, in its proper order. And is this not exactly the great obligation of which the Popes have constantly reminded Catholics for the past seventy years? If the Christian world of our time had not shown itself so frivolously heedless of

their voice, if the work of Catholics aware of the proper
realities and proper requirements of the social order had not
been everywhere opposed with such bitterness and suspicion,
Western civilization would not now be face to face with such
profound sufferings and the cruel trials it is undergoing today.
But I return to my subject and to the question of the penetration of Christianity and Evangelical truths into the heart
of social and cultural life itself. Special problems arise here,
concerning the three categories of civilization which we have
defined.

## II. *Civilizations of Pre-Mediaeval Origin*

With regard to civilizations of pre-mediaeval origin, the
principal difficulty consists in the fact that these civilizations
do not know (or perceive only in an imperfect manner, I say
this of Buddhism) the distinction between the things which
are Caesar's and those which are God's. Christianity should
teach them this distinction, at the same time respecting the
temporal structures proper to these civilizations.

The thing is all the more complex and difficult because
these great civilizations—Far Eastern, Hindu, Islamic—are
themselves honeycombed with deep conflicts and antago-
nisms, and are at the same time suffering from the processes
of disintegration and changes inflicted upon them by Western
cultural influences, frequently those which are most negative
and destructive (such as the idolatry of techniques, a disin-
tegrating religious modernism, materialism, and atheism,
Rousseauism, Marxism, racialism, and nationalistic worship
of the State).

At times the Far Eastern civilizations make use of these
influences in their own way in order to renew themselves in
accordance with their teleology and their own ambitions; at
other times, they rise up against these influences and try to

232         SCHOLASTICISM & POLITICS

throw them off, and Christianity along with them, imagining it to be a part of Western civilization and entailed to this civilization, not recognizing its transcendence and universality. We must admit that they are confirmed in this error by the prejudices and narrowness of spirit of many Catholics of the Old World who, like Mr. Hilaire Belloc, appear to believe that the Faith is Europe, or who imagine that the expansion of the Kingdom of God among peoples of the world consists in imposing upon them Western civilization with its various commercial and industrial, political, and military "benefits."

In a sense it must be recognized that the conflicts of civilization have their historic usefulness; it must be recognized that Western activism and imperialism have had the effect of obliging—though by the most unworthy means—the Oriental civilizations, which are themselves immobile or doomed to a kind of circular motion, to enter the movement, the great and terrible movement of history, which travels and advances in time (both for good and for evil). But at what a price! With what wastage, with what losses for the Kingdom of God! The Kingdom of God advances like a thief, profiting by the accidents of history, its shiftings, its scandals, and its crimes, because God draws good from evil. It would have been able to advance like a king of humility seated upon an ass's foal (the ass's foal is the Christian temporality), and hailed by hosannas, if the Christian West had been truly Christian in its own political life and in its relations with other civilizations.

The whole problem of missionary activity looms up at this point, appearing even more difficult—for different reasons—when it comes into contact with the Oriental civilizations we are here considering than when it is in contact with primitive societies. I do not have to go into this question here. I only wish to point out that Christianity here works as an agent of co-operation in three ways. In the first place, it teaches the Western civilization—in the measure that it learns this lesson—to respect and promote the human values of other civilizations and their historic vocation. Christianity is respectful of nature and its diversities. Although they have too often been practiced by Christians, methods which enforce conformity are not Christian methods.

In the second place, Catholicism—by the very fact that it itself affirms its own supernatural universality and dissociates itself from ethnical or cultural particularisms in which a certain naturalism, not always without concern for earthly interests, at one time undertook to bind it—bears witness to peoples of all colors and cultures not only of the transcendent catholicity of the Kingdom of God, but also, and consequently, of the natural catholicity (whatever may be its historical diversities) of reason and of the principles of natural law and the fundamental virtues of civilization.

In the third place, in the measure that it succeeds in penetrating the civilizations of pre-mediaeval origin with which I am dealing at this moment, it is clear that in aiding them, in their proper aspirations and claims, Christianity leads them toward collaborating in a fraternal manner with Western civilization, which despite its errors and setbacks, remains the heir of a Europe engendered by Christianity in the life of civilization.

Regarding the second point I have just mentioned, it seems to me advisable to stress one distinction of the utmost importance:

A while ago I recalled the words of Okakura: "Asia is nothing, if it is not spiritual…" The word spirit may be understood in two different senses: in a psychological and cultural sense, and in the supernatural sense of the "*pneuma*."

In the first sense it has to do with the higher natural activities of the human being, the *natural man* of which St. Paul speaks (without forgetting that these activities—as I recalled in the beginning in dealing with the natural virtues—can be elevated by grace in their own order). It is in this sense that each civilization is characterized before everything else by an irreducible and typical spirit. And if the Orient boasts a civilization more spiritual than that of the Occident, this has to do with the spirituality which remains psychological (even though the *pneuma* is not absent). And this means that in the Orient the things of natural spirituality have been pushed to a higher extreme of refinement and elevation, whereas by a curious phenomenon of differentiation, the Christian Occident, relying in a certain sense on the Church for the care of supernatural spirituality, has taken less care of the spirit in the order of nature and of civilization itself.

In the second sense of the word (in the proper and supernatural sense of *"pneuma"*), the word "spirit" refers to the infused gifts of the *spiritual man*, and in this sense there is but one spirituality of grace, which is spread by the Spirit of God upon all the members, visible and invisible, of the mystical Body of Christ, and which appears particularly manifested in the saints of the Church.

And I say that this Spirit of the Church does not destroy the characteristic spirit of the different civilizations, neither does it remain separate from them. But because of its really divine transcendence, it can penetrate and elevate, and insofar transfigure, but not destroy, the earthly spirits with which it deals. I would mention here the example of Father Lebbe, that missionary born in Belgium, who became a great Chinese man of letters and has now become a Chinese citizen, founder of two Chinese religious orders. It is Father Lebbe's greatness and his stroke of genius, in that ancient China whose culture and life he has made his own, to have understood the power of divine assimilation of the Spirit of the Church, regarding the spirit itself of Far Eastern civilizations. And Father Lebbe is not the only one who has understood this. The prominent Chinese bishop, Yu-Pin (who was once in the United States) has told me that China, after having experimented with various extremist ideas imported from abroad, found itself actually led, by its own characteristic feeling for the "golden mean," to a reversal toward its own spirit. And it was beginning definitely to understand that this spirit of its own traditional civilization could be saved only by the universal spirit of Christianity. It was just at the moment it was beginning to understand these things that a brutal military aggression, committed in the name of order (as is so much of the highway robbery which dishonors the world of today), tried to destroy China's attempt at a national revival. But it is not easy to stop a movement like this one, or to crush a people like the Chinese.

In short, the spirit of the civilizations of the Far East can come to renew and revive itself in accordance with the fleshly law of the *animalis homo* left to his own devices—I mean to say, by a political imperialism aggravating the most dangerous ethnical particularism; but it can also, on the other hand, renew itself according to the law of grace of the *spiritualis homo*, and by ascension into the religious world of the Incarnation, by which this spirit of Far-Eastern civilization, while remaining truly itself, will be purified and rendered more capable of universal communion.

And this is, indeed, the wonderful and terrible alternative which faces the world, in the West as in the East. Either civilizations—in the grasp of inexorable internal oppositions—will seek to rise up and to defend themselves without penitence of heart, according to the energies of this world and its prince, and in keeping with the law of darkness and sin which is that of politics *separated* from the gifts of Him who enlightens every

man who comes into the world; then the temporal community, or race, or nation, or State, or Liberty itself, will become
a devouring idol for man (in fact, they are that already). Or
*else* in allowing themselves to be penetrated by the holy forces
of the Kingdom of God, civilizations will be transformed,
and will receive into the core of the social and temporal order
itself, the life-giving influx which comes down from Uncreated
Love and which is promised to men of good will. And thus—
but after what settling of accounts—they would finally enter
into the fullness of their age and would aim at a heroic ideal
of brotherly love and an understanding of the dignity of the
human person, which may most appropriately be called, it
seems to me, the ideal of an integral humanism.

### III. *Western Civilization*

Let us now consider Western civilization itself. It is dominated, no matter what it may do, and even when it denies it,
by Christianity. From the point of view of the part taken by
Christians in the activities of civilization, I think one remark
may explain in part the lack of attention to pontifical directions upon which I commented a few moments ago. For the
Catholic, especially in countries of age-old Catholic culture
like France or Ireland, the atmosphere of Christian civilization, in parish and countryside, has so long been definitely
established, it is so natural and beyond discussion, that it
would seem almost an indiscretion or lack of tact to be especially concerned by it. May I be permitted to recall the words
of Bishop Freppel: *A quoi bon se faire de la bile pour Saint-Esprit?*
"Why on earth worry about the Holy Spirit?" A monk prays
in the perfect manner, said the Desert Fathers, when he does
not even know that he is praying. Christianity penetrated so
deeply into the natural structures of culture that there was
no need to know that they were Christian nor had to take

particular care that they be so. Let each man do his work where he is placed, without concerning himself about the rest, and all will go well. There was much of human virtue and dignity in such an attitude, but it also led to routine and negligence. In our civilizations of mediaeval origin, Catholics too long considered that it was enough for them insofar as social matters were concerned, to rest upon the structures of existing civilization (precisely because they were of Christian origin), without undertaking in this order any personal action of a properly social nature. We are now paying for this optimism, which—especially after the victory of the liberal and capitalist economy—too often led to egoism and sins of omission.

We have a great deal of lost ground to recover, in the midst of the crisis which Western civilization is now undergoing, in order to enter again into the role which Christian activity should play in the movement of temporal history and the social, political, and cultural transformation of the world. And yet it is on this condition alone that Christianity can expedite or animate revivals and changes which concern not only Western civilization itself, but all other civilizations, as well, in their action upon one another.

It is proper to recall here that, even if it remains dominated by Christianity, Western civilization has nevertheless suffered, in the very order of the "Christian" cultural forms on which it depends, certain terrible crises, of which the present catastrophes are but the logical and inevitable consequence. The first crisis was that of Lutheran immanentism; the second, that of Cartesian rationalism; the third, that of the optimism and individualism which sprang from Jean-Jacques Rousseau.[4] From these three great shocks (each,

---

4.    Cf. our *Three Reformers* (London: Sheed & Ward, 1928).

from the cultural point of view, a process both of growth and alteration in a Christian civilization, and, from the religious viewpoint, both a Christian phenomenon and one of the disintegration of Christianity), have resulted, on one hand, more and more intense and widespread impulses and movements of separatism; on the other hand, and at each step, efforts in the opposite direction of conservation and restoration, less charged with dynamism, but drawing their strength from the instinct of vital cohesion and recovery on the part of the cultural and religious forces that remain.

In fact, if we seek what constitutes in the modern age the spiritual entelechy of Western civilization, we will find, in the first place, Catholicism whose proper form is a transcendent one, that of the Church or the Kingdom of God. But its projections into the temporal sphere are mixed inevitably in this domain—the domain of the world—with forces and interests, more or less pure, of a sociological and natural order, and have moreover suffered for three centuries now the violent and constant action of adverse forces. These temporal projections of Catholicism have thus seen the structures of the Western world progressively escape, in large areas, from their radius of influence.

We find, in the second place, Protestantism of the Puritan and Anglo-Saxon type, the form of which was originally coextensive with the British Empire and its zones of influence or spiritual affiliation, and whose force has long been powerful, but now seems to have lost its mastery over human morals in vast sections of these parts of the world.

Finally, in the third place, we find democracy of the rationalist, Rousseauistic, French type, which represents a lower form, entirely secular and non-religious, of Christian energies, but remains inconceivable without these energies as its source and origin; its emotional and rational force also seems now to have lost mastery over a vast section of civilization long animated by it.

After many changes, the revolutionary dynamism of the forces which first produced the three great ruptures just referred to, has passed principally either into the totalitarian-communist movement which has succeeded in taking over as its laboratory a large part of the ancient Christian-Orthodox civilization and which wishes to win the world; or else into the totalitarian-Germano-racist movement which wishes to bring into subjection the ancient Western civilization and the entire world. It seems to me quite remarkable that the two great ruptures in civilization which we see today appear to have taken their direction from the religious ruptures which occurred in earlier times, and which *separated* from the Catholic community, first the orthodox Oriental world, and then the Protestant Germanic world.

## IV. *Attempts at New Civilizations*

I thus arrive at the third group of civilizations of which I spoke at the beginning. I did not say that they existed, but that they claimed or aspired to exist.

As every process of "generation" implies a "corruption," the engendering of new forms, laying claim to be the civilizations of tomorrow, implies the disintegration of civilizations of mediaeval origin. In fact, these new forms are attached to principles which, either in virtue of a philosophy of the world and of man, or in virtue simply of the totalitarian idea, are decidedly opposed to every expansion of Christianity in the temporal, social, and political domain.

I have no intention of making here a comparative examination of the various sorts of politico-social totalitarianism which confront one another today. It is well, however, to note that the word "totalitarian" should be understood analogically, and that it designates very different things. Used in connection with Italian Fascism it refers to the political totalitarianism of the State; used in connection with German National-Socialism, it refers to the biological and pantheistic totalitarianism of the "community of the people"; used in connection with Russian Communism, it refers to a totalitarianism with a different basis—dialectical and universalist—which, while making the absolute rejection of all transcendence the condition for the liberation of man, leads to a sort of monism of collective human labor. I note only that, considered in its abstract nature, the totalitarian principle, as such, lays claim to the entire human person—at least, in temporal and cultural values, but they count these values as supreme—for the social earthly community or for the State, and demands for that community the Messianic love which is due to the Kingdom of God alone.

Our common culture, common to Europe and America, is thus undergoing a process of fundamental rupture. I do not say that this rupture has taken place, I say that it is in danger of taking place. The traditional Western culture—with its original basis of Christianity and with the transformations and secularizations it has suffered, for instance, from the *Aufklärung* and the French Revolution, and with all the other alterations we might mention—now finds itself, precisely because it has been altered, facing fundamentally different forms which seek—as I have just noticed—to offer themselves as rising substantially new civilizations.

The form of civilization which is being worked out in Communist Russia firmly intends to become a fundamentally new culture. In their work on Soviet communism, the Webbs throw this point into particularly strong relief. There is here a potentially new civilization of which atheism will be one of the fundamental values.

So far as Italian Fascism is concerned, I do not believe it can be said that it represents—although it claims this—a form of civilization that is fundamentally new. It imposes upon Western civilization a tension which places this civilization in jeopardy, but it is supported by little else than the old politics of Machiavelli and the classic idea of the Roman Empire. But it seems almost inevitable that it will come under the sway of one or the other of its great totalitarian rivals—of the atheistic totalitarian idea or the racial totalitarian idea. For the moment, it seems to be especially subject to the latter.

And this latter totalitarianism—the racial and National-Socialist totalitarianism—tends in my opinion to introduce a form of civilization which is fundamentally new, whose religious co-efficient is just as incompatible as atheism is with the Western civilization of the present. The consummation of the rupture of our civilization will be effected by the triumph of this totalitarian idea as much as by the triumph of communism. I have observed, in the first chapter of this book, that the religious significance of racism is a demonic *paratheism*, as destructive and blasphemous as atheism, and perhaps more enticing, perfidious, and perverse. Racism's spiritual attitude is entirely opposed to the fundamental elements of traditional Western civilization. It sees in blood and in race the necessary vehicles of spirit and of culture; it seeks to nationalize science itself; according to the blood, from which it comes, thought will have an essentially different character. The natural universality of reason is a value which is directly denied and attacked by National-Socialism. It is the common denominator of Western civilization which is here in danger.

Thus, considered from the viewpoint of their spiritual principles, the Russo-communist movement and the Germano-racist movement rigorously exclude Christianity as an animating force—in any degree whatsoever—from the ethic of the temporal community, from civilization, from law, and from political and social structures. The penetration by Christianity and the Gospel truths into the heart of the social and cultural life, which we recognized at the beginning of this chapter as indispensable to the human fulfillment and perfection of all civilization, is rendered impossible by the two powerful movements of which I am speaking. One of the characteristics of these movements is that with them—insofar as the spirit from which they proceed is effectively realized—one crosses, in what concerns any Christian form of civilization, the threshold which separates progressive "alteration" from pure and simple rejection of the form.

If all that remains of Christian culture—though surviving in only a diminished form, by still retaining in some degree that sense of human dignity which Christianity has brought into the world—does not reassemble its forces; if the ancient Christian vitality of Western civilization does not rise again with vigor and purity under the effect of a renewal of the social-temporal conceptions vivified by the Gospel's spirit, one cannot see how Western civilization can resist the germs of death which are working within it. (It may be that it will pass through a kind of death in order to rise again.)

When we consider the frightful panorama of the nations, we feel obliged to make clear that spirit is humiliated today in an extraordinarily profound manner.

It is, indeed, true that spirit is punished for its own faults and oversights. What forces today are taking revenge on spirituality? The animal and elementary forces of vitality which chastise spirit for having too long failed in its own duties and in human realities. There is no other recourse for spirit but to descend, with the awareness of love, into the very depths of those elementary realities themselves. In this way a new Christendom may spring up. Never shall we renounce the hope of a new Christendom, a new temporal order inspired by Christianity. For the future advent of such a temporal order, two conditions appear forthwith so important as to need noticing.

The first condition concerns what should be called the reintegration of the masses. If it is true that the spiritual reintegration of the masses into Christianity is a primordial requirement for the healing of civilization, then it is clear that love rather than threats of violence must be extended to the masses. In order that the people may exist with Christ, Christians must exist with the people.

With the temporal reintegration of the masses into the political or national commonwealth, the concept of striving to make happy slaves is but an illusory solution. Although this temporal reintegration is difficult and slow, it is only to be *really* obtained, that is to say humanly obtained, by remolding social structures according to justice and human dignity, and with the free co-operation of the laboring classes, in order to go beyond the capitalist system and the social cult of material goods and material power.

The second condition for a new Christian temporal order concerns the question of means. If it is true that means must correspond to ends, then it is clear that to prepare a social order consonant with human dignity, no means unworthy of man can be used. Many times I have spoken of the purification of the means. Aldous Huxley has also denounced the folly of attempting good ends by bad means. Will Christians finally resolve to understand the proper law of Christian action? Or are they ashamed to be called children of light? The question is not one of condemning or rejecting the means of force and physical restraint, if justly employed; it is rather a question of recognizing the primary importance of those means founded on moral or inner energy, on spiritual firmness, on personal courage, risk, and suffering. It seems very remarkable that in the great dictatorships with all their power, a single man who can say "I do not agree" appears as an intolerable and extremely dangerous enemy. Why, if there is not in Conscience, Honor, Truth, Patience, and Love, a certain hidden strength that the totalitarian idols fear? We are stupid not to dare to improve the terrific resources of this hidden strength.

Finally, the question for what remains of Western civilization is one of becoming very conscious of its own principles, and of having very great confidence in its own means. If one does not dare to *be*, how can one *act* and *resist*?

I should like to conclude by saying that Christianity now faces an absolutely vital problem of *spiritual universality*, evoking in a way the problem which, in a superior and transcendent plane, Christianity solved in the time of St. Paul, in its escape from the claims of Judeo-Christian particularism. It also faces the problem which, upon the plane of temporal civilization, it solved at the time of the fall of the Roman Empire. Practically, this problem is solved only by an effusion of sanctity. It exacts a heroic detachment testifying to the primacy of the spirit. Above all must be affirmed the independence of the religion of Christ in regard to the regimes of earthly civilization and to the charge of established injustice which often encumbers these regimes; and also its absolute refusal in regard to the forms of idolatry which spring from race, class, or the nation, or state, when they are elevated into absolutes.

But it is not for an idealistic or angelic isolation that this detachment must be produced. The Sovereign Law of the Incarnation continues its influence here. While detaching the things of God's Kingdom from historical formations tending to bring into subjection that life which is freedom itself, that law of the Incarnation remains the law of superabundance and fruitfulness—the gift of self proper to love. And, consequently, the forces of Christianity must be involved again and anew in the flesh of humanity, to give birth, in the order of earthly civilization, to formations which are new and more pure.

Because Christian liberty is a pledged liberty, one which bears and transports the heavy mountains of history; because, and this is the very mystery of the Christian life, to the extent that this liberty becomes involved most deeply in history and the world, to that extent does it remain free; and bears witness to the fact that it arises neither from history nor from the world, but from the Living God.

# AFTERWORD

## *On Maritain's Political Philosophy*

The significance of Maritain's political philosophy will remain hidden to those who judge it by its acceptance in contemporary France. An impressive proof of its independent character is that it has been praised and rejected in the same camps. Until 1926 conservative rightist Catholics, taking advantage of the modernist crisis, claimed Maritain for themselves as the great philosopher of order and intelligence. He published many articles in the *Revue Universelle*, a periodical edited by Bainville, a friend of the head of *L'Action Française*, Charles Maurras.[1] The social and democratic Catholics then regarded him with some distrust.[2] But after 1926, when the Action Française was condemned by Pope Pius XI and Maritain accepted and emphatically defended this condemnation[3] (until this time he had been concerned primarily with speculative philosophy; henceforth he was to turn towards political philosophy), he was attacked not only by the Action Française, but even in the *Revue Universelle*.[4] The antipathy towards his work and public activities increased steadily among the rightist French Catholics, until it reached a climax during the Spanish Civil War. On the other hand,

Maritain now won more and more friends and admirers
among progressive Catholics. One of their writers, Vialatoux,
contributed to Maritain's *Bibliothèque française de la philosophie*.[5]
The periodical *Esprit* was strongly influenced by his personalism. The attitude towards Maritain's political philosophy was
often unfortunately determined by practical politics, though
Maritain himself insisted on remaining above all parties and
objectively grasping their particular spirit and psychologies,
as his characterization of the left-right mentalities in *Lettre sur
l'Indépendance* shows so impressively.

1.  Cf. Charles O'Donnell, *The Ideal of a New Christendom: The Cultural and
    Political Philosophy of Jacques Maritain* (doctoral diss., Harvard University,
    1940). This well-documented study is indispensable to all interested in
    Maritain's biography and relations to French intellectual, literary, and
    social movements. "Maritain contributed three or four articles a year to
    *La Revue Universelle* until the condemnation of L'Action Française" (p. 26).
    Later on he participated in and inspired the foundation of the democratic
    periodicals *La Vie Intellectuelle, Esprit*, and *Temps Présent.*

2.  Cf. P. Archambault, *Les Jeunes Maîtres* (Paris, 1926), pp. 81–116; on
    Maritain's political philosophy, pp. 106–111.

3.  Cf. *Primauté du Spirituel* (Paris, 1927) (English: *The Things That Are Not
    Caesar's* [New York: Charles Scribner's Sons, 1931]); the two volumes
    edited in collaboration with a number of theologians and philosophers,
    *Pourquoi Rome a parlé* (Paris, 1928) and *Clairvoyance de Rome* (Paris, 1929).
    As there was some hope that the Action Française would accept the
    decision of the Church, Maritain wrote his pamphlet, *Une Opinion sur
    Charles Maurras et le devoir des Catholiques* (Paris, 1926), which is several times
    quoted in *The Things That Are Not Caesar's.*

4.  Cf. O'Donnell, *The Ideal of a New Christendom.* He writes about J.
    Desclausais' article in the *Revue Universelle* of June 15, 1936, "sweepingly
    accuses Maritain of every heresy condemned by the Church. A charitable
    estimate of the attack would regard it as a canard" (p. 451f). Those
    interested in the various attacks on Maritain by rightist Catholics,
    adherents of Action Française, et.c, should read the documented accounts
    of Charles O'Donnell.

5.  Maritain's *Primauté du Spirituel* (French edition), contains a friendly
    discussion with J. Vialatoux, who later contributed a volume, *Essais de
    Philosophie Économique*, to Maritain's series and another volume, *Morale et
    Politique*, to *Questions disputées*, edited by Abbé Ch. Journet and Maritain
    (Paris: Desclée de Brouwer).

Is it possible to conclude from this change in Maritain's French audience that his political and social philosophy has changed too? Is it justifiable to oppose the Maritain of the first period, down to 1926, in which he fought particularly the errors of modern democratism, the author of *Antimoderne, Théonas,* and *Three Reformers,* to the Maritain of the second period, beginning with his polemic against the Action Française, after which he became the most prominent spokesman of those Catholics who looked for a new democracy under Christian inspiration and rejected all attempts forms of the past?

It seems to me that this distinction between Maritain's work only helps to illustrate the *unity of the central motives of his thought and activities.* Maritain has been a Thomistic philosopher since he started to write for the general public. After a youth outside the Church, after becoming a member of the circle around Péguy and after having been impressed by Bergson's lectures,[6] he became a convert under the influence of Léon Bloy.[7] Philosophy did not matter for Bloy, for he lived in the world of supernatural symbols and realities; but Maritain studied the works of St. Thomas Aquinas with the guidance of the Dominican Father Clérissac and accepted Thomism because for him Thomism is, in its substance, the expression of universal truth, able to incorporate the truth of all times and capable of being liberated from purely historical elements and additions. He has remained a Thomist.[8] His

---

6. Cf. *Ransoming the Time,* New York, 1941, p. 53.

7. Cf. Maritain, *Quelques Pages sur Léon Bloy* (Paris: Cahier, 1927).

8. I quote only one of the many passages from the work of Maritain expressing his fundamental philosophical attitude: "It took centuries of Christian work and effort for the mind finally to emerge into the integral universalism which truth requires. St. Thomas Aquinas is the great exponent of such universalism developed in the intelligence under the light of faith…. The philosophy of St. Thomas welcomes all being,

attitude toward the changing currents of thought, as well as
his attempts to understand present political and social problems in a more perfect and a profounder way, has always been
determined by his Thomism. It is not accidental that in *True
Humanism* the doctrine of the plurality of civilizations, which
destroys the acceptance of the Middle Ages as an obligatory
model for all times, is developed with the help of a Thomistic
terminology. Thomism is for Maritain neither a catalogue of
terms, whose meaning and application is fixed definitely, nor
an encyclopedia which has only to be consulted for the solutions of problems. The young Maritain emphatically opposed
all attempts to modernize Thomism, e.g., to let it appear as a
kind of Bergsonism and thereby to sacrifice its supratemporal
features.[9] But that is not a contradiction to the endeavors of
Maritain to demonstrate the vitality of Thomism by showing
how it leads to a deeper understanding of the trends of our
time.

It is not too difficult to grasp the foundations of Maritain's
political and social philosophy, which is determined by
Thomism. To use a simple formula: Maritain professes to
have a political philosophy, he does not hide it behind claims
to have a science without aims, based on pure facts or exclusively from practical activity. Political philosophy deals with
societies demanded by the nature of man. The decisive influence of Aristotle is obvious, hardly surprising for a disciple
of St. Thomas. The societies demanded by human nature
have, of course, not only an exterior, protective, or material

---

because it is absolutely docile to being. Its structure being as hard as steel,
it is as extensible as may be. Its discipline being the strictest possible,
it enjoys the utmost freedom." *The Things That Are Not Caesar's*, p. 104.
On Maritain's philosophy and its importance in general, cf. Gerald B.
Phelan, *Jacques Maritain* (New York, 1937).

9.    Cf. *Antimoderne* (Paris, 1927), p. 156–57.

function." They are necessary not only for life, but for a good
life, that is, for a moral and intellectual life. Here Maritain
goes—with St. Thomas—beyond Aristotle. A purely natural political philosophy cannot know the ultimate end of
man.[10] Aristotelian contemplation is not the beatitude of
the Christian religion. Revelation liberates political philosophy—as all philosophy[11]—from the limitations which are the
consequences of the factual weakness of the human reason.
Furthermore, it puts before the human reason realities which,
like grace and supernatural virtues, could never be found by
reason's own faculties.

One example may illustrate Maritain's views on Christian
political philosophy. Man as an individual, or as a part of
a whole, is subordinated to society.[12] Society is seen not as

10. Cf. *The Things That Are Not Caesar's*, p. 2ff.: "The subordination of politics
to ethics is absolute and even infinite, being based on the subordination
of ends; for the good of the state is not God Himself, and remains far, far
inferior to the supreme beatitude of man." And Maritain quotes from his
*Une opinion sur Charles Maurras*: "The subordination is such—it is indeed
infinite—that the strongest expression employed to indicate it will always
be exceeded by the reality. The Ancients, even Aristotle himself, did not
fully realize it, because they did not perceive with sufficient clarity that
the supreme good of human life is God Himself. Christianity was needed
to make that fully clear." Cf. also p. 126, where Maritain discusses the
superiority in kind of integral political science ("which if truly complete
must have reference to the domain of theology") to inductive political
science.

11. Cf. *De la philosophie chrétienne* (Paris, 1933). (The important introduction to
the Austrian edition written by B. Schwarz deserves to be translated into
English.)

12. Cf. *Three Reformers* (New York, 1934), and *Freedom in the Modern World* (New
York, 1936), p. 46ff. It is emphasized that the "person as such aspires
naturally to the social life.... There can be a society of pure persons,"
but "only in God... Everywhere else the persons who are members of
the society are also parts of it; that is to say, the society is not a society
of pure persons but a society of persons who are also individual beings"
(p. 49). A more recent formulation of the distinction between person
and individual is to be found in *Scholasticism and Politics* (New York, 1940),
in the chapter, "The Human Person and Society" (p. 59). Maritain's

something exterior and material, but as something necessary for the good, moral life. But society is, on the other hand, subordinated to man as a person—a man is not only an individual, but also a person. The salvation of the person lies beyond the temporal good of society, though a rightly ordered society is not in opposition to the end of the person, but a way of attaining it. The true temporal *bonum commune* is subordinated to the naturally and supernaturally supratemporal end of each person—but in its order it is supreme. This distinction between individual and person which was inspired by remarks of the famous Dominican theologian, Garrigou-Lagrange,[13] makes clear the limits of Aristotle, who could not grasp fully the notion of personality. Therefore, the relation between polis, the highest society, and the member of the polis fluctuated for him. On the one side, the polis was the good life, the end of man; on the other side, it was a means of making possible contemplative, theoretical life. This life, of course, did not transcend the world; there is for Aristotle no revelation, no supranatural order, determining the ultimate end of the person and making it necessary to regard the temporal *bonum commune* as supreme only in its realm, whose right order in itself is no ultimate end.

The whole importance of Maritain's Christian political philosophy can be realized fully only if it is studied not in its

personalism, for which the person is above stars, atoms, and society—as seen from below, ordained towards the temporal common good—does not regard the person as isolated being: "...the subjectivity of the person has nothing in common with the unity without doors and windows of the Leibnitzian Monad. It demands the communication of intelligence and love" (*Scholasticism and Politics*, p. 64.)

13.   R. Garrigou-Lagrange, *Le Sens Commun*, 3rd ed. (Paris, 1922), p. 332ff. "Par notre individualité, nous sommes essentiellement dépendants de tel milieu, de tel climat, de telle hérédité.... La personnalité, au contraire, vient de l'âme, c'est même la subsistence de l'âme indépendamment du corps."

most abstract formulation, e.g., in the distinction of individual and person, but in its connection with historical and temporal movements. Maritain's thought illuminates intellectual and historical types and developments which would remain unintelligible without it. Therefore, it is impressive and valuable also for those non-Christian or non-Catholic students who are unable to accept its last foundation, the Christian revelation, which does not destroy, but completes nature. In their eyes revelation appears only as a natural historical or psychological fact. They do not believe that God has really spoken to the world and to them.

All politics is based on specific images of man and on specific views of the ultimate end of human life. Scientism and positivism are also metaphysics—in spite of their denials. A political science based apparently and exclusively on statistics and empirical observations, unconsciously, and therefore uncritically, makes those decisions which determine the selection of the statistics and the direction of the observations. The fecundity of the Aristotelian–Thomistic philosophy in the hands of Maritain is manifested by the many insights into the history of ideas which can be found in the works of the French philosopher. Here we can observe a certain change in his attitude, some shift of emphasis in the points of view of the two periods. The younger Maritain—the Maritain concerned above all with speculative philosophy—was inclined to study the modern world in its movements of defection and apostasy.[14] He observed primarily the spiritual and intellectual secularization characteristic of modern times. He analyzed the transposition of aims from a superior to an inferior order

---

14. Cf. *Antimoderne* (Paris, 1922); *Théonas*, 2nd ed. (Paris, 1925; English translation, New York, 1933); *Trois Réformateurs*, new ed. (1925, English translation, 1934).

(e.g., the case of Rousseau for whom sentiment is the highest all-determining power). He noted the ignorance of human limitations (e.g., the case of Descartes who identified human knowledge with that of the angels). These studies, especially *Three Reformers*, have been misunderstood as expressions of a narrow-minded fanaticism, hating blindly and without discrimination. Some people noted only the ironical remarks and the polemics. But it may be of interest to point out that a prominent living French philosopher, glancing through the chapter on Descartes in *Three Reformers*, stated that he would not have anything to do with Maritain. Later, however, after a careful study of Maritain's works, he declared: "I am not at all sure that even we who admire him so much are fully alive to the lasting significance of his work."

Particularly important in this first period are Maritain's polemics against the modern belief in progress and against Rousseauistic Democratism.[15] The belief in automatic progress is rejected, because it misunderstands the ends of political and social life. Technical and material improvements alone cannot determine the ends. Rousseauistic Democratism is opposed because its sentimental equality makes all social order impossible. This criticism of modern dogmas (those of nineteenth-century Europe) has made Maritain appear to be an ally of the party of order. Owing to a misunderstanding, he was on friendly terms with some of its intellectuals, but in his

---

15. Against myth of progress cf. *Théonas*, VII and VIII; and for a more comprehensive analysis, *Freedom in the Modern World* and *True Humanism*; against Rousseau's democratism, cf. *Three Reformers*, III; and for particularly short and striking formulations, cf. *Ransoming the Time*, p. 16 ("...a pseudo-Christian error"); cf. also *The Things That Are Not Caesar's*, p. 132: "Democratism, or democracy as conceived by Rousseau... the religious myth of Democracy, an entirely different thing from the legitimate democratic regime...." But American Democracy owes "little to Rousseau" and is regarded very favorably by Maritain (*Scholasticism and Politics*, p. 90). The same chapter repeats the criticism of Rousseau (p. 93).

heart he remained always alien to this party. Even during the period when he was an appreciated contributor to the periodical of Bainville, *La Revue Universelle*, he rejected the belief in a political and social order fixed in itself[16] and he fought against belief in automatic progress and a Rousseauistic Democracy from the point of view of human freedom, because he regarded them as dangerous attempts to deprive the men of modern times of their true homes and their true spirit by abandoning them to non-human and subhuman conditions.

One can observe a certain apocalyptic trend in Maritain's writings, especially of this first period.[17] The world approaches a catastrophe. The dominant political and social powers completely ignore a true order. Most men are de facto bad. As St. Thomas puts it, they live only by their senses. There is an awareness of the true order in his political thought before 1926, but this appears in a more negative form, as a general interpretation of the secularization typical of modern times.

The period in which he actually entered the field of political and social philosophy is characterized by a more differentiating attitude towards the modern world, but without change in his fundamental principles. The primacy of the spiritual[18] is opposed even more emphatically to a belief

---

16.  Cf. e.g., *Antimoderne*, especially "Réflexions sur le Temps présent," p. 195. "Tout ordre n'est pas bon par soi seul (il y a un ordre chez les démons)."

17.  *Antimoderne*, "Reflexions sur le Temps present," p. 174: "A vrai dire, depuis le déclin du moyen âge l'histoire moderne est-elle autre chose que l'histoire de l'agonie et de la mort de la chrétienté? ... Jeanne d'Arc, si elle a réussi a delivrer la France, a échoué dans sa mission de rappeler la terre au respect du Droit chrétien."

18.  Cf. *The Things That Are Not Caesar's*, p. 4, where St. Thomas Aquinas (*ST*, II-II, q. 58, a. 5) is quoted: "Homo non ordinatur ad communitatem politicam secundum se totum et secundum omnia sua." Then Maritain continues in order to prove the superior character of the Church: "But in that order of eternal life the individual is no more self-sufficient— even less than in the temporal. By the very fact of being ordered to the

in a self-sufficient order, which makes a temporal form into a final end. A purely empirical investigation, as conducted by the Action Française, is described as unsatisfactory, incapable of replacing the missing true political philosophy. Maritain's Christian political philosophy, developing after 1926, emphasized more and more the dignity and the proper ends of nature and temporal history that of course is completely in the line of Thomistic thought.[19] What Maritain had begun in several works—*Religion and Culture, Freedom in the Modern World*—found its clearest expression in *True Humanism*, a series of lectures delivered in Santander shortly before the outbreak of the Spanish Civil War.[20] The careful student of its principles and fundamental attitudes will note that nothing essential of the first period is abandoned or altered. The Christian political philosophy remains. The negative aspects and movements of the modern world continue to be described and condemned; also Maritain's latest book, *Les Droits de l'Homme*, attacks Rousseauistic Democratism as sharply as *Three Reformers*.

---

beatific vision, he is parcel of a superior whole, of a State which is a more perfect unit than the terrestrial State...we need the terrestrial State for the normal development of our nature, not for participation in the essence of humanity itself, whereas none can be made to share through sanctifying grace in the divine nature without belonging either visibly or invisibly to the Church." Cf. also p. 125, Appendix: *Politics and Theology*. (Quotation from *Une Opinion sur Charles Maurras*.)

19.    With the rise of totalitarianism, Maritain insisted more and more upon the fundamental values of a democratic philosophy of life and society. Cf. his *Christianity and Democracy*.

20.    *Religion and Culture* (Paris, 1930; English translation, New York, 1931); *Du Régime Temporel et de la Liberté* (English translation, *Freedom in the Modern World* [New York, 1935]); *Humanisme Intégral* (English translation, *True Humanism* [New York, 1937]). *Ransoming the Time* contains the most important study on Equality, indispensable for the student of Maritain's attitude towards democracy and of his metaphysical opposition to all opinions which neglect the dignity of man.

But we observe two important developments: The insight that there are several ideals of Christian civilization appears and becomes more and more important. The civilizations are not equivocal, not absolutely different from each other, having only the name civilization in common. Nor are they univocal, that is, in substance identical. Their pluralism is based upon their analogical character—they realize in different ways and from different aspects the principles of the one supratemporal truth and reality. This insight is connected with a comparative description of the sacral medieval, of the anthropocentric liberal or absolutistic, and of the Christian-inspired humanistic ideals of civilization. We note here how helpful Thomistic terms are for Maritain. In medieval civilization the profane realm tended to be regarded as purely instrumental; in the coming Christian-inspired humanism it will be an independent but subordinated end (fin intermédiaire), whereas in the anthropocentric-determined civilization it is an ultimate end, either in an individualistic way or by making a temporal order absolute.

These descriptions of the spirit, of the ideal-typical attitude of different civilizations contain the most impressive rejection of the program: "We have to restore the Middle Age and its sacral civilization." The Middle Ages appear as an expression of a finished period, which has realized a definite form and order. To the accentuation of the organic unity and of the sacral Maritain opposes not the decadence of an absolutism closed in itself and of an anthropocentric individualism, but the personalism of a New Christendom. This New Christendom, the soul and heart of the true humanism, will recognize the existence of different religious beliefs and corresponding religious groups as a fact which has to be accepted. That, of course, does not mean a dogmatic toleration in which no dogma matters, because all can be true or all can be wrong. But the civil toleration does not exclude the orientation of all communities towards the temporal common good. Maritain believes that only the Christians who are citizens of the one supratemporal polis, the Church, know about the deepest foundation and ultimate finality of this common good, but it remains given to all groups, though in a more or less imperfect way, and not as an expression of a minimum of theoretical philosophical agreement, but as a common duty and work. The unity of the new civilization and its society will be determined less by exterior means than by friendship and the will to mutual understanding and cooperation. This Christian-inspired personalism is most different from a "religion of order" which regards exterior unity and acceptance of commands as decisive. It is at the same time opposed to an individualism which knows only societies mechanically united by interests, and which does not understand that persons can sacrifice themselves to the community just on behalf of other persons. Maritain's personalism is finally opposed to all kinds of totalitarianism which either deal with persons as a means and part of political and racial-telluric movements (Fascism and National Socialism) or, like Marxian communism, deny their intellectual and spiritual nature and therefore see their ultimate end in a material-economic order.

The dignity of the human person is the center of Maritain's New Christendom, destined to be the interior mover of the profane personalistic, pluralistic, and humanistic new civilization, and representing the form of worldly activity in our time by the members of the one church which is itself above all civilizations. Maritain's personalism permits him to appreciate democracy in a positive way. He no longer regards it in a traditional way as one of the political regimes nor does he identify it with an individualist Rousseauistic Democratism. Recognition of the rights of men which are based on Natural Law and on the Eternal Law of the Creator, is decisive for the democracy praised by Maritain. Active participation of all human persons in political life, control of the state by the people, and fraternal cooperation in common work under a leadership based not on inherited privileges and hereditary selection but on the necessity of having an authority to determine unity of action, are characteristic of this democracy, which is inspired by Christianity even though its members may not be Christians.

Maritain does not share the belief according to which special groups destined to exercise authority are the necessary expression of a supratemporal order. Authority can be exercised in different ways and under different forms. Maritain's democracy has not only a political but also, and perhaps primarily, a social character. It excludes antagonistic classes and does not hold the belief that the solution of economic and social problems will be brought about by substitution of the state for capitalists. Work for common tasks in communities, a kind of industrial democracy, appears to Maritain as a solution of the fruitless conflict between capitalistic and proletarian interests.

Speculative political philosophy has been connected by Maritain with an observation and interpretation of historical periods and temporal movements, which, as the author of the study *Freedom in the Modern World* himself emphasizes, have no character of necessity. Maritain does not believe in an immanent compulsory development of history. He hopes that the new Christendom and the civilization moved and vivified by it will become a reality—but this coming is not inevitable, only a possibility. A catastrophe also is a possibility.[21] Politics

---

21.  Cf. *Le Crépuscule de la Civilisation* (Montreal, 1940), lecture given in Paris, 1939.

does not belong to the realm of pure ideas and essences, but
to the realm of contingent existences. Maritain is neither a
utopian nor a cynic. He is not utopian because his concrete
ideal of civilizations seeks only to grasp possible trends, but
does not constitute an abstraction without relation to existing
conditions and forces. His ideal is not a construction beyond
space and time. Neither is Maritain a cynic, as are so many
disabused idealists or believers in supernaturalism, who abandons the evil world to the forces of destruction. He does not
separate the heaven of perfect principles from the realm of
imperfect contingencies.[22] He realizes that historical time
does not correspond to human time—one second of historical time can embrace whole human generations.[23] But he
believes that there is a justice in history which is the work of
providence, though, in the details of its realization, inaccessible to men. He rejects a perfectionism unable to understand

---

22.   Cf. "End of Machiavellianism," *The Review of Politics*, IV, 1 (January 1942),
      p. 6: "...the toleration of some existing evil—if there is no furthering of
      or cooperating with the same—may be required for avoiding a greater
      evil or for slowing down and progressively reducing this very evil. Even
      dissimulation is not always bad faith or knavery. It would not be moral,
      but foolish, to open up one's heart and inner thoughts to whatsoever
      dull or mischievous fellow." This article must be read by all students of
      Maritain's political philosophy.
23.   Cf. Ibid., p. 16: "In saying that evil and injustice do not succeed in
      politics, I mean a more profound philosophical truth.... The true
      philosophical answer [to the question: Evil succeeds?] consists in taking
      into account the dimension of time, the duration proper to the historical
      turns of nations and states, which considerably exceeds the duration of
      a man's life. According to this political duration...I do not say that a just
      politics will, even in a distant future, always actually succeed, nor that
      Machiavellianism will, even in a distant future, always actually fail." And
      p. 19: "...the ruler who sacrifices everything to the desire of his own eyes
      to see the triumph of his policy is a bad ruler and perverts politics, even if
      he lacks personal ambition and loves his country disinterestedly: because
      he measures the time of maturation of the political good according to the
      short years of his own personal time of activity."

the character of prudential decisions which have to take into account the conditions and the mentality of the environment, of friends and enemies; this perfectionism is very often only the hypocrisy of those who excuse their own inability to act by pointing out general imperfections or faults of others. On the other hand, he rejects a political amoralism incapable of understanding the ethics necessary for the good life of the community.[24] Political wisdom cannot be replaced by political techniques, nor the common good as political aim by power and expansion.

Particularly striking in Maritain's philosophy is its ability to unite supratemporal principles with a sense of concrete human and social problems, but always seen in their universal significance. Maritain sees temporal events primarily in their relation to a supratemporal order; that is demonstrated in a particularly moving way in his attitude towards France and towards the French catastrophe of 1940.[25] Sometimes he has been accused of being a French Nationalist, who ascribes to France attributes of universal human character. But nothing is more erroneous. Maritain regards the French nation *sub specie aeternitatis*, from the aspect of a French spiritual and intellectual mission, not replacing but representing and serving humanity. The French catastrophe appears to him as a consequence of a rupture between people and ruling groups. The people, in its substance incorrupted despite all weaknesses

---

24.  *End of Machiavellianism*, p. 17: "Success in politics is not material power nor material wealth nor world domination, but the achievement of the common good, with the conditions of material prosperity which it involves…these very conditions of material prosperity…are not and cannot be put in jeopardy or to destruction by use of justice itself, if historical duration is taken into account and if the specific effect of this use of justice is considered in itself, apart from the effect of the other factors at play."

25.  *France My Country* (French: *A Travers le Désastre*) (New York, 1941).

and human errors, committed the fault of a too passive indifference towards political decisions and activities. It tolerated the more or less cynical behavior of its rulers, who had either lost belief in their own principles, or accepted openly a cynical amoralism. Maritain is not interested in analyzing concrete events and concrete forces in their interplay and mutual relations, but in the understanding of the moral significance of general trends. His political, practical philosophy retains always a speculative character and its interest in concrete events remains a moral and spiritual one. Maritain does not seek to be a political scientist, but remains always a political philosopher. He regards not technical activity, but the good life—a life which, as Christian life, is elevated in the realm of grace—as the last aim of men and of all human societies. The political philosophy of Maritain understands the concrete character of all politics, bound to time and its contingencies. He is neither a practical politician nor an adviser in practical matters, though a philosopher of the political praxis. A political scientist is obliged to take Maritain seriously, for he must understand the principles and general directions which determine his studies and interests.

Maritain has a particular position among Thomists (and perhaps not only among them) on the ground of his unique gift for utilizing the principles of his philosophy in order to understand the present day. Technical terms like analogy, discussions about the hierarchy of types of knowledge, open up astonishing insights into realities which are of importance not only for specialists and philosophers but for everyone. Nothing is more alien to Maritain than a mechanical dialectic moved only by a limitless urge to dissect terms. His political philosophy is aware on the one hand of the metaphysical and the ethical and on the other hand of the contingent, practical character of politics. Maritain's own development proves that he is in touch with life without having submitted to a dictatorship of changes recurring in a perpetual flux. The principles of his philosophy remain always the same; their understanding and application is perfected more and more.

But the most profound cause for the impression made by Maritain's political philosophy upon everyone who is anxious to understand it and who does not *a priori* suspect Maritain as a particularly clever propaganda agent, is the fact that his philosophy transcends philosophy. The Thomist Maritain is not only the careful investigator of the structures and realms of being, whose unity as well as distinctions he tries to grasp. He is a man dominated and overpowered by the experience of reality. That unites him with those philosophers and great scientists who surely would not accept his interpretation of ultimate reality, but whose thought dominated their whole existence, and in such a way that their existence remained unexhausted by their thought. What gives Maritain a particular position is the fact that he is living in a great tradition, that his concepts are not only his concepts, and that he (as his Catholic students say) tries to participate in a wisdom which is not a created wisdom. During his first period, he seemed to be upset or impatient about the fact that the world was unwilling to accept the salvation which he himself had accepted. This anger and this impatience have become milder, have even disappeared. Maritain is today much more interested in the Christian background of all civilizations than in the description and condemnation of their negative moments, of their decay and apostasy. But his kindness conceals sorrow that the forces of evil in the world are stronger and more active than the forces of good. This sorrow over blindness and imperfections does not prevent him from feeling himself responsible for this world, this actual contingent world. The insufficiencies of the political praxis do not refute a political philosophy,

which knows the natural and—with the help of revelation—
the supernatural end of man and his civilization, whose variety is a proof of the supra-abundance of the Creator. The
Creator is reflected in the images not only of each man, but in
the whole of humanity and in all civilizations. No finite order,
no civilization, can exhaust Him, who is above the world,
beginning and ending in Him.

Maritain's political philosophy reaches its aim in contemplation, but a contemplation which is not an escape from
time and its struggles. The temporal common good is directed
toward the ultimate good. The terrestrial cities must help
the attainment of the Celestial City. Of course, the ultimate
end remains, even if opposed by terrestrial conditions. But
Maritain is not a sectarian regarding a world in which only
saints can really live as a normal situation. His religious belief
is not anti-humanistic, but a True Humanism—not rejecting but trying to develop fully all human and social possibilities. Not despair but hope of redemption is the last leitmotif
behind all his attempts to understand and to rescue society
and politics in our time.

*Waldemar Gurian*

# CLUNY MEDIA

*Designed by Fiona Cecile Clarke, the* CLUNY MEDIA *logo*
*depicts a monk at work in the scriptorium,*
*with a cat sitting at his feet.*

*The monk represents our mission to emulate*
*the invaluable contributions of the monks*
*of Cluny in preserving the libraries of the West,*
*our strivings to know and love the truth.*

*The cat at the monk's feet is Pangur Bán, from the*
*eponymous Irish poem of the 9th century.*
*The anonymous poet compares his scholarly*
*pursuit of truth with the cat's happy hunting of mice.*
*The depiction of Pangur Bán is an homage to the work*
*of the monks of Irish monasteries and a sign*
*of the joy we at Cluny take in our trade.*

"Messe ocus Pangur Bán,
cechtar nathar fria saindan:
bíth a menmasam fri seilgg,
mu memna céin im saincheirdd."

Made in the USA
Middletown, DE
28 June 2024

56366694R00159